THE MARUTI STORY

PRAISE FOR THE BOOK

'The inspirational saga of how a small car revolutionized Indian roads . . . *The Maruti Story* proves that Indians when empowered can change the course of history'—*India Today*

'[T]he book is a good source for the academically inclined and for researchers'—*Outlook Business*

'A detailed account of the making of Maruti, the sarkari company that got middle-class India moving . . . For anyone studying the evolution of India's automobile industry, this book is indispensable'—*Indian Express*

'The book is worth a read. Especially, if you love history'—*Business World*

'*The Maruti Story* is an easy-to-read, first-hand account of the birth of the country's largest car maker'—*Mint*

'Just like the Maruti 800, the original people's car of India . . . *The Maruti Story* is a simple, uncluttered kind of product. And it's a much-needed one as well'—*The Times of India*

'This book will definitely jog the memory of many a Maruti loyalist'—*Mail Today*

'Mr Bhargava's narrative . . . is lucid with a keen eye on detail'—*Business Line*

'*The Maruti Story* is an honest account of how individuals can and do make a lasting impact—positive and negative—on public sector enterprises in India and also how, given the leadership of a few committed professionals, an enterprise can attain global proportions beating all odds . . . For a large community of business managers, the book would be an insightful account of how a thought could be nurtured to become a world-class organization'—*The Financial Express*

'Read [*The Maruti Story*] for an insider's account of how the car had to navigate through political ideology and bureaucratic intransigence to become an icon'—*Down to Earth*

'A must-read, especially for those who are keen to know more on managing enterprises, policymaking and the unique Japanese way of doing things . . . Especially read it if you like business history'—*Free Press Journal*

'R.C. Bhargava, who has been associated with the [Maruti] project since its inception as a mere idea, deserves full credit for recording this for posterity'—*Deccan Herald*

'The book is more than the Maruti story for it has invaluable lessons and insights, relevant and applicable even today'—*The Week*

'The industrial development of India during the last forty years needs to be discussed in greater detail. The story of Maruti is inextricably linked with the emergence of India's manufacturing and industrial capabilities. R.C. Bhargava provides an extraordinary and rare insight into how a few determined entrepreneurs created an icon, navigating through the complex interplay of political ideology, bureaucratic influence, access to technology and entrepreneurial persistence. This well-documented insider's account is a must read for those who want to understand the process of India's industrial development'—Late C.K. Prahalad, Paul and Ruth McCracken Distinguished University Professor, Ross School of Business, University of Michigan

'A new industrial revolution and resurgence in India began with the birth of Maruti. It took time to understand the full, long-term implications in terms of not only automotive industry development and growth but also engineering, manufacturing and services. All of this unfolded with the growth of Maruti. R.C. Bhargava, an exceptional thought leader, administrator and manager—who has been with Maruti from its start and is now its chairman—has put together the Maruti story, which needs to be read by everyone interested in industrial development in India'—Tarun Das, former director-general, Confederation of Indian Industry'

THE MARUTI STORY

HOW A PUBLIC SECTOR COMPANY PUT INDIA ON WHEELS

R.C. Bhargava

with

Seetha

HARPER
BUSINESS

An Imprint of HarperCollins *Publishers*

First published in hardback in India by Harper Business 2022
An imprint of HarperCollins *Publishers*
4th Floor, Tower A, Building No. 10, Phase II, DLF Cyber City,
Gurugram, Haryana – 122002
www.harpercollins.co.in

This edition published by Harper Business 2024

2 4 6 8 10 9 7 5 3 1

P-ISBN: 978-93-5029-182-5
E-ISBN: 978-93-5029-286-0

Typeset in 11.5/15 Dante MT at
SŪRYA

Printed and bound in India by Replika Press Pvt. Ltd.

To Bhagwan Sri Sathya Sai Baba,
whose blessings have made me what I am,
and to my late parents for the values they inculcated in me

CONTENTS

INTRODUCTION

CELEBRATING THE FORTIETH ANNIVERSARY OF THE FIRST MARUTI CAR

Fourteenth of December, 1983, is a date I, and many others, will never forget. On that day, the first Maruti car was delivered by the then prime minister, Indira Gandhi, and Maruti started its journey, though nobody could have dreamt where it would lead. I felt as if I had conquered the world.

Why was this date selected for the launch of Maruti 800? When the government approved the memorandum of understanding (MoU) with Suzuki Japan in April 1982, we were told that cars had to be on the road before the end of 1983. Our counterparts in Suzuki were unbelieving when they were informed of the launch plan and they listed innumerable tasks that had to be done to get a car not only produced, but also sold and serviced thereafter. We agreed that the time given was unreasonable but explained that in the prevailing political situation, it was something that we, as management, could not argue about, and had to make our best efforts to deliver on schedule. Despite their strong reservations, Suzuki accepted the schedule. Knowing the Japanese commitment to meet targets, we started to think that we would still be Maruti employees in 1984!

I have described elsewhere in my book how we and Suzuki worked to complete all that was required, from legal documentation to setting up service workshops. Suzuki explained to us that the production in the initial three months would have to be on the basis of semi–knocked-down (SKD) kits. No components were available in India from any vendor. Even if someone started production, there was no time for testing and validating the parts. The erection of the weld and paint shops could not be done in the time available. The government allowed SKD kits to be imported on the same duty as had been fixed for completely knocked-down (CKD) parts. This invited criticism but Maruti Udyog Limited (MUL) did not benefit financially from early start of production. Cars made from SKD kits were expensive and not profitable.

The pressure to start in 1983 was purely for political reasons. In hindsight, this pressure helped us to create a culture of achieving targets on time.

We could only establish the assembly line in 1983 and this too required round-the-clock work. When it appeared to us that we would be able to assemble cars from SKD kits and that all arrangements for transport, sale and service would be ready, we discussed the actual date for the inauguration of the plant and the sale of the first car. This was a no-brainer. The late Sanjay Gandhi, who was the reason for this project being started by the government, was born on 14 December. Mrs Indira Gandhi, the prime minister, agreed to come to be the chief guest at the function.

Wednesday, the fourteenth, was a clear, fine day. No pollution in those days. We were all very excited but also tense as the prime minister was going to be there, and at least I felt that my career was on the line. Security arrangements, though nothing like what they are now, were still there. The minute-by-minute activities were rehearsed. The PM came elegantly dressed in a sari, some of us were introduced to her, and the event started. She first drove along the assembly line with the chairman, V. Krishnamurthy. Then speeches started. Mrs Gandhi became highly emotional when talking about the efforts Sanjay had made to make a small car. Osamu Suzuki, who was present, had to be explained the reasons for a prime minister almost breaking down.

After that the first car was handed over by the prime minister to Harpal Singh. Three more people received cars from her. The function ended and we all heaved a sigh of relief as there had been no glitches.

Forty years later, it is hard to believe what has emerged from that simple ceremony.

The automobile industry

A decade has elapsed since the publication of *The Maruti Story.* A new phase in the life of Maruti Udyog started after the government sold all its remaining equity holding in 2007. Sixteen years have passed since then and while MUL's leadership of the industry has remained unchallenged, much else has changed in the country, including in the automobile industry. This introduction briefly mentions these changes, how MSIL was affected and the company's plans for the next several years.

One had hoped that the liberalization of economic policies that took place from 1991 would lead to a new era in which the private sector would be encouraged to grow and become globally competitive, and the country would make good the lost opportunities of the past forty years. Alas, that did not happen till 2014. The distrust of the private sector continued and doing business in India remained as difficult as before. The importance of competitiveness, and the impact of government actions on it, were either not understood or not considered relevant, judging by the policies and practices that continued to prevail. The large number of scams and the growing corruption further added to the woes of the manufacturing sector. The importance of creating wealth in the country was not understood. Public sector companies, despite some moves towards privatization, remained underperformers and the structure governing their management was not improved significantly. Many of the brightest young continued to seek jobs, better careers and opportunities outside India. I, who had always been optimistic about our country's future, became somewhat of a pessimist by 2014.

The elections of 2014 and the policies of the new government changed the future outlook dramatically. I again became an optimist. The people had clearly voiced their strong desire for change and wanted the government not only to be clean, but also bring about faster development and create more jobs. The government under Prime Minister Narendra Modi committed itself to giving the highest importance to the manufacturing industry, recognizing that for a big country like India, this was the only way to meet the aspirations of the people. It decided to place trust and reliance on the private sector to achieve this objective—a departure from policies followed for sixty-four years.

Being aware of how difficult it was to do business and manufacture competitively, the government implemented numerous reforms designed to make manufacturing much more competitive. The enactment and implementation of GST to replace a multitude of complex central and local taxes has been of great benefit for industry. The government has brought in transparency in economic decision-making by increasingly using more technology and digitization. Opportunities for corruption and malpractices have reduced and in the last ten years, there has been no 'scam' in Delhi. A serious effort to eliminate 'black' money has been made. The political stability and the high level of trust that the government has built with a large number of countries has created a much more conducive climate for foreign investments to flow to India. Unfortunately, the Covid pandemic and other global events had a dampening effect.

Despite all these efforts, the rate of growth of manufacturing has been disappointing. The limitations of a government in increasing manufacturing competitiveness by the private sector have become quite obvious. Private sector leadership has to introspect and make the required changes in its style of management. The geopolitical changes in recent times have created vast new opportunities for manufacturing in India, but entrepreneurs have to take advantage of them. There are hopeful signs, especially from the younger entrepreneurs, who are now giving priority to the growth of their companies over their own personal interests. A good example is the recent partnership between Escorts and Kubota that could lead to this company becoming a global leader in the production of agricultural machinery. Direct foreign investment in some sectors of manufacturing is increasing, thanks to new and innovative policies. Will there be more Maruti-like examples in the coming years?

The automobile industry constitutes about half of manufacturing activity in India. It contributes over 7 per cent to the GDP of the country, rising from a mere 2.8 per cent in 1992–93.* The high level of competition in this sector, an outcome of the presence of most of the global manufacturers in India, has resulted in cars made in India being of global standards in terms of quality and technology. When Maruti started in 1983, nobody thought that cars could be exported to the developed countries.

---

* Research Unit, Press Information Bureau, Ministry of Information and Broadcasting, Government of India, 17 February 2023, https://static.pib.gov.in/WriteReadData/specificdocs/documents/2023/feb/doc2023217160601.pdf

Maruti started exporting cars in 1987 and export volumes should cross a million fairly soon. Maruti Suzuki India Limited (MSIL) is the leader with a 40 per cent share in Passenger Vehicle exports[*] and with a target of reaching 750,000 to 800,000 units by 2030–31.[†] Maruti is exporting cars even to Japan.

A major beneficiary of the development of a modern and large car industry in the country has been the automobile component industry. Component manufacturing became one of the fastest growing industries in the country. In 2022–23, its turnover was Rs 5.6 trillion ($67.5 billion) and exports Rs 1.61 trillion ($19.4 billion).[‡] The component industry creates very substantial employment opportunities. If the domestic car industry grows faster, it would enable the component industry to become more competitive and to invest more in strengthening engineering and developmental capabilities. It would be able to acquire a much larger share of the global market for automobile parts and accessories, which was $1,862 billion in 2022.[§] This is one of the areas where the geopolitical situation is specifically favourable to India.

The production of cars was adversely affected during the decade 2011–2020 due to numerous factors including the Covid pandemic and the global shortage of semi-conductors.[¶] Initially, during the period 2010–13, the fuel-pricing policy of the government caused a sudden and sharp increase between the prices of petrol and

---

* Society of Indian Automobile Manufacturers (SIAM)

† Maruti Suzuki Annual Report, FY 2022-23.

‡ ACMA, Press Release, FY 2022-23, https://www.acma.in/uploads/press-release/Annual%20Performance%20FY23%20Press%20Release%5b1%5d.pdf

§ ACMA, https://www.acma.in/

¶ Society of Indian Automobile Manufacturers (SIAM).

diesel, which resulted in the growth of the industry stagnating.* This situation was remedied in 2014 and car sales revived. The introduction of BS6 standards, followed by the Covid pandemic and the global shortage of semi-conductors, again caused a setback till 2021–22.† The industry has grown at a reasonable rate after that.

India is fast moving to bring cars made in India up to European standards in terms of safety and emission. Concerns about air quality intensified after 2017. BS4 norms had been in force in thirteen cities since 2010 and were enforced all over the country in 2017. It was then decided to skip BS5 and go directly to BS6 standards from 1 April 2020. CAFÉ II norms came into force in 2022. All these norms have their equivalent European standards.

The prescription of European standards of safety and introduction of BNCAP were designed to lower the very high accident and mortality rates from road accidents. Unfortunately, despite the excellent intentions of the government, death rates have not fallen.‡ There are several reasons for this. One is the absence of adequate training of drivers of motor vehicles, including two-wheelers and heavy commercial vehicles, before they are given a license. They also need to be tested in a transparent manner before issue of a license. State governments are responsible for this important requirement for ensuring the safety of all road users. Proper training and testing of candidates before issue of a

---

* Press Information Bureau, Government of India, Cabinet Committee on Economic Affairs (CCEA), 18 October 2014, https://pib.gov.in/newsite/printrelease.aspx?relid=110697

† SIAM, https://www.siam.in/pressrelease-details.aspx?mpgid=48&pgidtrail=50&pid=475

‡ Ministry of Road Transport and Highways, 'Road Accidents in India', 2022, https://morth.nic.in/sites/default/files/RA_2022_30_Oct.pdf#page=36

license is expensive, and therefore politically unpopular. This has to be weighed against the large number of lives lost every year.

Another requirement for reducing deaths is effective enforcement of traffic laws. Lack of modern infrastructure, corruption and lack of will to take unpopular actions is a hinderance. MSIL has used funds under its CSR programme to improve the process of improving driver training, issue of licenses and enforcement of laws but without state governments giving these activities higher priority results are unlikely to be satisfactory.

A big reason for accidents is failure of safety-related features on vehicles. While vehicles are mandated to be fully fit at the time of sale, regular and competent maintenance is required during the fifteen or more years that they operate. No regular and periodic testing of cars and two-wheelers, as in other countries, is so far required. The integrity of the fitness certificates given to commercial vehicles by testing centres is doubted by many. The enforcement of laws regarding plying of vehicles without having all fitness features in good condition is ineffective.

The importance of remedying these deficiencies will become increasingly important as the penetration of cars increases in the coming decade. State governments are likely to come under greater pressure to take effective action to increase safety on the roads as otherwise the fatalities on roads will continue to increase.

As a policy for reducing the carbon footprint, and reducing the dependence on imported oil, the government launched the National Electric Mobility Mission Plan in 2013. In 2015, the Faster Adoption and Manufacturing of Electric (and Hybrids) Vehicles (FAME-1) was launched to provide subsidies to help the faster growth of EVs and hybrids. The subsidies on hybrid vehicles were discontinued after some time. In the absence of a clear and transparent way of defining hybrid vehicles, there was suspicion of misuse of the subsidies. The GST on EVs was initially fixed at

12 per cent and later reduced to 5 per cent. FAME-1 was followed by FAME-2 in 2019.

The electrification of petrol-operated two- and three-wheelers was found to be easier and more acceptable to customers than for cars. In 2023, while about 82,000 electric cars were sold, the number of electric two- and three-wheelers were about 1.45 million.* Many car manufacturers are introducing electric cars but there are several obstacles to a faster adoption of electric cars.

Hybrid cars are gaining popularity, despite their high prices, which is partly the result of a 43 per cent GST levy. These cars give over 30 per cent fuel consumption benefits. Considering the high percentage of coal-fired energy in the grid, many consider that hybrids are a better intermediate solution for India. EVs would make a significant impact on carbon emission only when electricity-generation becomes far cleaner than at present.

Reports indicate that the acceptability of electric cars is slowing down in most parts of the world. Apple has cancelled its project to produce electric cars. Sales are slowing in many countries. MSIL has adopted the view that taking in consideration our resource endowment, economic parameters and ability to build infrastructure, the best strategy would be to consider the use of all available technologies for moving towards carbon neutrality. For example, we have a huge potential for developing biogas and ethanol from agricultural and animal waste as well as from urban waste. Biofuels would be clean, renewable, involve no imports, and would also help make the entire country cleaner. Ethanol use can be considerably enlarged. Hybrid technology should be used and, if possible, extended to smaller cars.

---

* Ministry of Heavy Industries, 'Sale of Electric Vehicles Registers a Growth of 49.25 per cent during 2023', 2 February 2024, https://pib.gov.in/PressReleaseIframePage.aspx?PRID=2001989

Electric-car use in India, on a large scale, requires not only very substantial improvement in the infrastructure but the generation of electrical energy has to shift from being predominantly coal-fired to clean sources. In the context of annual growth in demand for energy that would inevitably take time.

The regulations requiring two-wheelers to move to BS6 standards, along with cars, resulted in a very large reduction in their sale. This was similar to what happened with small cars and illustrates the price elasticity of demand for this category of buyers. The two-wheeler industry has begun to revive after four years of slow sales.[*] It is likely that as the economy continues to grow, and per capita incomes to increase, the more than 273 million two-wheeler owners will again be able to upgrade to the far safer and comfortable four-wheel vehicles.[†] It would be reasonable to expect that these customers would only be able to buy small low-cost cars, under about Rs 7–8 lakhs. Possibly by 2026, this could lead to a revival of the small car market.

The coming decade is likely to see GDP growth being between 7 per cent and 9 per cent a year, though I believe the potential of this country is higher. Policies that facilitate the growth of manufacturing in India will continue to be implemented. The younger generation of entrepreneurs are bound to realize the immense wealth that they can create for themselves and the country if they place the growth of their companies as the top priority, understand that maximizing the generation and

---

* SIAM, 'Auto Industry Sales Performance of March 2024, Q4(Jan– March 2024) and April March 2024', 12 April 2024, https://www.siam.in/pressrelease-details.aspx?mpgid=48&pgidtrail=50&pid=562

† Vahan Dashboard, 'Total Number of Registered 2 Wheelers in India', https://vahan.parivahan.gov.in/vahan4dashboard/vahan/dashboardview.xhtml, data sourced till 12 July 2024.

retention of internal resources is the key to growth and that strong teamworking would maximize their chances of success. The automobile and component industry is bound to be big beneficiaries of such an event.

Maruti Suzuki India Limited

The government sold its remaining equity in MUL in 2007, and the company became a listed subsidiary of Suzuki Motor Corporation Japan. MSIL could now function as a truly board managed company. This was a positive for decision-making and better management. However, doing business in India remained as difficult as ever till 2014 when the new ruling party was focussed on making it easier to do business and promote Indian manufacturing activity. The management culture of the company ensured that performance continued to be excellent throughout. SMC had recognized that MSIL was a company with the potential for materially impacting the future of the Suzuki group. The company had to be carefully managed and nurtured so that it could take advantage of the increasingly favourable conditions for growth in India. Cars made in India would also help in expanding Suzuki's global footprint.

The management structure of MSIL was modified so that both the board of SMC and its shareholders were confident that the company would continue on the path of growth and profitability. SMC knew that MSIL could not be managed from Japan and that Indians had to be fully involved in all aspects of decision-making and execution of strategies. SMC decided that the managing director and other executive directors would be persons deputed from SMC. Nakanishi, who had played an important role in SMC partnering government in 1982, became the first managing director. Since then, all managing directors have been Suzuki employees deputed from Japan. Executive directors on the board have also been SMC employees. This has given the Suzuki board and shareholders in Japan confidence that their interests in MSIL were being well looked after. The Indian involvement in management was achieved by appointing me as the chairman. My role was larger than what would be the case for most non-executive chairmen, especially because of my long association with Maruti and the relationship of trust with Osamu San. At the operational level, an Indian was appointed as the senior executive officer for each functional area. While the Japanese directors headed functional areas, these executive officers actually carried out operations. Being familiar with the conditions in the country, their task was to ensure that the policies suggested by Suzuki were modified to the extent needed to ensure that their implementation in India would be smooth and yield good results. They were responsible for communication with other employees, vendors, dealers, customers, media and government. They were permanent special invitees to board meetings and usually made presentations and answered questions. The results since 2007 show that this management structure has worked well.

Nakanishi, almost immediately after becoming the managing director, had to deal with the adverse impact of the 2008 global financial crisis, and then the loss of sales resulting from the government hugely widening the gap between petrol and diesel prices. This led to a sharp fall in petrol car sales in the country. MSIL was most affected as we did not have diesel cars in our portfolio. While the management was dealing with this issue, the Manesar plant had severe labour problems in 2011 and 2012. On the positive side, many important and significant initiatives were started during Nakanishi's tenure and they produced results after his departure. Perhaps the more important amongst them was the start of the Rohtak R&D facility; development of new car models in India; manufacture of diesel engines and cars, rapid extension of sales and service facilities to rural areas and smaller towns and obtaining land in Gujarat for further expansion of production capabilities.

K. Ayukawa succeeded Nakanishi as managing director and CEO on 1 April 2012. He left in 2022 after a highly successful tenure and assumed higher responsibilities in SMC. He was replaced by H. Takeuchi. Under Ayukawa's leadership, MSIL regained 50 per cent market share, something considered as very unlikely by many analysts in 2012. A unique arrangement was entered into with SMC to implement the project to expand capacity in Gujarat. Initially, MSIL had intended to make all the investments in the Gujarat plant. On the basis of a suggestion from Japan, this decision was changed, and SMC agreed to make the investments by bringing in the required funds as equity, entering into a contract-manufacturing agreement with MSIL and operating the Gujarat facility on a no profit–no loss basis. This arrangement created a win-win situation for both SMC and MSIL. Most analysts and some of the leading shareholders of MSIL had been very sceptical about the agreement but later realized how beneficial it was for all concerned. Since 2015, when the agreement was signed, MSIL sales have increased from 1.3 million units in 2014–15 to 2 million units in 2022–23. Profits during this period rose from about Rs 37,000 million to about Rs 80,500 million, and shareholders received Rs 90 per share as dividend in 2022–23 compared to Rs 25 per share in 2014–15. The price-to-earnings ratio of MSIL shares has increased from 30 at that time to 32 presently, as a result of which the share price had crossed Rs 12,500 compared to Rs 3,699 at the end of 2014–15.

The royalty payment system was revised during Ayukawa's tenure. The royalties are now denominated in INR and royalty rates now become lower after sales of a model exceeds a prescribed threshold. The work done in India in developing models that attract royalty is reimbursed separately. These changes have led to benefits for MSIL and also for SMC because of higher sales and profits. Ayukawa received several awards for being the best CEO in the country.

Hisashi Takeuchi has been the managing director from 2022. Many very significant decisions have been taken under his leadership and will be discussed later. Meanwhile, Osamu Suzuki decided to retire as chairman of SMC, and from its board in 2022. He was succeeded by T. Suzuki. Osamu Suzuki continues on the board of MSIL and has been designated as honorary chairman.

The production capacity and sales of MSIL have continued to grow, despite the temporary setbacks that the industry has periodically suffered. The installation of 750,000 car-manufacturing capacity at Manesar was completed in 2013. This has been augmented by another 100,000 units capacity in 2024. Reacting to the sudden increase from 2011 in the market demand for diesel cars, caused by the fuel policy, MSIL started to manufacture diesel engines, using Fiat technology. The Gujarat project, implemented by SMC, resulted in three lines of 250,000 cars a year being commissioned between 2017 and 2021. Exports have grown and 259,000 cars were exported in 2022–23.

A very significant event took place in 2017 when SMC entered into a business partnership with Toyota. Both companies agreed to cooperate in the area of new technology development and also share components and products with each other. This arrangement has the potential for making a significant difference to the future of MSIL. Toyota's sharing of technology with SMC would enable MSIL to use the shared technology for its growth. Already, hybrid cars are being sold by MSIL. Toyota in India is selling cars made by MSIL and thereby expanding total volumes. The export market of MSIL is growing also because of access to Toyota's network in other countries. SMC has established a fully owned R&D company in India so that it could use Indian talent to develop new technologies.

The R&D capabilities of MSIL have been significantly strengthened since it became a SMC subsidiary. A new facility, comparable to those of SMC in Japan, has been established in Rohtak, and that has enabled most vehicle and component testing to be done there instead of in Japan. The engineering resources of MSIL have been continuously enhanced and upgraded by training of engineers in Japan. It is intended that all work relating to ICE cars should gradually become the responsibility of MSIL, with support from SMC. In accordance with government policies, MSIL has been orienting its production and technology to meet the targets set for achieving carbon neutrality and improving the air quality. The production of diesel cars was discontinued in December 2019. MSIL was the first car company to introduce factory-fitted CNG cars. They proved immensely popular with the users and production often lagged behind demand. The sale of CNG cars reached 328,000 in 2022–23. In line with the policy to move towards using electricity as the fuel for cars, SMC took up the responsibility of developing suitable vehicles for the Indian and export markets. Electric cars would be produced in the Gujarat facility and the first model would be available in 2024–25. In all, six models are planned till 2030–31. These cars would, besides being sold in the domestic market, also be exported to Europe and Japan.

It is widely recognized that the penetration of electric cars in India would be slow due to a number of factors. In addition, coal-fired thermal energy constitutes about 75 per cent of the power consumed in the country. The reduction of greenhouse gases clearly requires that the internal combustion engine cars become more efficient. Fortunately, thanks to the SMC–Toyota alliance, hybrid technology has become available. MSIL has introduced hybrid cars, and they are proving very popular with customers despite their high price. The government appears to have recognized the value of hybrid technology for reducing the carbon footprint and may consider making tax modifications so that the growth of this technology could be faster.

India has a very large potential for producing biofuels like biogas and ethanol. These are renewable and clean and need to be promoted. Biogas and CNG are interchangeable as fuels and can be combined with each other. The acceptability of CNG has already been proven. MSIL has decided to help in the production and use of these fuels, including in our own production facilities.

MSIL decided to enter the small commercial vehicle segment around 2013–14. This was in response to the rapidly growing market for vehicles with 1 to 1.5 tonne carrying capacity, and the availability of a suitable product with SMC. Such vehicles were being used for operations within cities due to regulatory requirements. The Super Carry was launched in 2016. A separate channel for the sale of this vehicle was created and about 40,000 vehicles were sold in 2022–23.

The Covid pandemic provided MSIL with an opportunity to use its strengths to support the efforts being made by the government to deal with the unprecedented crisis. The company was able to make a significant contribution in increasing the production of ventilators and oxygen-generating plants by using its own as well as the experience and capabilities of its suppliers to help very small companies rapidly scale production volumes and help in saving lives.

3.0

The first phase of Maruti had ended when it became a listed company and a subsidiary of SMC. The second phase was the period that concluded with the end of the Covid pandemic and the semiconductor crisis. MSIL has now entered its third phase. The Indian car market has become the third largest in the world. This country is the only large nation that still has considerable scope for the growth of car production. The government has a very positive attitude towards the continued growth of the car industry and India becoming a large exporter of cars. The target of attaining zero carbon emission, the use of artificial intelligence and the geopolitical situation will require MSIL to be innovative and nimble in order to maintain its leadership role and take full advantage of opportunities that are arising. Maruti 3.0 will be no less challenging than the initial phase of the company. Takeuchi has been fully involved in developing the strategy for Maruti 3.0 and will have to see to its effective implementation.

SMC is fully aware of the future requirements and is working closely with MSIL to provide all the required support. The partnership with Toyota has already proven its value but I believe that MSIL and the Japanese partners would benefit to a much larger extent in the future. The R&D centre established by SMC in India would be supporting MSIL by making the required investments in developing new technologies. Most of the engineers in this company would be Indians. The major beneficiary of the results of the development work would be MSIL.

Not much thought was required to understand that reorganization and restructuring of MSIL was essential to deal with the new challenges before the company. The first step was taken when Suzuki Motors Gujarat, a SMC subsidiary, was acquired by MSIL with minority shareholder approval, by issue of shares of MSIL. SMC shares in MSIL increased from 56.48 per cent to 58.19 per cent. The paid-up equity of MSIL increased from Rs 150 crores to Rs 157 crores. SMC and MSIL senior management are working jointly to decide on further steps so that MSIL can efficiently produce, sell and service the large growth in the domestic and export markets.

Expansion of production capacity has been started with a project to create 1 million production capacity in Kharkhauda in Haryana state. The first line would be commissioned early in 2025 and full capacity is likely to be reached in 2027–28. Work is in progress in selecting another site where a capacity of another 1 million cars would be added. The work is expected to be started in 2024–25 and full capacity attained by 2030–31. SMC would also produce batteries for EVs in Gujarat.

The challenges in the future would be formidable. Selling over 3 million cars in the domestic market, comprised of twenty-eight models and with technology ranging from electric vehicles to hybrids to CNG to biofuels, would require MSIL and SMC to be highly flexible and innovative. The more stringent regulatory requirements would also have to be met. MSIL has always thrived in a challenging environment and I am sure will continue to do so.

MSIL plans to use technologies other than EVs to expedite reduction of carbon emissions. CNG car volumes would exceed 600,000 in 2024–25. The company also will be producing larger volumes of hybrids and cars using biogas and ethanol. These are clean and renewable fuels and do not have any import content. MSIL is considering to help develop the biogas potential of the country both for use as a fuel as well as for its own use.

The future for India, and for MSIL, is very exciting. The company has a great advantage in terms of its large volume of production, strong and committed supply chain and a vast network for the sale and servicing of cars. These will undoubtedly be of great value in introducing and localizing new technologies and rapidly expanding production and sales. A ten-million car-production goal in the future?

The journey of Maruti Udyog Limited, from the rather dubious circumstances of its birth to what it has become and what the future holds, is like a fairy tale with a very happy ending. The author has indeed been very fortunate to have been a part of this journey.

INTRODUCTION TO THE FIRST EDITION

The decade of the 1980s has been a watershed for India in many ways—putting it firmly on the path of modernization and technological advancement. At one end of the technology spectrum was the start of India's satellite programme, with the launch of the short-lived Insat 1A in April 1982. At the other end was the colour television, which made its debut in India in time for the Ninth Asian Games that were held in Delhi in 1982. And in-between, there was India's first modern car—the iconic Maruti 800.

The 800, as it is still known, rolled out of the factory of Maruti Udyog Limited in December 1983 and changed not just India's automobile industry but also the way people commuted and travelled. Maruti Udyog was established as a public sector undertaking (PSU) in 1981 to manufacture cars, following the nationalization of the late Sanjay Gandhi's Maruti Motors Limited in 1980. The Congress government led by Indira Gandhi decided that a foreign partner would be roped in and allowed 40 per cent equity share. It was perhaps one of the very early steps towards economic liberalization—a government committed to a socialist economic programme and swearing by self-reliance opening a window for foreign investment, that too in a PSU.

This was the first time that cars—considered items of luxury consumption and therefore at the bottom of economic priorities for resource allocation—were being manufactured in the public sector. Cars were being made by private companies but the existing two manufacturers—Premier Automobiles and Hindustan Motors—were languishing for want of better technology. There was a third manufacturer, Standard Motors, but it was hardly a player in the market and it formally closed shop years later.

Maruti Udyog established new standards of quality, productivity, industrial relations and customer care in the automobile industry and the manufacturing sector at large. It not only came to dominate the Indian car market within a short period of time but also showed that India could manufacture and export a sophisticated engineering product to the demanding markets of western Europe. Importantly, all this was done by a PSU at a time when the public sector was characterized by inefficiency and sloth. Why and how did this happen? This is a question that has often been asked, and this book will attempt an answer.

When the Maruti project was announced in 1980, there was a widely held belief that it would be stillborn. Not only did it come with a controversial political history, but it was also a PSU, which, in those days, were not expected to compete with private companies or be customer-oriented.

The record of PSUs has generally been poor, with few performing to their potential. This happened despite the tremendous advantages they enjoyed. Once the government approves a project, funding is not a problem, at least not for the approved investment. The government provides the equity as well as the loan amount at interest rates lower than what a bank would charge. It is much easier to procure land and get the required approvals from the state governments. Dealing with sundry government agencies becomes hassle-free. Where required, help or support from another ministry is usually forthcoming. Moreover, at least till the mid-1990s, PSUs attracted the country's best talent and were the employers of choice, especially for engineers. After all, government employment offered lifetime security and a better social status than working for the private sector.

The underperformance of PSUs, then, had to do more with the stifling environment of rules, procedures, government interference and corruption and, most importantly, the complete lack of motivation and involvement of the employees in the company.

A public sector company usually has enough money, at the time of start-up, to obtain the best of technologies and establish contemporary production processes and systems. Almost without exception, the Central government PSUs have not been handicapped on this account. Yet, PSU managements have not been able to create an environment where continuous improvements in productivity and quality take place and they are able to expand output and generate reasonable profits. One reason is that it is the government, and not the management, that takes key financial, technological and commercial decisions. A PSU does not have control over how it deploys its profits or internal resources.

The governance structure and systems of a PSU are very similar to those of a proprietorship company, where the owner has virtually total control over the management. In a PSU, the government is the controlling shareholder, holding normally 100 per cent of equity, unless a minority stake has been divested, a process started after 1991. Each PSU is under the administrative control of different ministries, depending on the sector in which it operates. The minister and officials of the ministry exercise the powers of the shareholder. Effectively, the minister—assisted by his officials—functions like the proprietor of a company.

This is where the similarity ends. In a private proprietorship company, the owner's motivation to run the company profitably is very high, since he has invested his own money. The company's professional managers also have a stake in its success, since they are assessed on the basis of its performance. On the other hand, the minister and his officers have no financial stake in a PSU; it is taxpayer's money that is invested. Their careers and fortunes are not affected by the inefficient working or the losses of a PSU, though they have full control over it.

Worse, usually officers in the ministry overseeing the PSUs have no experience of industrial or commercial working. They could learn on the job, but not only is their tenure on a particular desk quite short, they are also burdened with a lot of other responsibilities. That leaves them with hardly any time to gather the expertise required to effectively discharge their role as owners. There are exceptions, where a minister or a senior civil servant is genuinely concerned about improving the performance of a PSU and respects and supports the management. The PSU then benefits enormously. Sadly, the number of such instances is too small. Invariably, the blame for the non-performance of a PSU is passed on to its management, whose authority is severely curtailed. Obviously a system of management where authority is not accompanied with accountability cannot lead to sustained performance.

Such a situation also gives immense scope for a political party in power to use PSUs for its political advantage. PSUs usually have large budgets, give jobs and contracts, and thus become tools for exercising patronage. The gross overstaffing in most

PSUs is proof of this. Sometimes political funds are also raised through PSU contracts. There are numerous instances of PSU facilities being used for the personal benefit of politicians and bureaucrats. These actions hurt the performance of the PSU, but those exercising patronage—the politicians—are not accountable for its results. That responsibility rests with the PSU management, but it cannot refuse such requests unless it is willing to fall foul of the ministry. That is a risk few are ready to take.

Under the Companies Act 1956, the board of directors is fully responsible for the management of a company and has the authority to take all required decisions. Well-managed boards have competent outside directors, who bring expertise and experience from different spheres of business, and help in shaping policy and monitoring performance. In addition, if a company has diversified shareholding, the board is answerable to the shareholders at the time of the annual general meeting, when the accounts are approved. The shareholders also elect the directors. This accountability tends to check arbitrary actions and misuse of power by the management.

However, in the case of PSUs, all the directors are appointed by the ministry (since the government is the sole or controlling shareholder) and political considerations often determine the choice of non-executive directors. It is rare to find PSU boards with experienced outside directors who play a significant role in the management of the company. The position is not significantly different even in PSUs where the government has divested a part of its holding. It is not easy for a sovereign shareholder to be sensitive about the interests of minority shareholders.

The powers of PSUs boards are limited in many critical areas—approving capital investments, fixing the remuneration and conditions of service of employees (including performance-related incentives), entering into joint ventures, investing surplus funds and the like. Pricing decisions are frequently subject to approval by the ministry, which often intervenes, usually through verbal orders, in decisions relating to contracts and appointment of senior personnel, dealers and suppliers. The voice of the ministry representative on the board is the most important one and PSU boards rarely take decisions that are not in conformity with his views. Since most PSUs are dependent on the government for money, especially if they are not generating enough surpluses, their freedom of action is further curtailed by the conditions attached to the provision of funds. Not surprisingly, the boards make little difference to the management quality, and thus a major instrument of corporate governance is blunted.

In any company, the chief executive officer (CEO)—the chairman and managing director or just managing director in the case of a PSU—has to develop the management culture of the entire organization. The CEO requires a high degree of motivation, and the will, to create a performance-oriented organization. Unfortunately, the PSU operating environment is not conducive to this.

The CEO and the executive directors are appointed by the government on a contract basis, usually for five-year terms. On paper, the Public Enterprise Selection Board (PESB) is involved in preparing a shortlist of candidates for any vacancy and also recommending extension of contracts, but these recommendations have only limited value. Appointments to the board-level posts of a PSU have to be finally approved by the Cabinet Committee on Appointments, but if a minister is politically powerful he can always get his recommendation to prevail over that of the PESB. The minister and the secretary assess the work of the CEO and executive directors and write their annual confidential reports, which are highly subjective but form the basis of promotions and renewal of contracts. This further increases the power of the ministry.

PSUs are subject to Parliamentary scrutiny and control. However, it is the minister and the officers of the ministry who reply to Parliament questions and appear before Parliamentary committees. It is very easy for them to make a CEO appear in a poor light before members of Parliament (MPs), adverse comments from whom can have serious consequences for the career of a manager.

What does this mean for the top management of a PSU? The CEO and the directors are aware that their future is essentially in the hands of the minister and his officers, since they influence their promotions or extensions. Keeping key people in the ministry happy is, therefore, more important than performance. There are enough alibis for underachievement of targets, which are accepted as long as the ministry is favourably disposed towards the CEO.

There are other handicaps that PSU managements face when trying to run the company on commercial lines.

As with top managers in private companies, the CEO and full-time directors of PSUs are required to take commercial decisions, use the resources and facilities of the company to maximize benefits to it and its shareholders, and provide the best value for money to consumers. Also, in the course of their work, they have to enter into various contracts and agreements with individuals and firms. However, doing all this becomes very risky for public sector managers because, unlike their private sector counterparts, they are public servants and are subject to the provisions of the Prevention of Corruption Act (PCA), 1988, as they are dealing with public money.

Section 13 of the PCA, which defines criminal misconduct by

a public servant, specifies in sub-section (d) that a public servant would be liable if he:

(i) by corrupt or illegal means, obtains for himself or for any other person any valuable thing or pecuniary advantage; or
(ii) by abusing his position as a public servant, obtains for himself or for any other person any valuable thing or pecuniary advantage; or
(iii) while holding office as a public servant, obtains for any person any valuable thing or pecuniary advantage without any public interest.

The second and third sub-clauses are particularly problematic. When any contract is entered into with another party—whether for purchase or sale, or even for appointment as a dealer or a vendor—'a valuable thing or pecuniary advantage' has been obtained for that party. Thus, one of the constituents of a criminal offence will always be present when a PSU manager does any of these acts. The only other constituent to turn those acts into a criminal offence is that they involve 'abusing position as a public servant' or if, say, the contract was given without 'public interest'. It is these words in the law that hang like a Damocles sword over the heads of PSU managers and are used when the political system wants to pressure them. It is possible to allege, in respect of almost any commercial transaction, that it was done without keeping public interest in mind or by abusing one's position as a public servant. There is no clear definition of what 'public interest' is in a commercial transaction. Equally, there is no clear definition of what constitutes 'abuse of position' in such transactions.

The existing situation regarding 'public interest' in a commercial transaction is that as long as a PSU transacts all its business by strictly adhering to all prescribed procedures, and following precedents, it is considered to be working in the public interest. Yet, a large number of these PSUs lose considerable money each year, and execution of projects are delayed with considerable cost overruns. Much of this can be attributed to the managers being obsessed with ensuring that there are no procedural violations. The losses incurred are not considered by any authority to be detrimental to public interest. There is no thinking that the primary task of a PSU should be to achieve its approved objectives on time and to make profits. Surely by doing so it would be working in the public interest, even if some rules and procedures are violated, instead of by following rules but losing money. Procedures should not become an end in themselves. The boards of the companies should be able to look at any individual transaction to see if there was any wrongdoing. Unfortunately, this is not the case, and many, usually infructuous, prosecutions are launched using this provision. The situation with regard to 'abuse of position' in commercial transactions is very similar to that of prosecutions under the public interest provision.

The investigating agency has the discretion to decide who should be prosecuted using this section. It is true that the prosecution can only be launched after obtaining sanction of the government, if the officer is in service. However, once the officer retires, government sanction for prosecuting him is not required, even if the act was done when he was in service.

Once a charge sheet has been filed, alleging offences under these provisions of the law, the concerned officer has to spend years in court before it can be established that the transaction was a normal commercial one. In the bulk of cases, where these sub sections have been used, the accused officers have not been convicted. However, they have been subject to immense harassment. PSU officers are aware of this situation. How can PSU managers show backbone and resist improper requests from the ministry as long as the law is worded in a manner which makes it possible to classify most commercial decisions as crimes?

The requirement that PSUs should be audited by the comptroller and auditor general (CAG) has a similar effect. The procedures and processes for giving contracts or making purchases are expected to conform to the way work is done in the government. Audit is done accordingly. No exceptions because of the compulsion of commercial reasons are made in any important area. Results are judged on the basis of hindsight. This system places a premium on following rules, procedures and precedents because that is the safest way to take decisions. However, doing so means that nothing can change for the better and the same mistakes keep getting repeated. Making innovations carries the risk of adverse comments in the audit report, especially if the results do not measure up to expectations. The system does not recognize that in a well-managed and dynamic company, managers have to take quick decisions, and all of them cannot be the best possible. Bona fide mistakes tend to be treated as if they were mala fide. Over time, PSU managers have learnt that the best solution is not to take responsibility for any decision.

The powers of the board to function commercially and with the private sector gets further diluted by the fact that PSUs are 'Instruments of State' in terms of Article 12 of the Constitution. This means that all Fundamental Rights can be enforced, through the writ jurisdiction of courts, against a PSU (the Article does not apply to private companies). For example, a PSU has to ensure that in all decisions it takes the right of equal opportunity is not violated. Any aggrieved person who has not got a contract or an appointment or has not been promoted can challenge the decision of a PSU in court on the grounds that he was not given equal opportunity. This leads to a situation where decision making on contracts, appointments and the like takes much longer than necessary, since tortuous processes must be followed and immense paperwork generated so that it can be established that all Indian citizens were given an equal opportunity if ever the decision is challenged in court. As a result, often the commercial interests of the PSU are the casualties. A PSU must also pay heed to the Directive Principles of State Policy and build them into its management processes.

PSUs have also to comply with the directions they receive from the various Parliamentary committees which oversee their working. These include the committees on Official Languages, Scheduled Castes and Tribes, Assurances and the committee specifically meant to look into the working of PSUs. All this puts PSUs at a disadvantage vis-à-vis private companies, who are not subject to these laws and directions.

The government has recognized the need to give autonomy to PSUs. Under a policy initiative in the late 1980s, PSUs signed an annual memorandum of understanding (MoU) with the government. The PSUs would indicate the physical and financial targets they would achieve and the government would indicate what it would do to help them achieve those targets. In 1997, some PSUs were declared 'navratnas' and given more operational freedom. However, this did not really change the powers that the minister—and the ministry—enjoyed over public sector managers. It would be a rare CEO or director who would deny 'requests' from the ministry, even in these navratnas.

Apart from these, a major reason for the underperformance

of PSUs is the lack of motivation for employees and the absence of any system of performance-linked incentives.

Without doubt, it is the employees—from the CEO down to the shop-floor worker—who make the maximum difference to the long-term performance of any organization. Technology and manufacturing equipments, raw material and other inputs, production processes and systems can all be bought or acquired from others. However, employees have to be nurtured by the management. For the company to achieve excellence, not only must they acquire the necessary skills but should also have high levels of motivation that are sustained throughout their careers. Employees must become and remain creative and innovative. For this to happen, they need to believe that their future is intrinsically linked to the company's performance. Workers, in particular, need to understand that militancy and indiscipline in the workplace only hurt their long-term interests. For its part, the management, by its actions, needs to create and sustain these beliefs. This soft side of the management process is what differentiates the ordinary company from those that excel.

Does the public sector environment lead to the employees being committed to and involved in the prosperity of their companies? The honest answer is: no. Some PSUs do perform well in the short term, but few achieve long-term excellence, which comes only with employee involvement with the company.

The government works on the assumption that the salary paid is enough incentive for sustained high performance throughout an employee's career. These salaries—and annual increments—are much lower than in the private sector. Promotions are generally timebound and assured, so long as one has not made any serious mistake. All this does not create any motivation for enhancing performance and delivering results. Unfortunately, the way in which PSUs are managed—with the government periodically funding loss-making companies and promises made by the management to become profitable being overlooked—have convinced most employees that public funds are available to bail out loss-making companies and hence they can prosper (or at least retain their jobs) even if their company becomes sick. PSUs operate in a zone of comfort, and unlike private companies, do not have to worry about survival.

Managers have also learnt that exercising initiative is a high-risk, low-reward activity. But if any undertaking is to make continuous improvements, and reap the benefit of individual creativity, employees have to be encouraged to think of and try out new ideas. Mistakes will be made, but if every mistake is punished, people will stop trying to make improvements. This attitude carries over into decision making as well, with managers preferring to follow precedents and procedures, regardless of delays, since they will be held responsible if it later proves to be wrong.

Industrial relations is another bane of PSUs. Most PSUs have multiple, politically affiliated unions, whose relationship with the management is adversarial. PSU managements have done precious little to educate workers to change their attitudes and behaviour.

This was the environment in which Maruti had to operate from the time it was established in 1981 till 1992, when the government and Suzuki Motor Corporation (SMC) became equal partners and the company ceased to be a PSU. V. Krishnamurthy and I were fully aware of all these pitfalls when we took charge at Maruti, because of our long association with PSUs and the government. We were also clear that if the objectives set for Maruti were to be achieved, we would have to find a way to work within the public sector system and yet attain excellence. The rest of this book tells how this was achieved.

1

ASSEMBLING A DREAM

On 14 December 1983, a little white car, festooned with marigold garlands, drove out from a car factory located in a dusty town called Gurgaon, just outside the borders of Delhi and in the state of Haryana. At the wheel of India's first small car—the iconic Maruti 800—was a proud Indian Airlines employee, Harpal Singh, who was taking it towards his Green Park home in south Delhi.

Hours before, Prime Minister Indira Gandhi had, just before handing the keys of the car to Singh, made a short, emotion-laden speech. 'Perhaps, you living across the oceans,' she said, addressing the executives of Japan's Suzuki Motor Company, which had partnered with Maruti Udyog Ltd to produce the people's car, 'do not know the long history of vilification, falsehood, accusations and allegations that we had to face over it.' With tears in her eyes, she described the long hours her late son Sanjay spent every day, in a hot and dusty workshop, trying to develop an Indian small car, and translate his dream into reality. In between, her voice would crack, and she would sip water and dry her eyes.

In saying that she was summing up the long and tortuous history of India's first small car project.

Cars were Sanjay's first passion, one that led the son of India's Prime Minister to apprentice with the British car company Rolls-Royce Motors for three years from 1964 to 1967. On his return, he was fired with the idea of manufacturing a 'people's car'.

For the India of that time, strongly steeped in socialism and centralized planning, it was both a valid and an impossible dream. Valid, because motorization was essential for modernizing Indian industry and giving an impetus for economic growth. Impossible, because allocating scarce resources, including foreign currency, for developing private transport vehicles went against the deep-rooted beliefs of socialist planners, who did not recognize the fallout effects of a vibrant car industry.

At that time there were just three companies manufacturing passenger cars—Hindustan Motors in Kolkata (Ambassador), Premier Automobiles in Mumbai (Premier Padmini, better known in those days as Fiat after the collaboration with Italy's Fiat company) and Standard Motor Products India in Chennai (Standard Herald). The demand for cars far outstripped supply and in 1968, the waiting list for cars was as much as 82,000,* which meant that people had to wait for more than two years to get a car. The Premier Padmini was the preferred car, with a waiting time of up to five years. Bureaucrats used their influence to get special quotas to buy the car, use it for a few

---

*The Minister of Industrial Development and Company Affairs, Fakhruddin Ali Ahmed, in a statement to the Lok Sabha on 12 November 1968.

years and then sell it at a profit! The prices of cars were high by the standards of those days (in the Rs. 14,000 to Rs. 16,000 range in 1968), setting off demands from members of Parliament for nationalization of the three car companies! The logic perhaps was that in a government company, profit was not important and so cars could be sold cheaper. Quality was pathetic, prompting the government to appoint a Motor Car Quality Enquiry Committee in 1967.

Government policy had a lot to do with the condition of the industry. The main cause of poor quality was the lack of competition, and a huge gap between demand and supply. Manufacturers of cars, as well as virtually any other product, could sell whatever they could produce. Quality and customer service were irrelevant for ensuring that products were sold profitably, and often at a premium. A persistent shortage meant that the dealers could charge a premium—paid in cash—on the cars. The distribution of this unaccounted and untaxed money created a deep vested incentive for shortages to persist. While little was done by the government to put pressure on the manufacturers to increase output, reliance was placed on administrative orders to control prices.

The automobile manufacturing industry in India really dates back to 1948. Till then cars were only being assembled here, with G. Mackenzie & Co. making its debut in 1926 and General Motors India kicking off operations in 1928.* In 1953, the government took the first step towards making the country self-sufficient in automobiles. This was part of the government's

*'Growth Story—The Indian Automobile Industry', paper written by Dilip Chenoy, director general, Society of Indian Automobile Manufacturers, for *International Journal of Automotive Industry & Management*, Vol. 1, Number 1, 2007, Korea Automotive Research Institute, December 2007, page 49.

overall approach towards industrial self-reliance through import substitution. It accepted the recommendations of a Tariff Commission report on the development and protection of the automobile industry. The report said that in order to lower the costs of production, manufacturing should be concentrated in a few firms, which would execute a localization programme according to an approved time schedule. Assemblers who did not submit their manufacturing programmes to the government were to terminate their activities.* That saw the exit of foreign car assemblers.

The three domestic manufacturers who remained—Hindustan Motors, Premier Automobiles and Standard Motor—had to get their manufacturing programmes approved by the government.† They were given a phased manufacturing programme to localize the manufacture of components. While all of them were allowed technology import to manufacture a car, no further import of technology was allowed to upgrade the cars or change models. Foreign exchange conservation was the reason for this policy. Based on the Tariff Commission report in 1956, protection was granted to the industry for ten years. As with most timebound protection schemes, the period was repeatedly extended and no competition was allowed. This led to the situation where cars produced in India gradually became obsolete in terms of technology, consumed too much fuel and were of poor quality.

The following year, because of foreign exchange constraints, the government limited the types and makes of automobiles to be developed. Only three passenger cars were allowed. The

---

*The Automobile Industry of India, 1964-65, Association of Indian Automobile Manufacturers.

†Report of the Ad Hoc Committee on Automobile Industry headed by L.K. Jha, January 1960.

domestic car manufacturers did not invest in building any engineering base to develop models for the future. There was no motivation to do so, given the fact that their volumes of production were limited by their licences. These could be sold without any need to develop new models. Building development capability without external help was probably impossible, and the government policy did not allow such arrangements.

The policy was to discourage car use, since it was treated as an item of luxury. Thus high taxes were levied and manufacturers did not have a free hand to raise prices. It was only in 1973 that six-monthly price increases were allowed, but even this led to constant friction with the government. The only imported cars on the streets were those that belonged to the diplomatic missions. Diplomats, who imported these cars without duty, could sell them in India at very high prices. As a result, the government prescribed that diplomats would need to sell their cars to the public sector State Trading Corporation at their depreciated value, calculated according to a government-set formula. The STC later auctioned these cars and made large profits. The auction system could also be manipulated in special cases to ensure that selected persons could buy a good car at a low price. The cars made by Hindustan Motors and Premier Automobiles were indigenized in a few years and there was no need to import components for them. Only spares for foreign cars were allowed to be imports, and they attracted high import duties of over 200 per cent.

By the late 1950s, the government decided to look into the idea of manufacturing a small car in India. An Ad Hoc Committee on the Automobile Industry under economist-bureaucrat L.K. Jha was set up to look into the feasibility of manufacturing a low-cost passenger car in India. It was meant to cater to those whose monthly salary was below Rs. 1,000 and who could not afford to buy a car at the prices prevailing in those days. The target price was around Rs. 6,000 against the Rs. 10,000 price tag of the cars in the market. The committee (which promptly got dubbed the Cheap Car Committee and the Low Cost Car Committee) studied different models and manufacturers and did not rule out foreign collaborations. In its report, submitted in 1960, it set out the criteria that should decide the model and favoured one of the existing car companies manufacturing the selected model. The committee received twenty-four proposals from various firms, including the public sector Hindustan Aeronautics, French car maker Renault (which proposed to partner with Mahindra and Mahindra), Hindustan Motors, Premier Automobiles and Tata Locomotive and Engineering Co (Telco, which later was renamed as Tata Motors and would go on to unveil the world's cheapest car, the Nano, close to fifty years later). However, the tenure of the committee was over before it could ask for more detailed proposals and it is not known what progress was made in establishing the manufacture of a low-cost car.

The Planning Commission and the government also studied the idea of manufacturing a low-cost car in the public sector. At one point, the industries minister Dinesh Singh had told Parliament that a decision had been taken to start a low price car project in the public sector. In November 1970, the Cabinet decided on manufacturing a small car in the public sector and discussions were held with foreign car makers, including Renault, Ford and Nissan. However, the government estimated that the project, which would necessarily involve foreign consultants and collaboration, would require an investment of Rs. 57 crore. It was decided that this could not be a priority for the government, given the paucity of resources. Instead, private entrepreneurs wanting to manufacture a low-cost car would be welcome. Eleven letters of intent were issued which, if they came on stream, would have created an installed capacity of 1.56 lakh cars.* One of those receiving a letter of intent was Sanjay Gandhi.

The conditions under which the car would be manufactured were extremely tough. Foreign collaborations, consultancies and import of capital goods and components were barred. This was despite it being well known that there was no expertise available in India which could design and manufacture a small car with only local resources. India did not also have the capability to build the required capital goods. It is doubtful if even Henry Ford—founder of America's Ford Motor Company and father of the assembly line in automobile production—could have manufactured a car in India under these conditions.

Out of the eleven letters of intent, only three were converted into industrial licences. One of these was in favour of Sanjay Gandhi and the other two went to Manubhai H. Thakkar of Vadodara and Sunrise Auto Industries of Bangalore. The latter had plans for a three-wheeler passenger car.† Sunrise Auto rolled out a three-wheel car in 1976 and continued production till 1982, when it manufactured 126 cars, while there is no record of Thakkar having started his project. This procedure largely protected the government from any criticism of having favoured Sanjay Gandhi in issuing a licence to manufacture a car. On paper, at least, all those interested had been given an opportunity to undertake car production.

Ever since his return from Britain, Sanjay had been obsessed

---

*Discussion on motion regarding policy of government in regard to manufacture of car; Lok Sabha, 22 December 1972.

†Heavy industries minister Charanjit Chanana answering a question in the Lok Sabha on 12 March 1980.

with the idea of making a small car. He discussed his ideas with Captain Tillu, an instructor at the Delhi Flying Club (flying was his second passion) at the now defunct Safdarjang Airport in the heart of New Delhi, which he used to frequent. A workshop was needed to put his ideas into concrete shape. Tillu got some space in Gulabi Bagh, a congested locality in north Delhi, full of tiny sheds masquerading as workshops. Some time in 1966, Sanjay and Tillu set up a workshop in one of these sheds, with hardly any equipment, and hired two mechanics. In those lowly surroundings, both in the extreme summer heat and the chilly winters, the son of the Prime Minister would potter around with automobile parts from 8 a.m. to 7 p.m. Soon Sanjay wanted a bigger place and the workshop shifted to the premises of the Sylvania Laxman factory in the industrial area of Moti Nagar in west Delhi. While Sanjay worked to develop his concept of a small car, the process of getting a licence was under way. When it was clear that this would be possible, Maruti Motors Limited was incorporated on 4 June 1971. Some noted industrialists of the time were drafted as directors/shareholders—Raunaq Singh of Apollo Tyres, M.A. Chidambaram of Southern Petrochemicals India Ltd, Charanjit Singh of Pure Drinks (which was the bottler for Coca-Cola then) and V.R. Mohan of Mohan Meakin. A letter of intent to manufacture 50,000 cars a year and an industrial licence followed. All was ready to start India's small car project.

Sanjay applied for a plot of land in Gurgaon, situated in the neighbouring state of Haryana but bordering Delhi. The Haryana chief minister, the late Bansi Lal, was a Gandhi family loyalist, and he acquired and made available 297 acres of prime land to Maruti Motors Ltd for Rs. 35 lakh. Later, when the company went into liquidation, the acquisition of this land was one of the actions which was inquired into by the Janata Party government.

Construction work for the factory started immediately. A boundary wall quickly came up, along with a U-shaped factory covering 1 million square feet, and this was followed by a research and development centre. Meanwhile, Sanjay had developed a prototype of his car and it was shown at the India International Trade Fair in 1972. Another prototype was sent for testing to the vehicle research department of the defence ministry, which gave it a certificate of roadworthiness. The car was taken for a test drive across Jammu and Kashmir, Rajasthan, Haryana, Punjab and Uttar Pradesh. Seventy-three dealers were appointed, and each had to pay a deposit.

Commercial production of cars never started in Maruti Motors. It was an impossible proposition, considering the need to manufacture and procure all the required components, including an engine and a gearbox, locally. The equipment with the company could not be used to assemble cars, except in a totally manual manner. However, in 1976, Maruti Motors had furnished information to the government that the manufacture of cars had commenced from 7 July 1975 at the rate of 15-20 cars a month.* At this time the national Emergency was in force and Sanjay was all-powerful. This declaration could hardly be questioned by anyone.

Since the car business was not going to generate funds, some other source of income had to be developed. A new company, Maruti Heavy Vehicles, was formed to manufacture roadrollers. It acquired a Kolkata-based company, Agrind Fabrications, and went into business, diversifying into bus bodies later. With the imposition of Emergency in June 1975, Sanjay got preoccupied with politics, but Maruti Heavy Industries prospered. Getting

*Heavy industries minister Charanjit Chanana's statement in reply to a question in the Lok Sabha on 26 November 1980.

business was not a problem, with municipal bodies and state governments buying the roadrollers and many state transport undertakings placing orders for bus bodies. As long as the Emergency lasted, business flourished.

And then the Emergency ended. General elections were held in January 1977. The Congress was routed. The Janata Party, a coalition comprising a host of non-Congress parties, came to power. A slew of inquiry commissions were set up to look into the excesses of the Emergency. The operations of Maruti Motors and Maruti Heavy Vehicles also came under scrutiny. Even before the Emergency, the company was under attack from the opposition parties, with several discussions in Parliament on the change in the government's automobile policy to favour Sanjay and allegations about the allocation of land, among other things. Perhaps realizing this, all the directors, except Kapil Mohan (V.R. Mohan's brother), resigned from the board as soon as the news of the Congress defeat in the elections came in.

One of the inquiry commissions was devoted exclusively to Maruti. The D.S. Gupta Committee was given a thirteen-point term of reference, which included looking into all matters relating to the initiation, processing and clearing of the Maruti small car project and whether it was given any special preference in the matters of testing and clearance of the prototype of the car, contracts and agreements with public sector undertakings, and allotment of controlled commodities like steel and cement.

Labour trouble erupted at the factory. Kalra recalls that one day Sanjay was gheraoed by the workers for close to twelve hours. They wanted the government to nationalize the factory. They said they would allow Sanjay to leave only if he promised never to return to the factory. He agreed and left. From that day on, says Kalra, he never visited the factory.

The Gandhi family got preoccupied with legal cases and other political problems. With the orders for Maruti Heavy Vehicles drying up and commercial production of cars not a possibility, the company had no real source of income, but expenses on staff and maintenance of facilities continued. In order to restrict further increase in liabilities, shareholders Charanjit Singh and Sagar Suri asked for liquidation of the company. On 6 March 1978, the Punjab and Haryana high court ordered winding-up proceedings of Maruti Motors Ltd. Both the immovable and movable properties of the company passed into the custody of the official liquidator. According to the statement of affairs filed with the official liquidator, the company had recorded a turnover of Rs. 5 crore between 1 April 1976 and 22 July 1977, after which it remained closed.*

During the period the Congress was out of power, Sanjay had no time or means to pursue his dream project. However, Kalra remembers that he often spoke about it between 1977 and 1980. The luck of the Congress and the Gandhi family turned in January 1980 when the party returned to power with a huge majority. Sanjay, says Kalra, was excited about two things—the Maruti project and a single-engine two-seater Pitts S-2A aircraft meant for stunts that belonged to the Delhi Flying Club. He held discussions with Charanjit Singh, Sagar Suri and his younger brother, hotelier Lalit Suri, about whether they could arrange collaborations for Maruti with foreign car manufacturers. He planned to try for an amended licence to start a joint venture and revive the company. According to Kalra, attempts were made to find a collaborator, but the response was not good. This was no big surprise, given the state of the car industry in India and the political connotations attached to this project.

---

*Heavy industries minister Charanjit Chanana replying to a question in the Rajya Sabha on 20 November 1980.

In any case, fate had other plans. On 23 June 1980, the red-and-white Pitts aircraft in which Sanjay was attempting spins and dives crashed. He was killed instantaneously.

Mrs Gandhi didn't want her son's dream to die with him. Soon after his death, she called Arun Nehru, her second cousin's son, and member of Parliament, and asked him if it was possible to revive Maruti. The air was thick with rumours that other partners were planning to sell the land and these must have reached her. Nehru came into politics from the corporate sector and was heading paints company Jensen and Nicholson in Kolkata. He was called because Mrs Gandhi wanted an objective commercial assessment of the viability of the project. Nehru went through all the papers that were handed over to him. He already had a sense of the project, since he had visited it off and on with Sanjay and Rajiv Gandhi. Nehru said it was possible to revive the project, but it could be a success only if foreign technology was used and a joint venture was formed with the technology giver. He also voiced an opinion that a minimum production volume of 100,000 cars a year was required for viability.

This formed the basis for Mrs Gandhi to act. She decided that a government company should be established and given the task of finding technology, and entering into a joint venture to manufacture 100,000 cars a year. There was no opposition from within the government to this idea. No one would have dared to oppose her on such a sensitive matter. An ordinance was issued to acquire the assets and undertakings of Maruti Motors Limited which was later given legitimacy through the Maruti Limited (Acquisition and Transfer of Undertakings) Act, 1980.

The statement of objects and reasons said, 'looking at the present state of the car industry in the country, Government felt that it would be desirable to set up a public sector undertaking under the Central government for the manufacture of passenger cars, commercial vehicles. The purpose of nationalization was modernizing the automobile industry, effecting more economical utilization of scarce fuel and ensuring a higher production of motor vehicles.'

Maruti Udyog Limited was incorporated on 24 February 1981 as a 100 per cent government-owned company. The acquired undertakings of Maruti Ltd were transferred to the new entity from 23 April 1981. It is significant that the name of the government company was very close to that of Sanjay's defunct company. For a long time many people thought it was the same company, and did not realize that this was a public sector undertaking in which no member of the Gandhi family had any stake whatsoever.

The government decided that the Maruti project should be set up with a capacity to manufacture 100,000 passenger cars and 40,000 light commercial vehicles with a payload of 2 to 3 tonnes. It was also decided that technology should be obtained from a foreign collaborator. One other decision, not recorded anywhere, was that the products should bear the name 'Maruti'. In that manner Sanjay's dream would become reality.

The stage was now set for the next chapter in the life of Maruti. Little did anyone know that the project would go on to revolutionize the Indian automobile industry.

2

CREATING A PARTNERSHIP

The first board meeting of the new public sector company, Maruti Udyog Ltd, was held on 24 February 1981—the day the company was incorporated—in Room 174, Udyog Bhavan, New Delhi, which housed the Department of Heavy Industry under the industry ministry, the administrative ministry of Maruti. It was just a formality and the meeting only took note of the incorporation of the company.

A second board meeting took place on 15 April 1981, and took stock of the progress of the project. Two of the board members—humble joint secretaries at that time—would later go on to play significant roles in Indian economic management. One was Yashwant Sinha, who became India's finance minister thrice, and the other was D.R. Mehta, who became chairman of the Securities and Exchange Board of India. The board meeting also passed a resolution creating posts of a part-time chairman and a vice-chairman-cum-managing director. Work had already begun on identifying suitable persons for these positions.

Nationalizing the assets of Sanjay's Maruti Motors, and incorporating a new government company was easy. Achieving the objectives of nationalization would not be that simple. That this was weighing on Mrs Gandhi's mind was clear from a conversation she had with V. Krishnamurthy, whom she selected to play a crucial role in the company. 'The Congress party is under ridicule,' Krishnamurthy remembers her as saying when they met to discuss his assignment. She was probably referring to the spate of allegations that Maruti had been nationalized to financially benefit the Gandhi family. The issue was also hotly debated in Parliament, where it often figured during question hour. She had to set all speculation at rest by making the project succeed. Mrs Gandhi, despite having an aggressive policy towards nationalizing important economic institutions, probably realized the limitations of the public sector for achieving excellence.

She understood that getting the right people to manage Maruti would be a key factor for success and decided to get the best of the private sector and the public sector. From the private sector, Mrs Gandhi drafted Sumant Moolgaokar, the legendary chairman of Telco (Tata Engineering and Locomotive Company Ltd, now known as Tata Motors), as the non-executive chairman. Moolgaokar was a very respected name, and recognized as the doyen of the automobile industry. His association gave credibility to a project that was, at that time, seen to have been born in sin. It brought a person on board who knew the industry, even though Moolgaokar's experience was with commercial vehicles and not passenger cars. The government could hardly tap the two other passenger car companies—Premier Automobiles and Hindustan Motors—since they were rivals. Telco was only manufacturing commercial vehicles then and posed no threat. Significantly, the government had in the past started many companies to manufacture products about which it had no knowledge, but had never appointed the chairman and CEO of a private company to head it. This precedent was never followed again, though in a sense the arrangement was perhaps a precursor to the public-private-partnership system that, in the 2000s, was to become the most effective mode for implementing infrastructure projects.

From the public sector, she roped in Krishnamurthy, who had gained fame as the person responsible for turning around the unwieldy and slothful Bharat Heavy Electricals Ltd (BHEL) into an efficient, customer-focussed organization. A month or so after Maruti was nationalized, Krishnamurthy, who had been out of the government for several months, was summoned to meet Mrs Gandhi. She offered him the job of vice-chairman-cum-managing director of Maruti, in recognition of his outstanding managerial abilities, and ignoring the fact that she had approved the termination of his contract as secretary, heavy industries, a few months earlier. L.K. Jha, who was her principal secretary at that time and had, in the early 1960s, headed the Low Cost Car Committee, was with her. Krishnamurthy's immediate reaction was to refuse, since he had faced problems with the minister of heavy industries, Charanjit Chanana. However, Mrs Gandhi was not to be denied and Krishnamurthy had to give in. The first board meeting with Moolgaokar and Krishnamurthy present was held on 29 April 1981 at the Tata guest house on the posh Prithviraj Road in central Delhi.

When Krishnamurthy agreed to become part of Maruti, the brief given to him was simple and clear: get a car on the road by December 1983. That was just about two and a half years away. There was little time to lose. Krishnamurthy realized that the project wouldn't get off the ground with the usual government meandering and political interference that was part of public sector management. He hinted as much to Mrs Gandhi.

She told him to be in touch with Rajiv Gandhi, who would sort out any problem. Arun Nehru, who had served as the CEO of a private sector company in Calcutta, and was related to Mrs Gandhi, became the pointsman for the project. Between them, they took ruthless, hard decisions without wasting any time. This was again an unusual arrangement made by Mrs Gandhi in order to ensure that Maruti was successful. Similar arrangements were never made to ensure the success of other, perhaps far more economically vital, public sector projects. The arrangement conveyed a message to all politicians to keep their hands off Maruti, and to the civil servants that unnecessary obstacles should not be raised. The progress of the project later showed the effectiveness of the arrangement.

Realizing that people would be the key to achieving the task given, Krishnamurthy set about building his team. The first to come on board was D.S. Gupta, who was appointed staff officer. He was an MBA from the prestigious Indian Institute of Management, Ahmedabad, and had worked with Krishnamurthy for several years in BHEL. I came on board next. I had just ended a two-year deputation from the Indian Administrative Service (IAS) to BHEL as its director, commercial. Krishnamurthy and I had interacted when I was joint secretary in the ministry of energy. I was selected to be director, marketing and sales, but was initially appointed officer on special duty till the Cabinet Committee for Appointments cleared the appointment to the post of a director. The first meeting of the top management of Maruti—who were all new to the automobile industry—took place in July 1981 in Hansalaya building—notable at the time for being one of the city's tallest buildings—on Barakhamba Road, off Connaught Place, which was now the company's head office.

Besides determining the deadline for start of production, the government had also decided that Maruti should produce 100,000 vehicles a year, of which 50,000 units should be bought back by the licensor, so that foreign exchange outflow could be minimized. The heavy industries ministry had started the process of finding foreign collaborators in November 1980, writing to several automobile manufacturers in Europe and Japan and inviting them to submit their offers. While some companies had indicated their interest even before the letter was written, the general response was poor. Chanana had visited various European firms, British Leyland in the United Kingdom and Peugeot in France in late 1980 and early 1981. French firm Renault, German firms Volkswagen and MAN AG (which manufactured commercial vehicles) and Ford submitted detailed proposals. The ministry zeroed in on Renault as a possible partner and selected the Renault 18 (R-18), a 1647 cc engine car, a little bigger than the Ambassador. As a consequence Renault set up an office in India and posted two officers here. The R-18, launched in 1978, came in sedan and pick-up truck versions; the car was to be sold in India and Renault agreed to buy back the pick-up truck for export.

The new Maruti management found that there was need to collect more data before it could go ahead with the ministry's selection of the Renault product. Accordingly, a revised questionnaire was sent in July 1981 to those prospective collaborators, including Renault, who had responded positively earlier. Krishnamurthy was given broad hints by various people that the R-18 was the chosen car and it was pointless to look at any other car. One person involved in the negotiations with Renault told Gupta and me not to waste our time. 'A decision is not going to be taken here; it has already been taken in Udyog Bhavan,' he said. Krishnamurthy, however, had already been forewarned by Rajiv Gandhi that there would be many people who would say a decision has been taken but that Krishnamurthy should be very careful and use his discretion. In one of their meetings, Rajiv told Krishnamurthy about a hotelier waiting outside who wanted to be introduced to him. The hotelier, Rajiv said, would tell him that a decision on Renault had been taken. 'Listen with one ear and throw it out from the other,' Krishnamurthy recalls Rajiv telling him. Sure enough, the hotelier told Krishnamurthy, 'I believe you are looking at various cars, but it has already been decided that the collaboration will be with Renault.'

On receipt of replies to the new questionnaire, the Maruti team studied the economics of the Renault project—at what price the completely knocked down (CKD) kits would be brought in, the cost of the final assembled product (which worked out to Rs. 1.15 lakh including import duty and sundry costs)—and the terms and conditions for the buyback of the pick-up trucks, among other things. The result showed that the project would not be viable. The export price of the pick-up truck was even lower than the FOB (freight on board) price of the CKD kit in France. This meant that the price of the pick-up trucks exported from India would be lower than the price at which the CKD kits were exported from France. Besides this difference, Maruti would have to bear the cost of freight from France to Gurgaon, all production costs for assembling the pick-up trucks and again the freight cost to the port of export. Renault justified the export price on the ground that the price had to be competitive in south Asian markets, where the vehicles would be sold and where Japanese pick-up trucks would be the benchmark. While this was commercially valid, the Maruti management did not see any reason why pick-up trucks should be exported at a heavy loss, which would endanger the entire project. In addition, the cost of the car was also much higher than that of the

Ambassador and the Premier Padmini, and it was unlikely that Maruti could attain the desired volume of sales at this price. It was becoming clear that the Renault R-18 was not a good choice, and the buyback clause was likely to be a huge handicap.

I then proposed that Maruti commission a market survey to assess what the customers wanted, knowing which would enable the company to sell 50,000 or more cars a year. It was feared that in the context of the stagnant car market, it might not be possible to attain even such levels of sale. In addition, the findings of the survey could be used to convince the Planning Commission and the Public Investment Board about the viability of the project. It was also necessary to bear in mind that the Maruti project was supposed to make a small people's car and the R-18 did not fit the bill. The heavy industries ministry, however, was not very keen on a market survey, as it was felt that given the size of Indian families, the R-18 was obviously the right choice. Why waste time and spend money on a market survey? Nevertheless, we decided to go ahead with the survey.

We were also battling resistance from within regarding what Maruti should manufacture. Moolgaokar was opposed to the idea of the company manufacturing passenger cars, especially small cars, which he declared to be unsafe and unsuitable for India. These, he often told us, had no future in India and the Prime Minister should be persuaded that Maruti should manufacture light commercial vehicles (LCVs). In fact, that was the thrust of his conversation with me when I paid him a courtesy call at the Tata guest house. However, to his credit, Moolgaokar respected his limits as non-executive chairman and always conveyed his views to Krishnamurthy; not once did he go over his head to the powers that be.

In August 1981 the heavy industries minister, Charanjit Chanana, was replaced by Narayan Dutt Tiwari. It was widely believed that Mrs Gandhi was probably not satisfied with his stewardship of the Maruti project. Mrs Gandhi had full trust in Tiwari, who had immense administrative experience and would ensure that no hurdles came in the way of the project. At the same time, the secretary, heavy industries, K.S. Rajan, was replaced by D.V. Kapur, former chairman and managing director of the public sector National Thermal Power Corporation (NTPC). Kapur had earlier worked in BHEL, under Krishnamurthy, and had done an outstanding job in establishing NTPC from scratch. He had both technical and commercial experience and was seen as a good person to try and improve the functioning of a host of public sector industries under the industry ministry. I also had a good equation with him, as I had piloted the creation of NTPC as joint secretary in the Ministry of Energy. I was the ministry representative on the board of NTPC and had accompanied Kapur in negotiations with the World Bank, and when a foreign consultant was sought to be selected for the first NTPC project. This helped considerably in the initial years of establishing Maruti. Rajan continued as secretary, technical development. A few days into his job, Kapur recalls a senior official advising him, at a social do, to drop the idea of revisiting the Renault deal. Clearly, there was more than the usual interest in ensuring that Renault became Maruti's partner.

On 2 September 1981, the Maruti board was reconstituted and Arun Nehru was nominated as a director, overlooking a norm that members of Parliament should not serve as directors on the boards of public sector undertakings. Nehru was already involved in matters relating to Maruti. His presence on the board was designed to ensure that his association became closer, and board decisions would carry more weight in the government. Ignoring another norm that only joint secretaries of ministries should be directors of public sector companies, the secretaries of the ministries of heavy industry, technical development and finance were placed on the Maruti board. This too was a step taken to ensure that board decisions were accepted by the ministries without too much questioning. Implicit was the thought that Maruti should really be board managed and the role of the government should be minimized. This was the way to ensure that the December 1983 deadline was maintained.

The issue of what car to manufacture became somewhat acrimonious at one of the first meetings of the full newly constituted board, which I attended as OSD and special invitee. The board sat on sofas—there was no formal board table—at the Hansalaya office. Kapur recalls Moolgaokar saying, 'Gentlemen, before we start anything, I would like to express a strong view—Maruti should not manufacture cars.' There was a stunned silence. Then someone asked, 'What should it do?' Moolgaokar, Kapur remembers, said it should manufacture LCVs. Heated discussions followed. Kapur pointed out that, even assuming Moolgaokar was right, it would not be easy for the government to accept this view straightaway, considering it had committed to Parliament, while nationalizing Maruti, that the new company would manufacture a people's car. Moolgaokar was adamant and no other agenda item was discussed. At one point Moolgaokar even suggested that since he appeared to be the only contrary voice, the minutes should record his note of dissent. Kapur then blurted out, 'Mr Chairman, you will be creating history.' He pointed out there may have been instances of a chairman appending a note of dissent, but not in the very first meeting. He suggested that the note of dissent should not be put in.

In the event, the minutes of that meeting record that the board felt the company 'should produce cars and commercial vehicles in accordance with the decision of the government and that immediate action should be taken to collect all relevant information on the various options which could be examined by the board for selecting the specific models to be assembled/ manufactured by the company'. This was my bureaucratic experience cutting in to keep all options open and prevent a crisis! It was decided that a team from Maruti should immediately visit some manufacturers in Europe and Japan both to explore options and to 'convey the company's seriousness of purpose'. In the course of the discussions, the team could explore alternative options to enable Maruti to earn foreign exchange and ensure the active involvement of the collaborator in the working and success of the project. This included possible financial participation in the form of equity, so that the induction of appropriate technology and products could be negotiated at the most favourable terms to the company. If necessary, it was decided, the board could approach the government to change the parameters for collaboration—that the collaborator should not only give the licence to manufacture the chosen car but should also pick up 40 per cent equity in Maruti Udyog and buy back 50 per cent of the production. The board also gave the green signal to commission a market survey, which would provide data to help in the decision-making process, and also take up the preparation of detailed project reports.

The market survey, conducted by the Indian Market Research Bureau (IMRB), was a revelation and contradicted the logic that was used to justify the choice of the R-18. It showed that over 90 per cent of car usage in India was with less than four passengers; over 90 per cent of the usage was within the city and not for outstation trips; and the greatest value was attached to fuel efficiency, reliability and low price. None of these conditions—except reliability—was being met by the R-18. It was apparent the Renault project was not suitable; not only was it highly loss-making, it was also not what the consumer wanted. Only a small car would meet the needs of the Indian market. But what small car? In the pre-Internet age, Gupta and I made a start by studying several books on cars being manufactured in the world, including *World Cars*. We learnt that the United States was clearly not an appropriate source of technology, as no small cars were used in that country. Even in Europe, the choices were limited, with Fiat apparently being the best in making small cars. However, it was most unlikely that Fiat would collaborate on cars with Maruti. Not only was Gianni Agnelli, the head of Fiat, who had earlier visited India, not impressed with the idea of manufacturing cars here, but Fiat already had a relationship with Premier Automobiles, even though there was no active collaboration at that time. Japan seemed to have a number of small car makers, but the information available in the books was very scanty and incomplete. It seemed that there would be no way of determining the options available for manufacturing a small car in India without visiting the manufacturers.

A decision was taken to visit the bi-annual Frankfurt motor show to meet the European car manufacturers. In September 1981, Moolgaokar, Krishnamurthy, Gupta, an executive from Tata Administrative Services and I flew to Europe. Two British consultants joined us in Europe and they proved very useful, educating us on the automobile industry and the technical aspects of car design and performance. However, these consultants were not very favourably disposed towards small cars, and expressed a view that a small engine may not necessarily mean a car with higher fuel efficiency. They did not think that small cars being manufactured by Japanese manufacturers would be suitable for Maruti. At that time Japan was already giving the

European manufacturers a hard time and that may have had something to do with the consultants trying to keep Maruti away from Japan.

At the time of our visit, European manufacturers doubted the robustness of the Indian car market, as well as the merits of being a minority partner in a government-managed company. Their fears were not without basis. Though the Indian economy had grown 7.2 per cent in 1980-81, it was not seen as a very vibrant economy. The demand for cars had been stagnant for a decade. Cars were highly taxed and were considered a luxury item. The economy was still closed and highly controlled and the business environment for foreigners was not friendly. If the number of cars produced was small, royalties would not yield much income. The stringent localization conditions would mean that profits from the sale of imported components would be low. The world car market was going through a downswing at that time and European car makers were battling stiff competition from Japanese cars on their home turf. Getting into an unfamiliar, and what appeared to be an unattractive market, was hardly a priority.

During discussions in Europe the team found that all manufacturers were very uncomfortable with the buyback condition. The British consultants also advised Maruti's negotiators that a compulsory buyback condition would not work. If the quality and cost of the car were up to international standards, it would get sold without any written agreements. However, if they weren't, then no buyback condition would work as many reasons, including defects in quality and performance, could be found to abort an agreement. On the contrary, such a condition would only drive away potential collaborators. Krishnamurthy saw the logic of the argument and took up the matter with the ministry. The condition was dropped, but it was decided that components should be exported to make up for the outgo of foreign exchange in importing CKD kits.

In Europe, the Maruti team visited the Fiat headquarters in Turin, Italy, Peugeot in Sochaux, France, the Volkswagen plant in Wolfsburg, Daimler-Benz in Stuttgart and MAN AG in Munich, Germany. It also went to the Turin-based automotive design firm, I.D.E.A. Institute, with the thought of getting a car designed for Maruti. A concept design was shown to the team. This design and the Indica, which Tata Motors launched in 1998, are very similar. Not surprising since Tata Motors also used I.D.E.A. to design the Indica. However, the thought of getting the car designed had to be abandoned since I.D.E.A. said the tooling itself would take two-and-a-half to three years to manufacture. With a December 1983 deadline to meet, this was not a feasible option. The team did not go to the United Kingdom to visit British Leyland, as Maruti was keen on the Metro, which was a small car, but the company was not willing to offer that, arguing it was too sophisticated for India.

Discussions with Daimler-Benz and MAN were confined to commercial vehicles only. Daimler-Benz executives had earlier met Moolgaokar and Krishnamurthy in Delhi on 15 June 1981. The Benz team, which visited the Maruti factory and agreed to the condition of 50 per cent buyback of vehicles for export, suggested one of their light commercial vehicles for the project, but said their small car would not fit into the range of cars Maruti was looking for.

During the visit to Turin, the team found that the existing relationship between Fiat and Premier Automobiles would be an obstacle to any association with Maruti to make cars. Fiat preferred that Maruti collaborate with its fully owned subsidiary, IVECO, to make commercial vehicles. In fact, in an earlier meeting held in Delhi in May 1981, Fiat executives had indicated that a production volume of 100,000 vehicles was not an economical size and that it would require huge investments to modify European cars to Indian conditions. They, therefore, suggested that instead of producing an entire car in India, Maruti should produce certain components that were cheaper to manufacture here—but not the engine—while Fiat would produce components that were cheaper to make in Europe. Fiat also felt that the Maruti factory site at Gurgaon was not the best location from the point of view of exports since it was 1,500 km away from the nearest port. Fiat executives also pointed out that the company's experiences with licensing agreements in Brazil, the USSR (as it was then) and Spain were not very satisfactory.

Since, after the market survey, Maruti was looking for a small car, Fiat offered its Fiat 127, a super-mini car it had launched in 1971. It was, as senior Fiat executive Dr G. Calvi wrote to Krishnamurthy after the team returned from Europe, 'a car of great reliability and still the most sold model in Europe'. Importantly, it was available in a right-hand drive model and also a derived utility version—the Fiorino delivery van and mini-bus. This was shown when the team visited IVECO. But nothing came of this and Fiat was never a serious contender for a partnership.

During the visit to Renault, we explained our preference for a small car, and why the R-18 was not considered suitable. Renault did have a small car in its stable—the 782 cc Renault 5 (R-5), but it was a model launched in 1972. This was too old to be considered. Renault suggested the 1397 cc R-9, which had been launched that year. However, the price of the car was high, and Maruti could not have sold the car in India anywhere near the benchmark price of Rs. 50,000 determined after the market survey. Renault was also reluctant to invest any cash in the equity of Maruti.

Peugeot, which till that time was only producing large cars, was in the process of developing a small car. Code named M-24, it later became the highly successful Peugeot 205. The Maruti team test drove the car and liked it. However, it was to hit the market only in 1983. It would have taken a lot of time to adapt it for India and make all the arrangements for shipping CKD kits and transferring technology. It could not have been taken up for manufacture in India till at least the end of 1984. That didn't suit Maruti, since its deadline for start of production was the end of 1983.

Volkswagen was keen to collaborate and offered the Gol, an entry-level sub-compact car designed and sold in Brazil and launched in 1980 and a cheaper version of the Golf, as well as the Jetta, the sedan version of the Gol. Volkswagen explained that a buyback condition could not be accepted. However, they appreciated the government's desire to reduce the foreign exchange outgo and proposed to establish an engine-manufacturing facility in Maruti and to buy back the engines from Maruti. This proposition was the only one which seemed feasible. The team returned with the idea of going ahead with Volkswagen and Nehru approved the idea.

Meanwhile, British Leyland thought that India may not be such a bad market and, in November 1981, flew in its medium-sized Morris Ital—a 1275 cc car giving 11 km to the litre in city driving, which had been launched in 1980—along with a team of officials for discussions. The company also offered to sell its existing plant to Maruti to manufacture the car.

The idea of buying second-hand machinery had some appeal, given the high initial investment in putting up a plant—a serious issue for the company. The world automobile industry was going through a recession and many companies had cut back production and even closed their plants. The possibility of getting good machines at reasonable prices was, therefore, attractive. However, a big obstacle to this car was its price. And according to reports, the Ital had not been a successful model in the United Kingdom.

The Maruti team and the heavy industries ministry took stock after the Europe trip. Volkswagen had made the only firm and suitable offer. However, the Jetta's assembled cost in India worked out to Rs. 75,000, much higher than the target price. But time was running out and there were no other options. The Maruti management felt that the Japanese car options also needed to be checked out to see if something better could be found. Nehru felt a trip to Japan would be a waste of time as the Japanese response till then had not been very encouraging. While recognizing that Japanese companies might not be willing to come to India, the Maruti team and Kapur strongly felt all options should be explored before taking a decision. After all, going to Japan would cause a delay of only fifteen days or so.

Nehru agreed, and Kapur, Krishnamurthy, Gupta and I headed for Japan, timing our visit with the Tokyo Motor Show held from 30 October to 11 November. Initially, we planned to go via Australia to check out Ford's offer of the Laser. A senior Ford executive from Australia, Ralph Peters, had, on his own, exhibited great interest in the Maruti project. He visited Maruti in June 1981 and came again several times. Not only was he a source of considerable information to the management, but he seemed genuinely interested in helping the development of Maruti. Apparently he believed that the Indian market had good potential, and that Ford should get into this country. He proposed that Maruti consider the production of the Laser, a compact car sold by Ford in Asia and South America. He was the first to suggest that it would be better for Maruti to export components to Ford operations in Europe and the United Kingdom in order to reduce foreign exchange outflows, rather than think of exporting vehicles. Investing in the equity of Maruti would have to be approved by Ford headquarters in Detroit, and he was not sure whether the company would agree to being a minority partner with only 40 per cent stake; Ford had always been a majority partner in joint ventures. Just before we were to start on this trip, we were informed that Ford headquarters had nixed the idea of a partnership with Maruti. Obviously, Detroit did not share the vision of Peters, who was deeply disappointed and came all the way to India to apologize.

Sumitomo Corporation, one of the leading Japanese trading houses, offered to help arrange meetings and explain the Japanese way of doing things. There was very little contact between Japan and India till then and Indians were largely unaware of the Japanese way of doing business, except that it was quite different from the western style. Japanese companies were also a bit wary about India. There was virtually no Japanese investment in India, and most Japanese knew very little about the country. The idea of having a major trading company guiding the Maruti team was obviously a very good one.

In Japan, our team met representatives from Daihatsu Motors, Toyota Motors (which are part of the same stable), Nissan Motors, Mitsubishi Motor Company, Honda Motors, Suzuki Motors and Isuzu Motors (which manufactured heavy commercial vehicles) at the Tokyo motor show. The huge range of vehicles made in Japan was available at one place. For the first time we realized that not only did Japan make small cars, it also built variants for different market segments on the same platform. The possibility of expanding the market by reaching out to different users became apparent. This was the basis of the decision that collaboration with a Japanese company would be most advantageous as besides the small car, Maruti could also make the van and the pick-up truck. In Japan small cars were mainly used in the smaller cities. Kapur remembers that we did not see any small cars in Tokyo, except at the Auto Show. However, when we went to Kyoto and the suburbs we saw a large number of small cars on the roads, a majority of them of 547 cc engine capacity.

Toyota expressed disinterest in the Maruti project, since the company was already talking to Delhi-based conglomerate DCM for a light commercial vehicle venture. Apparently Toyota also had a policy of not having a government as a partner. Honda also did not show any interest. Suzuki Motor Corporation (SMC) too was very lukewarm and did not exhibit any real interest in getting involved with Maruti. Mitsubishi offered the 650 cc Minica. This came with the other variants on the same platform. Nissan offered the 1270 cc Sunny, launched in 1966 along with the 600 cc Subaru. This was manufactured by the automobile division of Fuji Heavy Industries, a part of the Nissan family. Daihatsu also exhibited interest and suggested both the 617 cc Cuore and the 993 cc Charade.

Daihatsu had earlier written to Maruti in June 1981 pointing out that its 550 cc and 1000 cc products were attracting a lot of interest in the world automobile market. Later in October, the late H.P. Nanda, chairman and managing director of Delhi-based commercial vehicles and engineering firm Escorts, wrote to Krishnamurthy saying that his company would represent Daihatsu in India and had the first option for manufacturing its commercial vehicles. He mentioned Daihatsu's 617 cc Cuore, which was claimed to give 22 km to the litre in city driving, but said this may not be suitable for Indian conditions. A week later, S. Sawada, head of Daihatsu's export division, wrote to me suggesting the 993 cc Charade (a derivative of the Cuore) as a possible product, since it was highly fuel efficient and equalled the performance of 1300 cc and 1600 cc cars.

It became clear to us that Japanese cars best fitted the idea of a people's car and were especially suitable for crowded cities and narrow roads. They could seat four persons, had luggage space and were more fuel efficient than other cars. Their cost in Japan, including taxes, was Rs. 30,000. Overall, they were a better choice than the European cars. We said as much at a stock-taking exercise with Tiwari and Nehru after our return from Japan. At that meeting, there was general agreement that the Morris Ital would not be appropriate. Cars larger and more powerful than the Ambassador would not, it was felt, be suitable for the Indian market. Any new car must be cheaper—and more fuel efficient—than existing cars. Foreign exchange constraints meant that it was important to keep fuel consumption down (most of India's fuel requirements are met by imports). The savings could be used to import CKD kits.

However, while in Europe the idea of buying back cars was not acceptable, Japanese companies were also uncomfortable about buy-back of components manufactured in India. There was an open question regarding the quality of Indian products. But, more importantly, Japanese manufacturers kept inventories of only three hours. The just-in time system could not really work if components were to come from India, unless inventories were held elsewhere in Japan. This would be too costly. It was then decided that manufacturers should be asked to make offers to produce cars under a licence agreement without insisting on a buyback clause involving either cars or components.

A few days later, I wrote to Daihatsu seeking offers for both the manufacture of the Cuore and its derivatives, as well as the 1290 cc Charmant. Later, I also asked them to make proposals without a buy-back clause, after which Daihatsu responded by saying it would like to study the Indian component industry first.

Around that time, Maruti got an indication that Volkswagen was no longer interested in proceeding further in collaborating with the company. Volkswagen's interest in Maruti had been exhibited at the level of a board member. However, the CEO, Toni Schmucker, rejected the idea when it came to him for approval.

After returning from Japan, we reported our findings to Tiwari and Nehru. The advantages of the Japanese products over what Europe had offered were obvious and, in any case, the one viable European offer from Volkswagen had been withdrawn. The thought that a Japanese car would most closely approximate Sanjay's idea of a people's car was politically very attractive. Both Tiwari and Nehru accepted the idea of going ahead with the Japanese, making a small car and not making commercial vehicles. At that point, Daihatsu seemed to be the best option available to Maruti.

This decision had an immediate fallout. The media was suddenly abuzz with the news that Moolgaokar was resigning as chairman. When Krishnamurthy told Moolgaokar that Maruti would be manufacturing a small car, and not making light commercial vehicles, Moolgaokar indicated that he wouldn't like to be associated with the project. The media speculations were not without basis.

Kapur soon got a sealed letter, which he had to open himself. When he did, he found it was a very brief resignation letter from Moolgaokar, citing no reasons. The first thought that occurred to Kapur was that the resignation had not come at an opportune time, since the winter session of Parliament was on and the noise over the nationalization of Maruti had not died down entirely. He told Tiwari about the letter when he met him in the evening. They decided that the matter should be kept under wraps till the Parliament session was over. The resignation was accepted with effect from 24 December 1981. No one involved in Maruti was surprised at the development. Krishnamurthy had briefed Mrs Gandhi and Rajiv about Moolgaokar's steadfast opposition to the idea of manufacturing small cars, and Rajiv had conceded that he should be allowed to go. The exit of Moolgaokar, recalls Nehru, sent out a very strong message—nothing would be allowed to come in the way of manufacturing a small car. The post of chairman was not filled till 1983, when Krishnamurthy became the chairman and managing director (CMD).

At its first meeting without Moolgaokar, the Maruti board decided that the production of passenger cars should be taken up first, and that of commercial models later. It completely ruled out the idea of producing a big car. The car to be produced, it decided, should preferably be below 1000 cc engine capacity and priced lower than other cars in the market. It authorized the management to evaluate collaboration offers and select the most appropriate one, which should meet the conditions of producing a people's car, minimizing the outflow of foreign exchange and ensuring the commercial viability of the project.

By now manufacturers came to believe that the project would be implemented and interest started picking up. In December, Mitsubishi sent a team to Delhi for discussions on the Minica and the 1245 cc Colt. The Minica had only two doors, and the experience of the Standard car had shown that such cars were not popular. Mitsubishi indicated its willingness to modify the design to make it a four-door car. January saw visits by Peugeot, Daihatsu and Nissan.

Talks with Daihatsu were proceeding well and were in an advanced stage. A team came to India on a week-long visit for negotiations with Maruti in the second half of January 1982. Maruti officials took Daihatsu representatives across the country to meet vendors and see their factories. Daihatsu offered a choice of the Cuore or the Charade for a small car in the first phase of the project and the Charmant in the second phase. They suggested the S65 model as the commercial vehicle derivative of the Charade for the LCV part of the project. The first year of operation would see the rollout of 15,000 cars and LCVs which would be increased to 100,000 over five years.

Daihatsu agreed to give Maruti a final offer containing their commercial and technical conditions by the middle of February. If it was going ahead with the venture, top executives would come for final negotiations by the end of February and an agreement could be signed by March. A collaboration appeared to be on the cards, well in time to meet the December 1983 deadline.

By mid-January, Daihatsu, Nissan/Subaru and Mitsubishi were the only companies in the running for partnering Maruti. British Leyland's Morris Ital was not found suitable. Renault had not supplied information that had been sought about the R-9. In any case, the car was above 1000 cc and, therefore, not acceptable. Though Fiat's 127 was below 1000 cc capacity and within the parameters set for the project, the price was too high. Fiat had also indicated that its capacity to render engineering and technical assistance was limited. Peugeot had a good car and its offer was the best among the European manufacturers. However, that company could not meet Maruti's time schedule. What further weighed in favour of the Japanese firms was that their cars had commercial spin-offs like vans and pick-up trucks while Peugeot's M-24 did not. It was decided to get final offers from all the firms and then take stock of the situation.

Little did anyone know of a completely new and unexpected twist in the tale that was going to surface.

One day, in February 1982, I was handed over a telex message in my office. My blood ran cold when I read it. The telex was from Daihatsu to Escorts, assuring the latter that it intended to manufacture a car with it, and that it was maintaining the relationship with Maruti only to understand the Indian automobile market, the relationship with vendors and dealers, and other matters. How it landed up at the Maruti office is a mystery that has never been solved. However, the upshot was that instead of getting the conditions of collaboration from Daihatsu, Maruti was virtually stranded without a viable partnership opening. The development was unexpected and left the management very angry. The government was also very upset both with Escorts and Daihatsu.

When all seemed lost, providence provided a solution in the form of SMC. A telex arrived within days of the Daihatsu fiasco, saying that SMC was very interested in the project and if it was not too late, it would also like to participate in the selection process. I telexed back saying Maruti was ready to talk, but SMC should send a team as early as possible, as time was running out.

This unexpected development was also one of those events which show how chance shapes events and destinies. An article had appeared in the 31 January 1982 issue of *India Today* which recapitulated the twists and turns in the Maruti saga since nationalization, the status of negotiations carried out till then with European and Japanese car companies, and carried a picture of the Daihatsu Cuore as the likely choice for Maruti. A SMC team was in Chennai in January-February 1982 in connection with the motorcycle project with TVS Motors. A director of SMC, flying from Chennai to Delhi to catch his flight to Tokyo, read the *India Today* article. He was horrified that SMC's arch rival, Daihatsu, was apparently walking away with such a big project and the SMC board was not even aware of this. He promptly alerted SMC headquarters, which lost no time in contacting Maruti.

Till then, SMC had not been in the picture as a potential partner at all. It later transpired that the letter which Maruti had written to Japanese car companies before the visit made in November 1981 had gone to the overseas engineering division instead of the overseas marketing division. This was treated as a routine inquiry and was apparently not brought to the attention of anyone in the top management of Suzuki. The Maruti team had met executives of the overseas engineering division at the Tokyo Motor show, and they obviously had no knowledge or understanding of the importance of the Indian project for SMC. The Maruti team had no way of knowing that it had met the wrong people, and did not pursue SMC after the somewhat cold reception at the motor show and the lack of interest exhibited by the engineers there. In fact, SMC should have been the company of choice, because it had all the variants of the small car, and was even then selling more small cars than any other Japanese manufacturer. A mistake at SMC's end could have proved very costly for both companies, but was remedied by sheer chance.

SMC quickly followed up my telex. S. Nakanishi, who was then a young executive in the overseas marketing department, and is presently the managing director of Maruti Suzuki India Limited, was the first to arrive. A day later, T. Aonuma, who was more senior and a manager in SMC's project in Pakistan, came to India for talks with Maruti and the ministry. They were told about the project, its political importance and support, and the very tight time schedule. An offer was needed urgently if SMC was to be considered. Nakanishi asked what price would make them competitive with others in the race. Some rough calculations on how the CKD price would translate into a retail price were done, and what our target price was so as to reach a sale volume of 100,000 units a year. SMC was asked to give a detailed commercial proposal in the next week or ten days. Within a few days, SMC sent what Kapur recalls as a three-metre-long telex with a complete proposal for collaborating to manufacture an 800 cc car. The price offered was more or less the same as what had been suggested in Delhi during discussions.

Around the same time, a Maruti board meeting on 5 March 1982 noted that Daihatsu had 'regretted its inability to collaborate with us on grounds of non-availability of manpower resources'. On 4 March 1982, Nanda had written to Krishnamurthy, in what seemed to be an attempt to make amends. He said Escorts and Daihatsu were in talks for a LCV venture but that he had made it clear, in the presence of a Maruti director, that Maruti should be given first preference for a collaboration on both a car and a LCV and Escorts would step in only if Maruti collaborates with another firm. 'Contrary to my understanding with them, they have decided not to collaborate with MUL which I do not consider is a good decision,' Nanda's letter said.

By then, British Leyland having been informed that the Ital was not acceptable and Maruti was looking for a small car, got back, offering the Mini, Britain's iconic, but old, two-door car. Around this time, Volkswagen too tried to get back into the race. Schmucker had retired in December due to ill health and was succeeded by Carl Hahn, a former Volkswagen executive who was heading the German tyre company Continental Tyres. Thanks to a joint venture Continental Tyres had with Modi Tyres in India, Hahn knew India and was keen for Volkswagen to have a presence. Volkswagen got in touch with Maruti again and there were several meetings between the management of the two companies. The last one was as late as 1 March 1982, where the Volkswagen team suggested that the project be developed in steps and a production level of 100,000 cars should be reached in a number of stages. A market plan, they said, could be developed based on the Polo-Derby family (Polo was another super-mini from the Volkswagen stable introduced in the mid-1970s, and the Derby was its sedan variant) and the Jetta-Golf. The two teams also had detailed discussions on franchising and the dealership network. Volkswagen was very clear that the project must keep the unique image that the company enjoyed. The company was told that a 50 per cent buy-back of production was not absolutely essential, though balancing of foreign exchange would be desirable. However, by the time Volkswagen reverted, it was too late.

Action was hotting up on the Japan front.

Two days after the 5 March board meeting, Krishnamurthy, Kapur, Gupta and I headed off to Japan, for final talks with Nissan, Mitsubishi, Subaru and SMC. We also met Daihatsu, in spite of what had happened, just to have alternatives to present to the government.

A meeting had been scheduled with the SMC president, Osamu Suzuki, at the Imperial Hotel in Tokyo. The meeting started early and had to finish by about noon, which was the Japanese time for lunch. Suzuki had an afternoon flight to the United States, where he had discussions scheduled with General Motors regarding the joint venture being negotiated between the two companies. Though it was just a preliminary meeting, where the Indian side explained the Maruti project, its objectives and the government's conditions, Krishnamurthy recalls that it was clear that there was a meeting of minds. Suzuki asked the Maruti team to stay on in Japan till he returned, so that they could have another meeting in Hamamatsu, the SMC headquarters.

Suzuki had become president of SMC in 1977. He was the son-in-law of the previous president and had assumed the 'Suzuki' name after marriage, as sometimes happens in Japan. He saw—what most others missed—that the Indian project could be crucial for the fulfilment of his ambitions and dreams to rapidly expand SMC, and keep it as an independent manufacturer. In hindsight, he has been proved more than right.

We then visited Mitsubishi headquarters in Tokyo. The meeting took place in a large hall where there was a long table. There were about forty senior Mitsubishi executives sitting on one side, strictly in accordance with their seniority protocol. On the other side were four of us. It was a unique, and overawing experience, and definitely created the feeling that Mitsubishi was too large a company with too many layers of management. Getting to talk to anyone near the top of the management pyramid would be almost like scaling Mount Everest. Later, when he was giving his assessment to Mrs Gandhi, Krishnamurthy remarked that the Mitsubishi budget was larger than that of the Indian government and it would be difficult for any of the Maruti executives to access even the second rung of the management.

That stood out in sharp contrast to the meeting with SMC at Hamamatsu a few days later. There were just four SMC representatives, including Suzuki himself. The immediate sense that Krishnamurthy got was that this was a manageable organization, where Maruti could get access to the top leadership. What impressed him was Suzuki's quick decision making. It was also apparent that Suzuki was very cost conscious. The offices were not even air-conditioned. It had nothing like the beautiful guest house with a huge garden, in the centre of Tokyo, which Mitsubishi had used to entertain the Maruti team.

The discussions with SMC revolved around the nitty-gritty of the proposed collaboration—whether it would be possible to manufacture a car of the quality of Japanese cars at the target price of Rs. 50,000 and whether the quality could be maintained, given the working culture of the public sector. Suzuki had his apprehensions and he voiced them. SMC had a plant in Pakistan in those days and Suzuki was unhappy with its performance, which he blamed on the work culture. He was disturbed about workers regularly reporting late for work, frequent absenteeism and the break for prayers five times a day. If Maruti wanted the same quality as was being achieved in Japan, within the proposed price, he made it very clear that it must be prepared to work the way SMC did.

On the Air-India flight back to India, Gupta and I spent the entire time evaluating the proposals from the various companies. The management was racing against time, and wanted board and government approval to the choice of a partner as soon as possible. The CKD import price of the Suzuki SS80 (which later became the Maruti 800) was the lowest of all the European and Japanese models (Renault's R-9, Peugeot's M-24, British Leyland's Mini, Nissan-Fuji's Subaru and Mitsubishi's Minica). SMC also offered the best terms for training Maruti personnel in Japan and had quoted the lowest charges for its experts who would be sent to India. The evaluation showed that SMC's offer was financially the best, and this was recommended to the Maruti board. An additional point in SMC's favour was our impression that it would not work in a bureaucratic manner and would help Maruti become a quality, low-cost manufacturer.

Both the board and the government agreed with the evaluation made by us and approved the proposal to sign a non-binding memorandum of understanding (MoU) with SMC. This would then be followed up with further negotiations to finalize the legal documentation.

With a firm proposal more or less in hand, Maruti decided to apply for a composite licence of 140,000 passenger cars and commercial vehicles. Though the plant capacity was intended to be only 100,000 vehicles a year, the company decided to apply for a licence for a higher number to cater for future expansion, a common practice in the days of licensing, since the process of getting a licence was a cumbersome one. We knew that, at that point of time, getting a licence would be a piece of cake. It decided that the company should first manufacture the 800 cc passenger car, followed by the van and the pick-up truck.

On 1 April, Suzuki came to India with a team of executives. He met Prime Minister Indira Gandhi, Tiwari and other top government functionaries, visited the Maruti factory and had further discussions on the collaboration. Earlier, Nakanishi had submitted a report on the Maruti project, which went to the SMC board and led to the project being approved. A formal and detailed MoU between SMC and Maruti was signed on 14 April 1982. SMC agreed to provide technical collaboration and licence to manufacture an 800 cc car, the Carry van and a pick-up truck and a four-wheel drive. Apart from a lump-sum payment of $2.4 million, Maruti would pay royalty of 2.15 per cent. SMC agreed to pick up an agreed stake in the equity of Maruti, subject to a cap of $25 million.

The decision of SMC to partner the government in the Maruti project was in many ways surprising and did not follow the usual Japanese procedures for taking investment decisions in a foreign country. Those days, India was not on the radar of most Japanese corporations as a destination for investment. Generally, Japanese companies invested in foreign companies after they saw successful investments being made by the bigger Japanese firms. SMC, at that time, was hardly a leader. India's political closeness to the erstwhile USSR and the strong socialist thinking in industrial policy were contrary to Japanese beliefs. Normally the Japanese make their own market survey before taking any major investment decision. No such exercise had been undertaken by SMC. The giants of the Japanese automobile industry, like Toyota, Nissan, Mitsubishi and Honda, were not in India. Being a minority partner in a government company was itself seen as a recipe for disaster. The embassy of Japan in India was understood to disfavour the project. Suzuki took the decision to enter India in less than two months after the first meeting—surely an all-time record. Not surprisingly, the reaction in Japan was less than positive. Business circles were sure the venture would fail and that SMC would withdraw in a few years.

The decision to partner the government was clearly a top-down decision taken by Suzuki himself, based on Nakanishi's positive report. The speed of decision making was a result of the pressure from the Indian side as well as the dynamism and ability of Suzuki to take truly entrepreneurial risks. When asked as to why he took what appeared to most people, including the Japanese embassy in India, as an unwarranted risk, Suzuki explained that he always believed that it was people who determined how any project performed, and everything else was secondary. He said that at the time of the first meeting with Krishnamurthy and me, he was convinced that he could work with us and ensure success. If he did not have this feeling, he would not have asked the Maruti team to stay back till he returned from the United States. I wonder how many people in the world could take a decision to invest $25 million on this ground. Suzuki showed that his faith in the importance of people as the basis for doing business was better than the technical evaluations which companies made and which showed that India was not a good place to invest money.

Negotiations on the details of the joint venture agreement now started in full earnest. Work also started on preparing a project report needed for Maruti to obtain the necessary government approvals. The process involved getting the project report approved by the Planning Commission and the Public Investment Board, before it could be placed before the Cabinet Committee for Economic Affairs by the Department of Heavy Industry. The licence and joint venture agreements were also to be approved by the ministries of finance, law and heavy industries.

The May 1982 project report estimated an investment of Rs. 221.935 crore, with a debt-equity ratio of 60:40. It involved the manufacture of 40,000 cars, 40,000 vans and 20,000 pick-up trucks, all with an 800 cc engine. The plant was expected to reach full capacity utilization of 100,000 vehicles by 1988-89, by when the indigenization levels would reach 95.7 per cent.

Maruti projected the demand for passenger cars at 105,000 by 1989-90, which was lower than the figure of 200,000 set out in a report of a working group of the Development Council for Automobiles and Allied Industries in August 1981. The working group was set up to estimate production targets for the 1980s. Two months later, a sub group had scaled the demand projection down to 150,000. Maruti's projection of 105,000 was worked out on the basis of the demand for new cars (which was assumed to grow at a compound growth rate of 5 per cent a year) and the replacement demand for cars that were older than twenty-five years at a rate of 17,460 cars a year.

However, the Planning Commission found the replacement demand too optimistic considering that only 69,247 cars had been replaced since the 1950s.* The Project Appraisal Division

---

*Note of the Project Appraisal Division of the Planning Commission, 25 June 1982.

of the commission pointed out that the materialization of the demand would depend on the price of the car and tax and duty concessions would be needed to reach the target price proposed by Maruti. The commission picked holes in other parts of the report as well, pointing out that the estimates of capital costs, operating cost and working capital were 'fraught with uncertainties'. Maruti pointed out that these estimates were prepared with the involvement of SMC personnel, who were experts in this area, and the chances of overruns would be consequently low. It was also pointed out that all projects had some factor of uncertainty in the estimates, as evidenced by the record of cost and time overruns in almost every single public investment in projects. The late Sukhamoy Chakravarty, a noted economist, who was economic advisor to the Prime Minister, also wrote a note saying the country should not fritter away foreign exchange resources on a project like this.

Several meetings were held with Planning Commission officials to get them to give the green signal to the project. Apart from the formal meetings, Maruti executives working on the project report shuttled between various desks of the Project Appraisal Division to sort things out. While some progress was made, time was running out. Ultimately, Maruti could only get around this problem by pulling the right levers, with the help of Nehru.

In the summer of 1982, Suzuki sent a team with a few cars of each model for testing in Indian driving conditions. The cars could be imported after going through the process of getting an import licence. This was not easy and required some telephone calls to be made. It was also clarified that cars would be needed for marketing purposes as the customers would need to see the product before they could be expected to book the cars in advance. They were driven by Japanese technicians from Kolkata to Delhi and then to Shimla, Mumbai and other places, covering a total of 10,000 km over different terrains. There was huge public interest in the cars wherever they went. This was very encouraging for Maruti and Suzuki. The test running itself led to several modifications in the cars to suit Indian driving conditions. These included higher ground clearance, stronger and more durable horns and more sturdy shock absorbers.

After the Japanese had completed the test runs, Maruti received requests from various automobile magazines and others for being allowed to test drive the cars. Maruti was willing to do so in order to spread knowledge about these cars. One of the persons given a car to drive was Major Ravi Kapur, who drove the car to Shimla. On his way back, he was blinded by the lights of an approaching truck and crashed into the back of a truck parked on the roadside without any warning lights. Two persons travelling with Major Kapur were killed, while he himself remained in coma for several months. Fortunately he recovered fully.

Meanwhile, Krishnamurthy, Gupta and I went again to Japan to negotiate the various agreements that had to be signed. We spent much of June and July 1982 in Tokyo and Hamamatsu. That is where we got our first taste of Suzuki's famed cost consciousness. Summer in Japan was sweltering hot, but there was no air-conditioning in SMC's offices in Hamamatsu. Suzuki explained that air-conditioning was not good for health! Fresh air was much better. The clause-by-clause negotiations were carried out by Gupta and myself with the SMC team led by one of its directors. Periodically, I would report to Krishnamurthy and take directions. Discussions would start at 9 a.m. and continue till late night. Progress was slow, as everything I said had to be translated into Japanese and what the Japanese team said was translated into English. Every few days both teams moved to Tokyo so that all the clauses agreed between SMC and Maruti could be discussed with the former's lawyer in Tokyo, M. Yanase. The final versions of the agreements were drafted by him.

We had been warned that the Japanese were very tough negotiators. Not only did they do their homework very well and were fully prepared on facts and figures but they had enormous patience. The opposite negotiating teams were at times beaten because they were not able to match this patience. We also understood that the Japanese saying 'we understand' or nodding their head did not mean that they had agreed to what was said. Agreement required the Japanese team leader to specifically say what he had agreed to. Our negotiating strategy took account of these factors. We were determined to show no impatience and to sit in the meetings as long as necessary. We would also do our homework thoroughly. The SMC side was impressed by the fact that we were negotiating, even with Yanase, without any lawyer. But what made perhaps a bigger impact was my ability to do mental calculations faster than they could using a calculator!

Initially, SMC had expressed grave doubts on Maruti's time schedule of finalizing the agreements within a couple of months so that they could be cleared by the government and signed on 2 October 1982. They mentioned that negotiations with General Motors on similar agreements had started many months earlier and were unlikely to end for many more months. I, however, insisted that this time schedule had to be followed if the deadline of starting production in December 1983 was to be met.

SMC was not willing to take 40 per cent equity in Maruti, as desired by the government, as it said it did not have that much spare cash. A limit of $25 million had been set in the MoU. The initial estimate for the project was about $220 million and 40 per cent equity meant that $88 million would be the total subscribed capital. Suzuki agreed to subscribe 25 per cent or $22 million. In a meeting in the Maruti office in Hansalaya, I explained to SMC the additional benefits a minority shareholder obtained under the Companies Act, if his equity was 26 per cent. SMC immediately agreed to increase their share to 26 per cent. In order to meet the government requirement of 40 per cent equity, SMC agreed to take an option to go up to 40 per cent within five years.

The benefit to Maruti from explaining the benefit of taking 26 per cent equity was gaining the trust of SMC. It made no real operational difference because under the terms of the joint venture agreement, and the major policy decisions agreement, Maruti could not have ignored or overruled SMC's views on any major matter. The project would have already failed if a situation ever arose where the government and SMC opposed each other in a shareholders' meeting over a special resolution. However, my pointing out the legal rights which would accrue to SMC helped in building the feeling that we would work in a fair and transparent manner. Trust and confidence between partners is the key to the long-term success of any joint venture, especially where technology and production know-how is entirely with one partner.

SMC was, not unnaturally, worried about the possible dangers of working as a partner in a government company. To allay its fears, a clause was added that the joint venture would be operated with the objective of fully achieving the purposes of the licence agreement and the project, as well as making profits. Generating profits was never an objective set for public sector companies; managers were not rewarded for making profits or punished for making losses. The insertion of this clause was to drive home the fact that Maruti should not be like other public sector undertakings and generating profit would be an important objective. At the same time, the observance of the terms of the licence agreement would help in maintaining quality standards and a proper management structure, without resulting in overstaffing.

The groundwork was beginning in Delhi as well. Strategies for vendor development, marketing and distribution of the vehicles and registration of customers were finalized. The board, at one time, suggested that Maruti should be a holding company and a separate subsidiary—which would be a joint venture with SMC, with a debt-equity ratio of 3:2—should be incorporated for the implementation of the project. The subsidiary would have a 40 per cent foreign equity holding, held either entirely by SMC and its subsidiaries or with up to 10 per cent by the International Finance Corporation (the private sector lending arm of the World Bank). Of the remaining 60 per cent, MUL would hold a maximum of 40 per cent, while financial institutions or the public would hold the rest. The board had a sound rationale for this. SMC was an unknown brand in India at that time. Besides, Maruti was also supposed to manufacture commercial vehicles, which were not part of the SMC range of vehicles. A subsidiary structure would have given Maruti the flexibility to work out other arrangements for commercial vehicles.

Suzuki, however, was not keen on the idea and at a meeting with Krishnamurthy in August indicated that SMC would prefer to have equity of Maruti Udyog and not of a subsidiary company. Krishnamurthy agreed but indicated that the decision may have to be reviewed if there was a legal complication in SMC investing directly in Maruti. There wasn't—40 per cent foreign investment was allowed in Indian firms—and finally, Maruti issued equity to SMC to the extent required to give it 26 per cent stake in the enlarged equity base.

At one point, the government considered piggybacking on Maruti to get SMC, given its expertise in manufacturing two-wheelers, to help revive the ailing public sector Scooters India. Scooters India was based in Kanpur and Tiwari, who hailed from Uttar Pradesh and had been chief minister of the state, was keen on reviving it. If SMC agreed, then Scooters India could come under Maruti, which would be a 100 per cent holding company, with Maruti Suzuki manufacturing cars and Scooters India, a separate subsidiary company, making scooters. The two companies would have a common chairman and a few common directors. SMC engineers went to Lucknow and studied the company. Not surprisingly, Suzuki did not find the idea acceptable, and the proposal was given a quiet burial (to the unexpressed relief of the Maruti management as well). Privately, Suzuki said that putting money into Scooters India would be like pouring water into a bucket without a bottom.

Maruti had worked out a total investment of $226.82 million in the project. One of Suzuki's strengths was the ability to cut capital costs. True to character, he wanted this brought down to $200 million. One of the ways to do so was to make the production totally manual. However, Maruti was strongly of the view that some amount of automation should be introduced, particularly where it would result in better quality. Krishnamurthy had to argue this matter with Suzuki and finally conveyor belt systems, a couple of robots, automatic painting guns and some other machines were included in the project. At the same time, Maruti agreed to keep the project cost at $200 million. The equity subscription was made on this basis by both parties. Suzuki was very doubtful of the cost-control capabilities of Indians. Later, however, Maruti with the help of SMC engineers, surprised him by completing the project in Rs. 180 crore ($180 million).

Krishnamurthy also tried to persuade SMC to help Maruti in raising finances for the debt portion of the investment. Interest rates in Japan then were much lower than in India. However, SMC was not in favour and currency risk was one of the main considerations. Suzuki did not also want to stand guarantor for any loan. As it happened the yen appreciated very sharply and if MUL had taken a yen loan it would have been very costly. Suzuki indicated that he would like to sign the joint venture agreement only after financing arrangements were tied up. This resulted in the government providing the loan funds, as was usual for government projects.

The pricing and mode of payment for the CKD kits and imported components was another tricky issue. While the initial CKD price, expressed in US dollars, was available in the offer made by SMC, the question was how prices would be determined in the future. It was decided that there should be a price escalation formula based on the cost of the key inputs used for manufacturing a car. The Japanese government published data on the movement of prices of all such materials and so an authentic source of information was available. Suzuki produced a formula to determine the cost of the CKD parts. I suggested an extra input—the impact of labour productivity (for which indices were also published). SMC agreed to include this factor in its formula and it was incorporated in the Sales and Purchase agreement.

The result worked very much in Maruti's favour. For the ten years that the licence agreement was valid (1982-1992), while material costs went up, labour productivity also increased. The net impact, according to the formula agreed upon, was that there was no increase in the CKD price. I had made this suggestion because I had seen in BHEL that price escalation formulas almost invariably resulted in annual increases in the price of imported inputs, and that improvements in productivity were all in favour of the producer.

SMC wanted to deal with the issue of exchange rate fluctuations, since the CKD price was expressed in dollars whereas costs in Japan were in yen. Suzuki suggested a formula which would result in both parties sharing the impact of a change in the dollar-yen rate. This provided that if the dollar remained in the 210-240 yen range, the dollar price would remain unchanged. However, if the yen weakened beyond 240 to the dollar, SMC and Maruti would share the gain. If it strengthened beyond 210 yen, there would be a 50-50 sharing of the loss.

This was to prove valuable in the long run. After the first two-three years, the yen strengthened very sharply against the dollar, even reaching the level of 80 for a short time. The result was that SMC's sale price, expressed in yen, started falling as the yen appreciated. Over the years, SMC received far less yen for a component than they had received in 1984. If the price of the CKD kit had been expressed in yen, or if this formula were not incorporated in the agreement, Maruti would have had to pay a much higher amount as the dollar price each year would have reflected the change in the exchange rate. Despite the obvious benefit to Maruti resulting from the sharing of the exchange risk, during 1995-97 the government frequently asserted that SMC was making enormous profits from the sale of CKD parts, whereas the fact was that it was making a loss. Calculations of the yen earnings for components, given by me, were just ignored by the bureaucracy.

After three months of tortuous negotiations, the agreements were finally ready to be processed. SMC had its own legal department while Maruti hired Delhi law firm J.B. Dadachanji. The law ministry also had to vet the agreement. A problem cropped up at that stage. An additional secretary in the ministry, apparently piqued at what he felt was my brusqueness, raised objections to some of the clauses. Time was running out and finally, law minister Ashoke Sen's intervention was sought. An early morning meeting was arranged between me and law ministry officials and the matter was sorted out.

Finally, at 12 p.m. on 2 October 1982, bang on deadline, two agreements got signed, with the government, SMC and Maruti being the signatories. One was a licence agreement on technology transfer between Maruti Udyog and SMC. The other was a joint venture between the Government of India and SMC. A third agreement was signed between SMC and Maruti and covered the sale and supply of CKD components for the ten years of the licence period.

A piquant problem arose after the signing ceremony. The agreement was to be toasted. But 2 October—Mahatma Gandhi's birth anniversary—was a dry day. Maruti, therefore, booked a suite at the public sector Ashoka Hotel and champagne bottles were somehow procured and duly uncorked.

It was a moment to celebrate. The people's car had finally been put on the road to realization. And it was also time to get down to work. There was little time to lose. A car had to roll out of the factory in exactly fourteen months.

3

GETTING STARTED

Anyone seeing the glitzy malls, the high-rise condominiums, plush housing colonies and steel-and-glass towers housing the India offices of some of the largest multinational companies would find it hard to believe that Gurgaon, a satellite town of Delhi and the epitome of new India, has a very ancient history.

Its origins can be traced to the time of the Mahabharata. It is said that the village was given by the Pandavas as gurudakshina (donation to a teacher) to Guru Dronacharya. Guru Gram got distorted over time to become Gurgaon.

It is also difficult to imagine that only twenty-eight years back, in 1981, Gurgaon was just a small town in the largely rural state of Haryana, set amid a flat, dusty and barren landscape. There was no industrial activity worth the name, with the Maruti factory Sanjay Gandhi had set up in the mid-1970s being the only prominent landmark. Agriculture too was nominal, since the area faced a serious water problem. Things started looking up for the small town only in the early 1980s when real estate developer K.P. Singh started buying tracts of land from impoverished villagers for his company, DLF, to build posh housing colonies. That was also around the time the public sector Maruti Udyog started operations and several automobile ancillary units started coming up in the vicinity. Today, the auto and auto component industry in Gurgaon and surrounding areas is larger than in any part of India, producing goods worth Rs. 28,000 crores. With close to 500 large and medium-sized factories and over 8,000 small-scale units, Gurgaon generates over 200,000 jobs a year and is the second highest contributor to Haryana's tax revenues, after the industrial town of Faridabad, on the south-eastern border of Delhi.

When Maruti Udyog was established, the site on which the by-now defunct factory that Sanjay Gandhi had built was overrun with weeds. When Suzuki first visited the factory, he was startled to find that the place was swarming with monkeys. Tongue firmly in cheek, I told him that the monkeys were there because Maruti was another name for Hanuman, the mythological monkey god, and the faithful servant of the god Rama! I explained to him that it would not be possible to kill or hurt the monkeys. They would go away on their own at the appropriate time. And this is exactly what happened. Hanuman was the son of the wind god and, though it is not clear if Sanjay Gandhi had this in mind when giving the name Maruti to his company, the name turned out to be appropriate for a 630 kg car that was to signify lightness and speed, in contrast to the ponderous, slow image of the 900 kg Ambassador and the 700 kg Premier Padmini.

The fact that the land and factory building of Sanjay Gandhi's Maruti was transferred to Maruti Udyog considerably reduced the difficulties in starting production by the end of 1983. Acquiring land is always a very difficult and time-consuming process, as the procedure often gets held up by court orders. While the location in Gurgaon was not ideal by any means, especially if Maruti was to export cars in the future, the proximity to Delhi and being on the national highway was a big advantage. There was also a sense of dismay when the building was inspected. It was literally coming apart at the seams. The roof was extremely weak. The concrete on any roof has to be supported by steel girders. What passed off for these girders in the factory were thin steel coils, similar to those used in parks to border flowerbeds and pathways, and often not welded together. Expansion joints (metal joints so that the roof doesn't crack when it expands in the heat) had not been provided in the roof. As a result, the RCC (reinforced cement concrete) roof had developed big cracks and leaked heavily whenever it rained, leaving those present wondering whether they were inside or outside. There was no proper provision for rain to drain off from the roof as the sloping was improperly done. The skylights had cracked and it was a minor miracle that the building was still standing. It was a clear case of professional negligence by those who had designed and constructed the factory building.

The project report had been prepared so that production of vehicles would start in October 1983, and sales from December 1983. In those three months, 192 vehicles would be produced and a little over 2,000 vehicles would be assembled up to March 1984. The first cars had to be produced from SKD (semi-knocked down) kits—that is, the entire painted body, along with most of the components, were imported from Japan, and these were assembled at the plant, using a very few Indian-made components. The general operation sequence of car manufacturing starts with huge steel coils being cut into rectangular sheets. These are then stamped in the press shop into the various parts that make up the outer car shell—the floor, bonnet, doors, roof, and the rear portion. These parts are then welded together in the welding lines to form the body in white. This name is given because at that stage the car shell looks like it is made of stainless steel. The welded body gets painted in the painting booths so that the car looks attractive, and is also protected from rusting. The painted body then goes to the assembly line where all the components, including the engine and the transmission, are fitted. At the end of the assembly line, the car is complete, and it is started and driven to the test area. Here it undergoes rigorous and exhaustive testing to ensure that there are no defects, including leakage of water, malfunctioning instruments, or any inadequacies in performance.

In the SMC system of project management, all the constituent shops of a car factory are not constructed simultaneously. In our case, the last stage—the car assembly and testing line—was set up first. After this had stabilized, it was followed by the paint and weld shops. When these shops were working well, the press shop was commissioned. The decoiling and slitting facility to handle the steel coils was the last to come up. The idea was to make sure that when any facility was commissioned, the downstream facility for using its output was already fully functional. That ensured that no capital expenditure incurred would remain unutilized for want of a downstream user facility. This approach to installation of capital equipment ensured that in Maruti there was no equipment installed that did not reach 100 per cent capacity utilization within six months or less of its installation.

Suzuki also decided that initially the production capacity to be installed would be 40,000 units a year, and it would be increased to 100,000 later. This was another example of how SMC reduced cost as underutilized equipment meant waste, especially in India, where interest costs were high. This concept of installing capital equipment in a step-by-step manner was not practised in India, especially in the public sector. The discussions about why SMC was following this system made engineers and managers aware of the cost of unutilized capital investments, and was an excellent start to inculcating a culture of cutting costs at all times.

Before the assembly- and testing-line equipments could be installed, it was necessary to undertake the civil and electrical works. The most critical obstacle was the condition of the roof. Not only had the heavy leakage to be stopped, but the roof itself had to be strengthened so that it would not collapse. On more than one occasion, wooden poles had to be used to shore up the roof, while repairs were carried out, so that portions of it would not fall down. It was a minor miracle that no serious mishap happened, though there were several narrow misses.

To advise on what could be done about the roof, a structural consultant, Dr Murthy, was hired from the Indian Institute of Technology, Delhi. After carrying out a study, he was clear that the roof could not take any additional weight. Stopping the leakage and the correction of the slope so that rainwater would flow to the drains could not be done using conventional technology or materials. One option was to remove the existing roof and re-erect it properly. The process would take two years to complete, and cost Rs. 16 crore. The time schedule did not permit this option to be seriously considered.

The other alternative was to first properly weld the steel supports and strengthen them to the extent possible. Thereafter, foam cement, which is light in weight, could be applied on the roof to seal the cracks and provide correct slopes for the water to drain out. Expansion joints could also be provided. These measures could be implemented much faster and would cost only about Rs. 1.91 crore. This option was accepted and work commenced at full speed. SMC engineers also visited the site in the searing May heat to supervise the work. They spent hours at the factory site and two of them fell ill. After that, a jeep with an icebox full of Thums Up would follow them all the time!

Work was slow because there were no plans, structural designs or calculations of the work done in Sanjay's time. That led to bizarre situations. While digging up the floor, in what was to be the paint shop, the labourers found a solid block of concrete under the floor. There was no indication of this existing, and no one could explain what it was for. It took a couple of weeks to break it up, and this delayed the schedule for completing the civil works.

Even after the repairs, the roof had no load-bearing capacity and, therefore, cranes and other load-bearing equipment could not be fixed on it. A separate steel structure had to be put up for this purpose. This was not the ideal way to build a car factory, but there was no other alternative.

The Maruti top management was clear about two things—all deadlines had to be met and there would be no compromise on the quality of the car. It wasn't an easy task, considering the problems and obstacles the company had to face. The economic environment of India in the 1980s was hardly business-friendly, even for the private sector. The public sector—to which Maruti belonged—was even more constrained, its hands tied by various laws, rules, regulations and procedures applicable to government companies. No concessions could be allowed in this respect, despite the fact that Maruti was being dealt with in a special manner. The management had to work within the system and yet introduce a work culture which would be radically different from that prevailing in government companies. Cost and time overruns just could not be allowed to occur. Employees had to become result-oriented and not cite compliance with procedure as an alibi to justify failure to meet targets. Continuous improvements in productivity and quality and recognizing the importance of customers had to become the way of life for all employees. This was the real challenge in the initial years of the company.

Krishnamurthy had been very successful in turning around BHEL and making it a highly profitable organization. BHEL produced equipment for generating and distributing electricity. Even though BHEL was perhaps the best-run government company, the State Electricity Boards, who were its customers, had numerous complaints about quality, delays in delivery and responsiveness of the company. The organization had multiple labour unions, all politically affiliated, and it would be hard to claim that workers were involved in making improvements to quality and productivity.

The challenges facing Krishnamurthy in Maruti were very different, and despite his reputation as a very capable manager, many people were sceptical about his ability to make Maruti a success. Manufacturing automobiles, and making Maruti profitable was a different ball game compared to BHEL, which had almost a total monopoly in providing power equipment, and more or less a captive market. State Electricity Boards had no choice but to place orders with BHEL. They did not have the option not to install generating capacity as the Five-Year Plans required them to do so. BHEL had only to produce equipment according to the Plan targets. On the other hand, cars were to be sold to individuals and there was competition from two well-established and politically powerful companies. Making good quality competitive cars would not be enough, as the market size for cars had also to be enlarged rapidly. A nationwide sales and service network was required and components had to be developed by hundreds of vendors. Japanese standards of quality had to be attained. This was a daunting task. But Krishnamurthy and I both had a strong motivation to succeed. Krishnamurthy had to uphold his reputation as being one of the best managers in India. I had topped in the 1956 batch of the IAS and was in a good position to become the Cabinet Secretary if I had stayed on in the government. If Maruti failed, all those who had advised against my leaving the IAS would have been proved right, and I would have thrown away a good, secure career.

It was one thing to be determined not to allow time and cost overruns and another to make this actually happen. The reasons for such overruns—an intrinsic part of projects executed by government companies—is not lack of competence on the part of the managers or a lack of will to achieve their targets. The problems faced in project execution are related to the systems which need to be followed and the fear of vigilance inquiries if procedures are circumvented in order to save time and cost. Often, the delays and cost overruns happen because the projects have not been prepared in a precise and knowledgeable manner. Maruti had an advantage in this area because the Japanese had a very good idea of costs of equipment and machinery, and the projects estimates were prepared in great detail. I also had over twenty-six years of working in the government and was very aware of how to manage the paperwork to ensure that there were no serious problems with audit and vigilance.

The project implementation schedule was prepared in great detail and the work to be done each week had been identified. It was still necessary to monitor progress and find a way of making up slippages if they did take place. Accordingly, Krishnamurthy formed a project review committee which he headed. This group of officers met every Tuesday from 9.15 a.m. till lunch, in the toolroom that once served as Sanjay Gandhi's office and was to become the hub of Maruti Udyog's activities in the initial months. Punctuality was stressed and the committee would start work exactly at 9.15 a.m. The workers also saw how strict management was on the issue of punctuality, and the message was not lost on them. The culture of adhering to deadlines and not allowing even a few hours of delay was inculcated through the working of this committee. Excuses were just not tolerated.

~

For almost a year after Maruti Udyog Ltd was formally incorporated, it functioned with minimum staff—the top management and some secretarial staff. Recruitments at the senior- and middle-management level started only after February-March 1982, when the choice of the collaborator had been almost made. Managers had, almost without exception, to come from the public sector or the government, since Maruti could not offer more than government-determined salaries for the public sector As a result, Maruti recruited several senior executives from BHEL, the Railways and other public sector undertakings. Recruitments for factory operations began after the joint venture was signed, though engineers were signed up earlier for the civil works, so that work on the factory building could start.

Maruti took a conscious decision that as far as possible, it would not hire people working with the car companies operating in India, because they would come with the baggage of the work culture in their organizations, something the management was very clear it didn't want. If the entrants to the company were new to car manufacturing, they could learn how to work according to SMC systems from the beginning. If engineers and managers were hired from Indian car companies, they would first need to unlearn their past experiences, and that itself would take time and cause problems. Thus Maruti opted largely for fresh engineering graduates, with a sprinkling of experienced persons from other automobile companies like Eicher Motors and Tata Motors, which were seen as being more professionally run. All persons at the executive level were interviewed by me before they were finally selected. Surprisingly, Maruti did hire a couple of persons from Scooters India, despite the performance of that company, and they did a good job in Maruti.

Public sector companies are seen by politicians as opportunities for providing employment to their supporters. In a country where jobs are fewer than those seeking employment, it is very difficult for any politician to refuse to recommend persons who come to them for help in finding employment. The more enlightened politicians would, however, tell the head of the public sector undertaking that while it was the minister's job to make recommendations, it was the job of the PSU to take decisions on merits and see that the company's interests were not hurt. However, it was expected that the person who came seeking a job or some other favour was made aware of the fact that the politician had spoken about him and that the recommendation would be given weight. Unfortunately, the number of such enlightened politicians has declined over the years.

The Maruti management was aware of this reality and worked on the principle that if the recommended candidate was as suitable for a job as any of the others, he would be preferred. At the same time, those making recruitment should not be given total discretion in making selections, as they would find it hard to resist pressure from politicians. Thus, it was decided to frame recruitment rules that minimized the element of discretion. It was decided that only first-class engineering graduates would be eligible to apply for the job of a graduate engineer trainee with Maruti. They would have to appear in a written examination, conducted by an outside agency, and only those who qualified would then be interviewed for final selection. Thus the discretion element was only with respect to those who came through the examination.

For workers, where the pressure was even more, it was prescribed that the minimum qualification would be a two-year trade certificate from an Industrial Training Institute. Such persons would again have to appear in a written examination, to be conducted by an outside agency, and those who cleared this would be interviewed. Later, when enough apprentices were passing out from Maruti, recruitment was limited to those who had done well as apprentices in the company. These recruitment rules were endorsed by SMC and Maruti could tell politicians that the Japanese would not allow relaxations in the system. The number of posts to be filled in each category was also approved by SMC. As a result, Maruti could recruit on merit, and also prevent overstaffing, the bane of most public sector companies.

Soon after Maruti started production, the Haryana government demanded that all recruitment of workers should be made from people living in the state, especially those from areas near the factory. However, Maruti argued that this was not possible as Maruti was a national project and it could not adopt a sons-of-the-soil recruitment policy. To its credit, Haryana did not insist on enforcing its stand. There was, however, pressure from the families of those whose land had been acquired when Sanjay started his project. Every effort was made to ensure that at least one member of each such family was given a job in Maruti. The problem lay in obtaining authentic records of whose land was acquired. Besides, in the period of about fifteen years since the time of the land acquisition, families had grown and split, and now each branch wanted employment. Over time, Maruti could work out a solution which satisfied everyone.

In terms of the recruitment policy, workers were mostly hired from within a 200 km radius of the factory, but this included states other than Haryana. Maruti also made a conscious effort to hire workers from other parts of India, including from the south and the west. Workers in Maruti actually come from all parts of the country. The first lot of supervisors and workers joined around April 1983.

Meanwhile, construction at the factory was proceeding rapidly and equipment had started arriving from Japan. Maruti had got special permission for customs clearance of the capital goods at the factory itself, so that they were not stuck in the ports for days, as was common. The first consignment consisting of components of the conveyor system—on which the cars moved as they were being assembled—arrived at the Chennai port and caused a bit of drama. A Maruti executive had been stationed at the port to receive it and he informed me that the container was on its way to the factory. Two days before it was to reach came the realization that the doors of the factory were too small for the 40-foot container. It was mid-December but Amitava Nandy, who was in charge of projects, and M.M. Singh, who was executive engineer, spent an entire night in the winter drizzle, shored up by a packed dinner from Nirula's restaurant in Connaught Place, over 30 km away, supervising the breaking of the wall to create a passage for the container.

~

As equipment started arriving, Maruti was faced with a serious problem of power supply. The plant needed 20 MW of power at full capacity. Power supply in Haryana was marked by frequent and long cuts and huge voltage fluctuations. Continuity of power supply was necessary in a car-manufacturing operation, especially in the paint shop. Steady and correct frequency was also essential as Maruti was using a lot of sensitive electronic equipment, having gone in for full computerization from day one—among the early companies to do so.

An arrangement was thought of under which the factory could have a second independent source of supply from the Delhi grid. This would mean a transmission line from Bijwasan on the Delhi-Haryana border. The Central Electricity Authority (CEA) sent a proposal to the Department of Power in the Ministry of Energy and a broad agreement was reached at a meeting in which representatives of the Delhi Electric Supply Undertaking (DESU) and the Haryana State Electricity Board (HSEB) were present. However, things didn't move and it was learnt that the secretary, Department of Power, did not approve the recommendations and sought further discussions with the CEA. It was later agreed that the factory would get the second line from the Badarpur Thermal Power Station, also in Delhi, to meet emergencies. Though this arrangement was implemented, the problem of fluctuating frequency remained, as it was common to the entire Northern Regional grid. Electronic equipment could not work on the grid and Maruti had to install a 5 MW capacity diesel generator to ensure uninterrupted power supply, with steady frequency. Suzuki was not happy at this additional cost, as the need for stand-by diesel generating sets was never felt in Japan.

This state of affairs continued for a little over two years. By then Delhi too was experiencing power shortages, and it was clear that the situation was likely to worsen over the years. Relying on the Badarpur plant for power, over the long term, was not going to be a good option, especially when power needs would increase with expansion of production capacity. The demand for cars was growing in a manner that it would have been unwise not to think of increasing production beyond the initial planned 100,000 units. It was also obvious that Maruti would not get priority over the needs of Delhi in being supplied power. Increasing diesel-generating capacity was one option, but a better one came by chance. In 1984, the public sector Gas Authority of India (GAIL) had been set up and Vineet Nayyar (who later moved to the private sector to play key roles in software giant HCL, and then Mahindra Technologies) was the first chairman and managing director. He too was from the IAS and a friend of mine.

One day, over lunch, Nayyar complained that GAIL had made investments in gas pipelines, primarily for fertilizer units, but these were not coming up. A great deal of gas would thus remain unsold and the pipelines underutilized. I immediately said Maruti would install gas turbines and enter into a long-term contract to take whatever gas could be made available. GAIL and Maruti engineers worked out that gas for generating 60 MW could be made available. In those days BHEL was able to supply 20 MW turbines and it was decided to install three of them in a phased manner. Suzuki agreed to this investment, recognizing the long-term benefit of having adequate power supply. Getting approvals of the concerned ministries took considerable time and effort, but ultimately the IAS network proved useful.

In May 1991, GAIL and Maruti signed a contract for half a million cubic feet of gas per day and Maruti put up the three gas turbines between December 1991 and December 1997. Multiple fuel capability was provided as, at times, the pipelines would be shut down for maintenance. This proved of considerable value, not only during the shutdown periods, which were comparatively small, but also in 2002, when supply was discontinued for a long period, as the gas was needed in Delhi for supplying the needs of commercial vehicles. The courts had decreed that commercial vehicles in Delhi should be all converted to CNG and there was a considerable shortage of gas till GAIL could arrange to increase supplies a year later.

Having so much captive power generation proved to be of immense value in the years ahead. The Gurgaon site, where originally a production of 100,000 vehicles was planned, was, twenty-five years later, in 2007, producing about 650,000 vehicles. This growth would not have been possible without our own supply of electricity. If diesel had been used for power generation, the cost would have been enormous, as oil prices increased over the years. Maruti could recently also move the aluminium foundry for the engine blocks from Manesar, which is a short distance away, to Gurgaon.

There was enough power for all of Maruti's needs as well as for the various joint ventures for components that had come up in the meantime within the factory complex. To maintain production in the Maruti factory, it was equally important that the vendors also maintained matching levels of production. The joint venture companies established by Maruti were being hampered by the inability of the Haryana grid to supply electricity. The HSEB had a long waiting list for companies seeking new power connections, and no priority was being given to the joint venture companies. If these JVs did not get power, and could not start production, it would have hampered Maruti's production. The obvious answer was to supply power to the joint venture companies from Maruti's own generation, but the HSEB objected to this, as the law in those days did not allow power from captive generation being sold. This law was designed to shield State Electricity Boards from competition and to preserve their monopoly position. In conditions of severe power shortages all over India, and the Boards being unable to increase generation adequately, the law was really against the interests of the national economy. Meanwhile, the problem was solved by Maruti establishing a subsidiary company and transferring the gas turbines to this subsidiary. Then the joint venture companies subscribed to the equity of the subsidiary, and so became part-owners of the gas turbines. Getting power from the gas turbines became legal.

Maruti had surplus power at night, because it worked for two shifts only, and HSEB wanted this surplus power. Maruti was willing to make supplies to the HSEB, provided it was assured of getting paid. A suggestion was made that the sale value of the power be adjusted against the Central sales tax that Maruti had to pay to the state government. However, the Haryana government did not agree, and said that taxes payable to the government could not be adjusted against dues of a statutory Board. HSEB assured Maruti that they would make regular payments but wanted the power to be supplied at the cost of generation. An arrangement on this basis was finalized in the interests of good relations with the Haryana government and worked quite satisfactorily.

~

While work on installing all the production facilities and developing vendors was going on, the marketing and sales system had also to be established. The first issue was the names for the various vehicles to be manufactured. In January 1983, Maruti's advertising agency—Rediffusion—suggested Legend or Aries for the car, Car-o-Van or Mascot for the van (Car-o-Van was to denote the multiple uses of the vehicle), Carry for the pick-up truck and Jimny for the proposed four-wheel drive vehicle (both these names were being used by SMC). There was considerable debate on these. However, it was finally decided, with the approval of the government, that the company's flagship product, the car, should be called 'Maruti 800'. This would help to build the Maruti brand, a name Sanjay had adopted. The van would be called the Maruti Van.

By then, Maruti had flown in ten vehicles of each model for marketing-related publicity. The cars had to be flown in to save time. We had to display the vehicles all over India, then invite customers to make bookings, do the computer allocation for determining the order of delivery, inform the customers of their priority and start sales by December 1983. Getting an import licence for these vehicles was not easy, since there would be a foreign exchange outgo. Though SMC agreed to supply these vehicles at a concessional price of around $2,000 each, still, with freight, the total bill would come to a little under $70,000, a large sum in those days. The Directorate General of Foreign Trade raised objections about why so many cars needed to be imported. In a reflection of the public sector mindset, no one thought marketing was a necessary activity. However, Maruti could convince the authorities that India was a big country, and it would be physically impossible to display one vehicle of each type in the major cities, within the limited time available, with a smaller number of vehicles. The import licence was issued. Roadshows were organized in different cities. Indian Oil agreed to become a partner of Maruti in these roadshows and made available their facilities. In turn, it became the supplier of lubricants and fuel to the factory.

The displays were held at different venues in various cities, varying from Indian Oil Corporation (IOC) petrol pumps to five-star hotels and parks. Young trainees recruited by us were deputed to present the cars to the public. Maruti got drivers from the Automobile Association of Upper India as well as from some dealers to drive the vehicles from place to place. The displays at each site lasted for about three days. I joined in many of these shows and held press conferences at some venues. Generally media reporting was extensive and we could get a great deal of free publicity for our vehicles.

At a press conference in Kolkata, sceptical journalists mocked that the Maruti 800 would disappear in the city's famed potholes during the rains! The following year, after the monsoons, at another press conference in Kolkata, I asked them what happened to the car. The journalists admitted that the Maruti 800 was the only car which could keep running even when the roads were flooded. They wanted to know why. The reason, I explained, was that the distributor in SMC vehicles was waterproof, whereas in the Ambassador and Premier Padmini water splashing from the road would enter the distributor and bring the car to a stop. After a heavy rainfall, it was quite usual to see large numbers of stalled cars on the road, with drivers desperately trying to dry the distributors.

For the roadshow in Srinagar, I flew from Delhi and went to the Raj Bhavan, the governor's residence, along with the young engineer in charge of the team, to show the cars to the governor, B.K. Nehru. The cars were supposed to be displayed the same evening at the plush Nedous Hotel in the city. Just before the display was to start, there was rain and strong winds and the whole arrangement of lights, placards and other paraphernalia went haywire. The engineers worked hard to put the show together. At the same time, I took on the role of a salesperson and explained the features of the vehicles to prospective customers. Later, at the suggestion of the local dealer, I directed the engineers to take the cars the next day to Sopore, famous for its apple orchards, where an impromptu roadshow was organized.

The interest from the public was enormous. This was the first time after several decades that people had seen any vehicle different from the Ambassador and the Premier Padmini. The finish and the paint quality were vastly superior to those vehicles, as were the fuel consumption and other performance data.

A few of the cars imported for the roadshow, not required by the engineering department and for vendor-component testing, were allotted for use by senior officers of Maruti. They evoked a lot of interest on the road. At every traffic light halt, people would stare and often come up to whoever was driving and ask questions about the car and when it was to hit the market. When V.K. Mathur, who had joined from the government as the general manager for projects, was driving one of these cars, he found awestruck occupants of a Mercedes staring and pointing at the car. N.D. Tiwari's first question on seeing the car, when Kapur took it to Udyog Bhavan, was, 'Where will you put the holdall?' The holdall carried the bedding and was in those days an intrinsic part of all travel, whether by road or train. He was shown the boot at the rear, but he felt it was too small. He suggested that provision be made for a luggage carrier atop the car, as was the case with other Indian cars. Maruti did develop a luggage carrier suitable for the car, but it never became popular. People started travelling without carrying their bedding!

~

The price of the vehicles was critical to increasing the total car market size to over 150,000 vehicles within five years, so that

Maruti could sell 100,000 vehicles. The IMRB survey had said that the demand for the small car would depend on its price, and had suggested that it should not be above Rs. 50,000. The project report had indicated that Maruti should try to market the car—which sold in Japan for the equivalent of about Rs. 20,000—at a little under Rs. 40,000. This was based on various market-related considerations. Most salaried people took loans to buy cars. Private companies did not give car loans of more than Rs. 40,000 to employees, while the government and public sector companies gave only Rs. 30,000. Given the cost of servicing loans in those days, and the salary of government employees, the project report had estimated that any amount over Rs. 30,000 would cast a high burden on most individuals, and adversely impact sale volumes. In addition, the cost of renovating and reconditioning old Ambassadors and Padminis was only Rs. 25,000. People could prefer that option to buying a significantly more expensive new car, as in fact was happening before Maruti came into existence.

Selling the car at Rs. 40,000 wouldn't have been too difficult, given the cost of production. The project report estimated that when the annual production reached 100,000 vehicles, the ex-factory cost of the car and van would be Rs. 32,423 and that of the pick-up truck Rs. 29,563. It suggested that the ex-factory sale price be fixed by adding 7 per cent profit to the cost of production of the vehicle in 1988, when the plant achieved full capacity. The excise duty would be extra.

At a board meeting on 2 March 1983 it was decided that the car and van would be priced at Rs. 45,000 and the pick-up truck at Rs. 43,000, inclusive of central excise, central sales tax and the dealer's margin. The final price for the customer would include actual transport costs, dealer's commission and local taxes. In arriving at this price, the board had looked at some international studies, which said a low-cost car would be considered affordable if the price was twelve times the average entry-level salary. The management stretched this to fifteen times and worked out the Rs. 45,000 figure on the basis of the average monthly salary of Rs. 3,000 of a Class I officer of the government.

The production cost of Rs. 32,423 had been arrived at by assuming an import duty of 25 per cent plus 5 per cent surcharge on the CKD components and a 40 per cent plus 5 per cent duty on capital goods. This was the rate of import duty then prevailing on specified components for commercial vehicles, required to be imported to enable manufacturers to increase production of these vehicles. The country had been experiencing a shortage of commercial vehicles and black marketing of vehicles was rampant. Thus increasing production of commercial vehicles was in the public interest, but the ability of the vehicle manufacturers to do so was limited by the production capacity of local vendors of some critical components. Importing these components was the only answer.

However, the import duty levied on automobile components, including car parts, was very high—over 120 per cent. This was because car components were not being imported to manufacture the Ambassador or the Premier. They had been fully indigenized. Components were being imported only for use as spare parts for the limited numbers of imported cars which were being used in India. These cars were often bought by the very rich at astronomical prices. Costly spare parts posed no hardship to them. On the other hand, a 120 per cent duty on imported components would considerably increase the cost of production of the commercial vehicles using them. The government recognized the need to differentiate between the components needed to produce commercial vehicles and those required for use as spare parts in costly imported cars.

Accordingly a 25 per cent import duty was fixed for the components to be actually used for commercial vehicle production. Maruti argued that the same logic should apply to the import of parts to be used for the production of its vehicles. At 120 per cent duty, no vehicle could be produced at a price which would sell in the market.

Krishnamurthy went to see the finance minister, Pranab Mukherjee, with two proposals—that the customs duty on imported components should be reduced to 25 per cent for the components to be used for production of vehicles, and that the excise duty should be 15 per cent. Earlier, Maruti had also proposed that customs duty on imported capital goods be waived, as this would bring down investment costs by Rs. 37 crore and reduce production costs by Rs. 740 per car when peak production of 100,000 cars was achieved. This proposal was rejected.

Mukherjee wanted to know on what basis Maruti was making that demand. Apart from referring to the same logic being behind the reduction of duty on components for commercial vehicles, it was explained to him that the car, being much more fuel efficient than what was available in India, would save petrol and thus foreign exchange. Further, without achieving volume sales, the objectives of nationalizing Maruti could not be achieved and the project would fail. Since the car was using new technology, it would take time to develop components locally, and so imports were necessary. Even the phased manufacturing policy (PMP) approved by the government recognized that five years were required to reach 92 per cent local content. It was also shown that in many countries, small cars attract lower excise duty. Maruti, on its part, would keep costs to the minimum as well as pass on any tax benefits to the consumer. Krishnamurthy asked what the government could do to keep the price at Rs. 45,000.

The arguments were accepted but an appropriate system to give effect to what was needed had to be evolved. An across-the-board cut on duties on the import of automobile components would have adversely affected government revenues, as spare parts for imported cars would also have got the benefit. There could also have been an adverse impact on the local automotive component industry, though this was unlikely, as import of components required an import licence. It was decided that the benefit of reduced import duties would be given for components to be used to manufacture vehicles which met specified standards of fuel efficiency. The logic was obvious. A lower customs duty was justified to attain savings in the consumption of imported fuel. The standards would be fixed by the government, and the Pune-based Automotive Research Association of India (ARAI) would test and certify if vehicles met these standards. The duty fixed for fuel-efficient cars was 40 per cent (25 per cent basic customs duty and 15 per cent special customs duty).

Hindustan Motors and Premier Automobiles cried foul and said the government was unduly favouring Maruti, only to be told that they could get the same concession if they also met the fuel-efficiency norms. In reality they were not importing components any way. Later they developed new models which met the fuel-efficiency norms and could thus avail of the lower duty. The system of linking customs duty with fuel-efficiency was given up in 1993. The excise on fuel-efficient cars was fixed at Rs. 5,906.25 per car till February 1986.

SMC felt the price of Rs. 45,000 would result in losses and wanted a higher price. Maruti, however, had worked out its strategy and done its calculations. The company expected to generate large funds from the scheme proposed for the advance booking of cars, by asking for a deposit of Rs. 10,000 per vehicle.

The customers would be paid 7 per cent interest on the deposit. Gupta and I had devised this scheme and Krishnamurthy had approved it. I explained to Suzuki that the money collected from bookings could be used for working capital requirements, doing away with the need to borrow at high interest rates. Moreover, the company could also invest surplus funds and earn interest. The scheme of taking a deposit for booking a car and mobilizing a large amount of cash was beyond anything SMC had ever experienced. It was used to selling cars in competitive markets and the idea of people paying 20 per cent of the price in advance and then waiting for years to get delivery appeared bizarre. They had not factored in the absence of any working capital or an enormous amount of interest income when preparing their estimates of the cost of production of cars in India. After some arguments, SMC accepted the price of Rs. 45,000.

The booking scheme generated about Rs. 140 crore, far more than what anyone had expected. The bulk of the money was invested in public sector undertakings—which agreed to pay close to 14 per cent interest—and a small amount with the Housing Development Finance Corporation (HDFC), which agreed to provide home loans to Maruti employees. Public sector companies were preferred over banks, not just because they gave higher interest on the deposits but also allowed Maruti to withdraw the money at short notice whenever it needed funds. One of the consequences of this system was that Maruti was a profitable company from the very first year of its incorporation while normally a car company takes three to four years to break even.

When sales started the ex-factory price of the car was fixed at Rs. 47,500, including excise duty of Rs. 5,906.25 per car. The customer price in Delhi, after including transport costs, dealers' margin and sales tax was Rs. 52,500. This price was maintained for nearly three years.

~

In March, the first lot of shop-floor employees—five supervisors for the assembly line—joined and were sent to Japan for training the very next month, after a week's lessons in basic Japanese. None of them had ever been abroad. I decided to talk to them about how to conduct themselves in Japan so that they created a good impression about Maruti.

I spent some time discussing the differences between the Japanese way of working and what we do in India. I particularly emphasized the importance of punctuality and hard work. I wanted to make sure that the training was effective through close monitoring. I received weekly written reports, and sent back guidelines and observations. In Japan, the trainees first learnt Japanese and then were familiarized with their industrial culture, before starting on the job training. It was an exciting time for them, being in a totally different environment and culture. The training was subsidized by the Japanese government under the Association of Overseas Technical Scholarships (AOTS).

SMC had, from the very beginning, emphasized the need for intensive training at all levels, if the objective of emulating its levels of productivity and quality was to be achieved. The Maruti management was repeatedly told that employees could not be expected to do their job correctly, and make improvements, if they were not educated on what to do and how to do. In many cases the lessons would need to be repeated and managers must have patience if an employee did not fully learn the first time. Taking disciplinary action, or threatening action against employees who made mistakes, would not yield results in the same manner as training and patience would. It had to be recognized that many of the workers were coming from an agricultural background and needed to learn a totally new culture. Most executives too would need to learn a new work culture and new practices. The help of AOTS was taken in order to reduce the burden of training costs. This Japanese government initiative proved extremely valuable in implementing, over many years, training for a large number of employees, and enabling Maruti to achieve high standards of productivity and quality.

All licence agreements provide for training in the factories of the licensor. The number of training man months is usually specified and the licensor charges an extra amount if more training is required. While the agreement with SMC had the usual clauses outlining training in its factories, the understanding was that it would accept a larger number of trainees without charging any extra money. SMC was aware of the foreign exchange situation of the government and how difficult it would be to get additional foreign exchange allotted for training.

Engineers, managers and supervisors were regularly sent for training in batches. Maruti had to obtain clearances from the government each time, as foreign currency was required. It was a constant tussle to convince the government of the value of training in Japan, since there was always the suspicion that Maruti was sending too many people for training, and often training was considered to be just a foreign junket. It was hard for people in the ministry to understand that changing a traditional work culture was an arduous task and could only happen through education and training. The fact that AOTS was meeting part of the training cost helped in persuading the government to release foreign currency. Close to 230 persons were sent to Japan for training during the first five years. The money spent on training gave a higher return than investment in any other facility. Unfortunately, not many investors in India give as much attention to training managers and workers as they should.

In 1988-89, it was decided that SMC would also accept workers for training. These workers would be deployed on SMC's production lines for a period of six months and would be paid wages. Selection of workers for training would be based on seniority and performance. Since going to Japan was a huge attraction for the workers, this scheme became a means of motivating workers to achieve higher standards of performance, so that they could qualify for selection. The employees' union also took interest to ensure that selection was made as objectively as possible. It was decided that selection of supervisors from the ranks of workers would be made from those who completed the training in Japan and did well. This scheme operated for fifteen years, during which time 979 workers went to Japan for training.

By the time the first batch of supervisors returned after three months' training around July 1983, the first SKD kits—painted panels—had arrived, packed in special plywood crates. The quality of the plywood was excellent and Maruti earned good money by its sale. The plywood later found its way into Delhi's markets for use in furnishings. Across Delhi, signs saying 'Maruti Ply sold here' sprang up.

With the arrival of the first kits, the supervisors now had to learn how to actually assemble cars. The tools used by SMC were all new to the Indian supervisors, who were only used to hand tools and had never handled sophisticated electronic and hydraulic instruments. The very first car was assembled by L.K. Gupta and his team of four supervisors in August 1983 in the toolroom. This was a training kit, which was to be promptly dismantled and assembled all over again. The car was to be driven by me at 8 a.m. The assembly was to be over by 6 p.m. the previous evening. However, progress was slow because of the lack of systems and this was the first experience of assembling. It was midnight when all the bolts were tightened, torqued and marked OK.

With a sense of satisfaction at having assembled the first car, Gupta cranked the vehicle to test it. It didn't start. They did not know what was wrong. It took them the whole night and the morning to find out that the carburettor had malfunctioned because of shipment by sea. In all, it took them seventy-two hours of work before I could drive the first vehicle. That experience highlighted the problems which could occur during sea shipment. Correctives were applied and the problem never recurred.

Even as training in assembling cars was going on, the doors of the factory were being modified. Dust is a perennial problem in Delhi and its surrounding areas, especially in summer, when dust storms are common. The Japanese, who didn't want a speck of dust on the shop floor, found the doors did not fit properly and would not keep the dust out. That amused many of the Maruti personnel, who wondered how one could avoid dust in India. The solution was to install air washers and to keep the air pressure inside the factory more than the pressure outside so dust would not come in. In addition, at every entrance there was a wet pit and employees had to walk through this so that the dust on their shoes would get cleaned. Caps had to be worn inside the shop floor so that dust and hair would not fall inside. These were all new practices and a good lesson in not assuming that a problem had no solution.

After training in manual assembly, the supervisors started

training on the assembly line. During the first few months, cars were assembled by being placed on trolleys, which were pushed from station to station—the normal practice in India then. The Japanese gave process sheets, which were placed at each of the forty workstations, explaining in detail what each person was required to do. All this was completely new to the Indian employees. It was not easy to make them accept the discipline of meticulously following the process sheets and not doing work according to their memory. Mistakes invariably happen when an employee thinks he has mastered his job and starts ignoring the laid-down process sheet.

After a few months, the conveyor system was installed, which avoided the need to push trolleys. Suzuki had agreed to the use of conveyors after a small spat. When SMC first made the layout for the factory, it was without a moving conveyor and the car shell would move on a trolley from station to station. For a cost-conscious SMC, this was an ideal way to keep capital cost low in a country with abundant supply of cheap labour. Even the project report had spoken about the trolley-based assembly till a production volume of 25,000 vehicles was reached. The project report had projected a production rate of over 25,000 cars from the second year. The high interest exhibited all over India in the car made it abundantly clear that demand would not be a constraint on achieving higher levels of production. Moreover, if the Japanese work culture was to be introduced, it could not be on the basis of old technology. So Krishnamurthy insisted that conveyor systems be introduced from the very start. The Japanese agreed to his views after some arguments.

That wasn't the only issue relating to manual versus automated equipment to be used. Another was about using multi-spot welding machines in the body shop, for the assembling of the underbody of the car, instead of the conventional equipment where a number of welders made one weld at a time. The underbody of a car goes through considerable wear and tear and a high level of reliability and accuracy in welding was important. However, the machine was expensive and Suzuki felt it would be cheaper to have fourteen welders instead of the machine. He was also not prepared to introduce welding robots at this stage. The Maruti management was keen that employees get exposed to the concepts of modern production technology right from the beginning. Suzuki argued that robots were not required when labour in India was cheap. He then made one of his rare mistakes by saying that the other two car manufacturers in India were not using this kind of advanced technology. Krishnamurthy immediately retorted that if the Maruti factory was to be like that of the other car manufacturers, then it didn't need SMC. 'Let us call the whole thing off,' he said. Modernizing the automobile industry and bringing in the latest technology into the country was one of the main reasons for getting a foreign collaborator for Maruti. Faced with such firmness, Suzuki had to step back.

During the commissioning of the project, I noticed an anomaly in the layout design in the Daifuku floor conveyor, which conveyed welded car bodies to the paint shop. The conveyor was installed on the floor and, because it was three feet high, it hindered operations and operator movement, affecting productivity. I spoke to our engineers. The maintenance head of the area, M.M. Singh, assisted by V.K. Arora, constituted a team which virtually redesigned and changed the whole concept and modified the equipment and reinstalled the imported conveyor system below the floor. This facilitated smooth operation.

In the first phase of the project in 1983, the civil and structural work and preparatory work for installation went on almost round the clock. The project team worked in close coordination with the Japanese equipment suppliers and their local contractors. Krishnamurthy would frequently visit the shop floor late in the evenings, arriving unannounced, and reviewing the progress directly with project engineers. He was always concerned about the well-being of the staff working on the shop floor and would invariably ask about their health.

One major challenge was to install the heavy vehicle inspection equipment, supplied by Anzen of Japan, in large pits in the floor. The Japanese were quite concerned about how this would be done. In the evening they went home, expecting to do the job next day. However, the contractors for the installation, Josts Engineering, employed a crack team of riggers from a particular region of Punjab headed by one Joga Singh. They completed the job by the skilful use of forklifts and rollers. When the Japanese returned the next morning and saw that the huge equipment was resting well in the pits, without any telltale signs of overhead slings, they enquired as to how it was accomplished. Before either K.S. Johar or V.K. Arora, who were the project leaders, could answer, Joga Singh saluted and announced: 'Sir, we brought huge blocks of ice and filled the pits with it, rolled the equipment on the ice. In the night, the ice melted and the machines went down and settled in the pit automatically, while we slept.' Everyone had a big laugh.

In October 1983, the weld shop had only a main body-assembling jig where all the sub-assemblies coming from SMC had to be assembled. It was not possible to make more than twenty bodies per shift. Our own technicians and supervisors made small modifications on the line, like adding more balancers for holding welding guns, and made a small sub-assembling jig. With this the production went up to forty-eight bodies per shift. This was one of the earliest instances of our engineers making improvements to enhance productivity and total production capacity. Such efforts eventually led to production reaching 140 per cent of installed capacity.

The side body was coming in an assembled state from SMC and would suffer many dents during transit. Two SMC persons taught our people how to repair them. Most of the tools used by the Japanese were given Indian names, with the small circular asbestos sheet used for controlling the spread of heat during repair named 'chapatti'. This led to our workmen getting more involved and they quickly learnt the work and became experts.

~

As compared to the Premier Padmini and the Ambassador, Maruti had got its pricing right. After the roadshows, where it had played up the fuel-efficiency angle, the company was confident of getting a good response from the public.

That was borne out by the bookings, which opened on 9 April 1983. By 8 June, total bookings crossed 135,000 vehicles, giving Maruti an assured market for three years and raking in over Rs. 133 crore. For Maruti, it was a vindication of sorts. Suzuki had been highly sceptical of the idea, wondering why anyone would pay such a huge deposit for a car that had not been manufactured. Foreign car manufacturers could perhaps not understand the kind of car-starved market India was in those days, when people had to wait for years to buy a car or even a scooter. 'This, more than anything else, has vindicated our judgement and decision to go in for the present product mix,' Krishnamurthy exulted in the first annual report of the company, 'we are now confident that the vehicles which we have selected for introduction in the Indian market best meet the requirements of the Indian consumer.'

When the booking scheme was devised it provided that the order of sale of cars would be determined using a computer-generated random number programme, designed by the information technology department of Maruti. Even well-educated Indians had no concept as to what this programme meant. Given the very high number of bookings, and the consequent premium that the cars were expected to command, senior mediapersons and others were certain that the delivery order would be manipulated. Transparency and objectivity in a public sector was not expected. However, the IT department had discussed the programme and convinced me that even they could not rig the programme. The order of delivery of cars to be generated was determined by the exact nanosecond when the key was pressed to start the programme. It was impossible for this to be controlled by anyone. Every time the key was depressed a totally different order of names would be generated.

A grand ceremony for the draw was organized on 17 September 1983 at the Hotel Maurya Sheraton. The vice-president, the late M. Hidayatullah, who was the chief guest, started the generation of numbers by pressing the 'Enter' key. When the lists appeared—a different one for each city—it was apparent that there was no rigging. No VIPs were at the top of the list in Delhi. An employee of Indian Airlines would get the first car. The credibility of Maruti—and of the allotment process—was established. Doubts were never expressed again when, in the future, new bookings were made and allotment lists prepared in the same manner.

The names of the allottees were sent to the dealers. Maruti prescribed a detailed sale process so that the allottees could be informed shortly before their cars were due for delivery and they could arrange funds and pay the dealer. Usually money was paid a couple of weeks before delivery took place. The benefit to dealers was that they did not need any working capital, and thus their costs were lowered. Maruti had to closely monitor the system to ensure that dealers followed the prescribed process and that no one jumped the queue. It had to be also ensured that dealers paid the interest due to the customer on his deposit money. Often some dealers neglected to do so and had to be pulled up.

Meanwhile, members of Parliament started demanding a separate quota for themselves, a demand that frequently surfaced in starred and unstarred questions as well as special mentions. The board rejected this demand when the heavy industries ministry wrote to it, but decided to keep a 5 per cent manufacturer's quota for allotment to customers in the commercial interests of the company, or where payment had been made in foreign currency, or for export, or to government organizations. Such special allotments were being made by other automobile manufacturers also. However, soon after this system was introduced, a non-governmental organization working on consumer issues, Common Cause, objected to this quota, but the board decided not to change its policy. In 1984, a writ was filed in the Supreme Court and the Court stayed the operation of the quota. One consequence of the writ was that I had to cancel a planned long weekend trip to Shimla. This was to be my first holiday after joining Maruti almost four years earlier. Instead, I had to go to Chennai to brief the Attorney General, so that a reply could be filed in court.

After several hearings, the Supreme Court, in 1986, allowed the use of a manufacturer's quota, but laid down detailed guidelines as to how cars were to be allotted from the quota. All the classes of persons who could be allotted cars from the quota were defined, as well as the number of cars for each category. The principle of first-come, first-served, in terms of eligible applications received for allotment of a car, was to be observed. The process became mechanical, and no discretion needed to be used. The benefit was that there was no pressure any more in the matter of allotting cars. The basic purpose of using the quota to promote the commercial interests of Maruti could, however, not be served. This was the first lesson in understanding that being a government company entailed court scrutiny of what private companies treat as normal commercial transactions. Later, Maruti was to realize that there were many areas where being a public sector undertaking created disadvantageous situations as compared to private companies.

The first car produced by Maruti was donated to Lord Venkateswara, the presiding deity at the Tirumala temple in Tirupati. The donation was not made by the company, as Maruti had already formulated a policy that it would not make donations to anyone. It was feared, not without reason, that if any donation was made, either in cash or in the form of a car, there would be endless demands and refusing them would create many enemies. It was easier to say that policy, framed at the instance of the Japanese, prohibited the company from making donations. The decision to donate a car to the deity at Tirupati was taken by vendors, dealers and employees, who paid for the car. The subsequent success of the company, and all those associated with it, showed that the humble offering pleased the gods!

~

The industry practice when Maruti started operations was that cars and other vehicles were driven from the factory to each dealership for being sold. Customers, therefore, never got a brand-new car but one that had seen some wear and tear after having been driven for varying distances, which could be as much as 2,000 km. Under the prescribed maintenance schedule, cars were required to undergo the first free service after 500-800 km and the lubricating oil had to be changed. This was important as in the initial running of the engine, the oil got contaminated rapidly. Technically, the warranty of a car could be cancelled if a customer did not get the vehicle serviced within the prescribed mileage. Yet, till Maruti changed the practice, the mileage for the first free service started after delivery! Cars were driven well beyond 800 km without any change of engine oil. The manufacturers just overlooked this. Clearly, this was technologically quite wrong and the engine would suffer some damage when cars ran for 2,000 km without an oil change. Additionally, the cars were often roughly handled by drivers and this also affected future performance of the cars. The icing on the cake was that the car manufacturers charged customers transportation costs which were more than what the companies were actually spending!

Among the first decisions the Maruti management took was to change this system and give customers brand-new cars. One of the options was to transport cars in railway wagons. This was quite common in the developed world. Special wagons were used for transporting cars, but such wagons did not exist in India. Maruti estimated that it would need around 200 special rail wagons to start with. It approached the Indian Railways, but the response was not very encouraging. The Railways took the stand that Maruti must pay for designing and building the special wagons and own them. The Railways would charge for the haulage of the wagons. The wagons would have to be designed by RITES, a public sector railways consultancy company. RITES indicated that it would take close to three years for the first lot of wagons to be made available, but the time could be shortened if Maruti compromised on the design. It was not considered feasible for RITES to buy the wagon design from a foreign country. The time schedule indicated was obviously unsuitable for Maruti's requirement of selling cars from December 1983. In addition, Maruti was wary about making any investment, since the Railways had not indicated the tariffs for transporting the cars through the special wagons, and were not willing to give any guarantees about wagon utilization or turnaround time. The movement of cars could not thus be planned and the customers would have no idea about when they would get their car. The entire approach was not very commercial and showed little concern for meeting the needs of a customer. The fact that this could be large business for the Railways was not appreciated. Besides this major risk, there were several other issues including the construction of a siding in the Maruti factory. It was clear that the option of using the Railways would have to wait.

The only option that remained was to move cars using road transporters. The quickest and easiest way was to get long-bodied trucks and convert them to load up to five cars in each. The design was worked out by Maruti. Transportation contractors were selected who would own the trucks, get them modified to carry cars and vans, and undertake the job of transporting them to the dealers. Dealers were encouraged to undertake the transport of their own cars, as it was felt that they would be better motivated to move the vehicles safely and quickly. At the same time, workshops which could do the job of converting the trucks into car carriers were identified. The conversion job had to be done on a priority basis as a large number of trucks were required and the need grew as production volumes increased. Maruti engineers were constantly chasing the contractors and the workshops to increase their productivity and output.

Facilities had to be designed and built, both in Maruti and at the workshop of each dealer, for loading and unloading the vehicles. The unloading had to be done at the workshop because after receipt of the vehicles, they had to undergo a pre-delivery inspection before being sold. Initially moveable ramps were used, but these would get damaged and slow down the process of unloading vehicles. The answer was to build permanent ramps. It was important to reduce the time for loading and unloading, and avoid damage to vehicles in the process. The shorter the turnaround time of the trucks at each end, the lower would be the costs, and more importantly, the trucks could do more trips. One of the tasks of the concerned department in Maruti was to monitor the journey time of the trucks and if there were delays, find the cause and apply correctives.

Damage to cars during transit was a problem that had to be tackled. One reason was bad driving habits, including over-speeding. Drivers had to be educated and, in some cases, fines had to be imposed on the transporter. Overhanging branches of trees on the highways were also found to be damaging cars and a wire mesh had to be put on top of the trucks to protect the cars.

The consignments were initially insured with general insurance companies. A few years later, as the extent of damage came down while the volume of cars being transported increased, Maruti calculated that it might be cheaper for the company to bear the cost of damage. This reduced the total cost of transport and created a further incentive for the company to monitor and reduce damage costs even more. External insurance did not create any such incentive within the company.

In the beginning, the trucks were returning empty. Soon other car and two-wheeler companies started using these trucks, wherever possible. It was not unusual to see trucks which carried Maruti cars coming back loaded with Bajaj scooters or Premier cars. The transporters also started to carry steel or other commodities on the return journey. However, Maruti had to ensure that the attempt to get return cargo did not result in the trip time becoming longer than what could be accepted.

Maruti continued to look for better ways of transporting vehicles. One option was to use tractor-trailers, which are used to carry forty-foot containers. They needed to be modified, so that they could carry seven or eight cars. No design for such a vehicle was available in India. In any case, there was need to customize the car carrier to suit the dimensions of the vehicles Maruti was manufacturing. An Indian structural engineer, K. Rangaswami, who had been working in the United States for many years and had decided to come back to India, offered to design trailers to carry the cars. He worked on a contract basis, with a success fee. He did an excellent job, and Maruti started using trailers designed by him in 1984.

The option of using the railways came up again after a few years. By then the railways was facing the heat of competition from road transport, and was trying to become more commercial in its working. By sheer chance a college mate of mine was appointed as head of commercial operations in Northern Railway. He telephoned me to discuss the transport of cars by rail. During discussions it emerged that the railways had old passenger coaches that were no longer fit for their designated use. These could be modified and used for carrying cars. The book value of these coaches was zero and only a small amount of money was needed for carrying out the modifications. Maruti now had a benchmark of costs and insisted that the per car cost of transport should be competitive with road transport. It took some time for the bosses in the Railway Board to agree, but finally this mode of transport also became operational.

The problem of wagons sorted out, it was now time to press for a dedicated railway siding. Maruti had been loading its cars from the Delhi Cantonment railway station, 10 km away from its factory. The cars had to be driven there and this was complicated by the presence of a powerful driver's union in Gurgaon. The union had strong political backing and charged very high rates because of its monopoly position. Drivers who were not members of the union were not allowed to operate. After considerable efforts Maruti could get a dedicated siding at Gurgaon itself, which saved cost and damage to cars.

As the start-up deadline neared, pressure increased on everyone. One October day in the factory, Krishnamurthy and I handed out promotion letters, one of them to Nandy. Half an hour later, feeling on top of the world, Nandy encountered Krishnamurthy in the corridor. Krishnamurthy took him to a corner and said, 'Your project is delayed. If you feel you can't do it, hand over your resignation letter and I will relieve you immediately.' The assembly of cars was behind schedule because the testing line, on which cars are tested after they come off the conveyor belt, was getting delayed for want of a good electrician. Nandy knew that apart from the why of a problem, we also wanted to know how it could it solved. More than that, we just wanted it solved.

Nandy then went to Gurgaon town, found five electricians and tested them at the factory. He found one whose work was satisfactory and he was put on the job, with Anzen Electricals, the electrical contractor, helping him out. The man later became Maruti's main electrical contractor. The assembly line was completed and on 19 November the first car to be assembled on the line rolled out. It was Indira Gandhi's birthday, a fact Krishnamurthy made sure to mention when she came to launch the first cars on 14 December 1983.

Before the assembly of cars could start, Maruti's employees understood what Japanese work culture really meant. A. Shinohara, who was the director production, would not allow the assembly line to start unless all the equipment and the shop floor were absolutely clean. A lot of dirt had accumulated during the process of erecting the equipment. Initially Maruti employees thought that sweepers would do the cleaning. But in Japan there are no sweepers and everyone does his own cleaning. Shinohara picked up a broom and a bucket of water and started cleaning the shop floor! Maruti employees could hardly refuse to do the same. For the next ten days the cleaning work continued, with Shinohara as the leader. Assembly operations started when he was fully satisfied. He explained to all that the first requirement for quality work is absolute cleanliness and each person must keep his work area clean. The same principle was extended to the offices. The lesson was well learnt and when Krishnamurthy or I saw a nut or a piece of paper on the shop floor, we would pick it up. With cleanliness in mind, designated areas were provided where tea and snacks were served. No food could be taken outside these areas. Of course, smoking was a big no-no inside the factory. Nobody was even allowed to bring in a matchbox because of the many highly inflammable materials inside a car factory.

~

With the message going out loud and clear that no delays or sloppiness would be tolerated, there was little evidence of slackness. The sacrosanct deadline was finally met. On 14

December 1983, Sanjay Gandhi's birth anniversary, Mrs Gandhi formally inaugurated the factory. It was the first time she was stepping into the factory; she had seen it from outside just once. In a voice choked with emotion she said: 'This small car has a very long story.' She went on to describe Sanjay's dream of building small cars and all the efforts he made and hardships he endured in trying to make his dream a reality.

She pressed the button that started the assembly line and the first car for sale rolled out. She personally gave the keys to the first ten allottees of cars from all over India, the first being Harpal Singh of Indian Airlines.

4

CAPTURING THE MARKET

Along with Harpal Singh, close to 800 customers in Delhi and Mumbai also became proud owners of India's first modern car. Initially, sales were restricted to these two cities, but by March 1984, they had been extended to Kolkata, Chennai and Chandigarh, practically exhausting the first year's production of 852 cars. The response was enthusiastic. Suddenly, a car became a much more affordable symbol of upward mobility. The 800, in some respects, became both a status symbol and a social leveller, as it was found parked both outside the cramped houses of grocery shopowners in congested localities as well as the driveways of industrialists. It also led to a new sense of freedom for women. The wife of one big industrialist told me that now she could move around on her own, whereas earlier she always had to rely on a driver. The Ambassador and the Padmini were not so easy to drive, and there were always some questions about their reliability on the road. As time elapsed more and more women started to drive themselves, as the 800 gave them the confidence that the car would not have problems.

The demand was huge, and the pressure to increase production was immense. There was a large premium on the car and despite Maruti's efforts to ensure that there was no black marketing, there were many complaints of this happening. The sales system adopted by Maruti insulated the company from allegations of sharing the premium, as cars were made available to customers in accordance with the computerized delivery list. Nevertheless, it was not a happy situation, and the management realized that the only answer was to increase output. Within a few months of starting production, the factory was rolling out a hundred cars a day. 'Such a rapid rate of build-up of production is unprecedented in the Indian automobile industry,' Krishnamurthy exulted in the first annual report for 1983-84. The two private sector car companies, even after being in existence for over thirty years, had not exceeded a combined production of about 130-140 cars a day. Better still, the company was also able to generate profit from the first year itself—a good Rs. 1.7 crore—though the project report, approved by the government and SMC, had projected losses up to 1987-88. Car production is capital intensive, and companies break even only after about three years. Maruti was able to make profits because of the interest earning on the Rs. 133 crore of booking deposits, and the absence of any working capital borrowing. This interest income helped to meet the higher cost of production, mainly due to a stronger dollar, which pushed up the cost of importing the CKD kits and steel.

While the efforts to rapidly increase the production of the 800 were in full swing, preparations were also going ahead to ensure that the van was launched by the scheduled date of December 1984. This meant developing and homologating (testing to see if the vehicles conform to various local regulations and then certifying for sale) a whole lot of components which were different from those used in the 800. New dies had to be procured, and a separate welding line installed for putting together the white body of the van. The painting line for the car and the van was common, but a new assembly line was also needed for the latter. Thus civil works, equipment procurement and installation and training of workers had to be carried out along with assembling the 800. SMC was well versed in such activities and ensured that both sets of activity proceeded as scheduled. The van was launched by N.D. Tiwari on 14 December 1984, exactly a year after the 800.

Within months of the launch of the 800, the company came to know that SMC was introducing a new model of this car (SS80) in Japan towards the end of 1984. This new model had not been in production when the collaboration was being negotiated. This was not surprising, as models are frequently changed in competitive markets. However, when the specifications of the new model were studied, it was found that while all the external dimensions remained the same (as they had to meet the law which gave concessions to small cars in Japan) clever design had created a larger cabin space and more legroom for the passengers in the rear seat. Krishnamurthy and I were convinced that this extra space would greatly enhance the long-term acceptability of the car for the Indian users, and felt that SMC should be persuaded to manufacture the new model in India.

In June 1984, Krishnamurthy made a presentation to the board and sought a decision on whether to switch to the new model. The issue was that Maruti and the vendors had already spent a substantial amount of money on the tooling for the old model as well as for its components. Since some of the components of the new model would be different, those vendors would have to write off the cost of the tooling and Maruti would have to compensate them. A quick decision was needed so that the appropriate press dies could be ordered. The board voted in favour of changing the model and Krishnamurthy left for Japan, along with the director production, to discuss this matter with Suzuki.

However, the response in Japan was not very enthusiastic. Suzuki did not want the model to be changed, not only because of the need to write off investments made by Maruti, but also because it would require SMC to again prepare and send all the documents for the transfer of technology. This would be a great deal of additional work. In addition, there would certainly be some delay in the localization of components. However, Krishnamurthy explained at length why the new model was much more suitable for Indian needs and that its introduction would enable Maruti to increase market share rapidly. He also very forcefully stressed the importance of Maruti products being technologically as up to date as possible, since this was a national project. He took a firm line, banging on Suzuki's table to stress his point that Maruti did not enter into the collaboration to produce old models. As in the case of the conveyor for the assembly line, and the multi-spot welding machine, Maruti's firmness paid off. Suzuki agreed to introduce the new model of the car, appreciating the long-term benefit to the company from having a better product. Once the decision was taken, SMC worked overtime to speed up the process and the first new model car was sold in June 1986. By that time the car was priced much higher, at Rs. 63,900, due to an increase in taxes and input costs.

The customers who had booked for the old model retained their priority for the new model. In September 1986, fresh bookings were invited for the new 800, as the old list was running out. So high was the acceptance of the car that 157,000 people booked for it despite restrictions being imposed on the number of bookings a customer could make, and knowing that delivery of the car could take a long time. This response convinced even the diehard sceptics that Maruti was going to be a success, even as a government company. Component makers realized that becoming a supplier to Maruti would give them volumes never thought possible, and it was a business opportunity of a lifetime. Becoming a Maruti dealer became an even more attractive opportunity and the pressure for becoming a dealer increased manifold.

Maruti was called upon to take a difficult decision soon after the first bookings had been made. The pick-up truck, a purely commercial vehicle that was part of the original project along with the 800 and the van, got a very poor response—bookings of just 2,000. In the project report, the pick-up truck was expected to account for 20 per cent of total production. The booking response showed that the customers did not want this vehicle, and manufacturing it in small volumes would not be viable. The company realized it had made a serious error of judgement in not recognizing that petrol-driven commercial vehicles could never compete with diesel-driven ones, as the government-determined price of diesel was much lower than petrol. SMC had estimated that the pick-up truck would be very successful because of good experience in other Asian countries. In Pakistan, it was used for rural transport, after being fitted with a canvas top, and sold in large numbers. However, India had a vehicle called the Tempo, which carried a load slightly more than the pick-up truck and ran on diesel. The highly value-conscious Indian customers immediately realized that the pick-up truck would always lose out to the Tempo, because of the Tempo's lower operating costs. Realizing that the truck would be a failure, Maruti decided to drop its production and to write off the costs incurred till then in tooling and other related activities. This experience was a reminder to Maruti on the importance of correctly assessing the behaviour of Indian customers, and the dangers of transferring experience of other countries to India, without careful examination.

~

In December 1984, exactly a year after the 800 was launched, Maruti rolled out its van. There were two versions—one with a high roof and the other with a flat roof. The high-roof van, it was thought, would be particularly useful for those who wanted to use the vehicle both for carrying passengers as well as for commercial use. In Japan, for example, dry-cleaners and florists used it for making home deliveries. It was hoped that such usage would also develop in India. These expectations were not fulfilled to the extent hoped. Maruti also tried to popularize the van for carrying children to school and a version was developed for this purpose.

After a good initial response, the sale of the vans started to drop. One reason was that the vehicle did not have an engine in front, but it was placed under the front seats. As a result, the van had a flat front, instead of a bonnet like most cars. The driver and front-seat passenger were unhappy at there being no buffer for them in case of a collision. Accidents did occur, and it was seen that the vehicle was no more dangerous than cars and over time, this feeling of insecurity faded away. The van also tended to overturn if corners were taken at high speeds. This was more likely to happen with the high roof version than the flat-roof model. Maruti had to educate drivers that the van did have a higher centre of gravity, and hence it was important to take corners at lower speeds.

With sales of the van remaining below expectations, Maruti asked its advertising agency, Rediffusion, to rework the marketing strategy in 1988. A market survey done by Rediffusion showed that many potential customers thought that owning a vehicle which was being primarily projected for commercial use was infra dig. The name itself had a commercial connotation. Rediffusion recommended that the vehicle be repositioned as a car which provided maximum space at minimum cost. This approach was accepted. In December 1987, the vehicle's name was changed to 'Omni' and it was widely advertised as the most economical and spacious passenger vehicle in the market. The advertising campaign concentrated on the space it provided for people and baggage as well as its suitability for weekend travel. The campaign also focussed on dispelling myths about the safety of the vehicle. The new pitch worked and sales rose 21 per cent the very next year. The advertising campaign became a national-award winner. However, production of the high-roof version was given up, as the demand for this version remained very low.

In 1990-91 Omni sales suddenly dipped by 4 per cent, followed by another 9 per cent in 1991-92. This time it was found that the users were not finding the rear seat comfortable enough, and the suspension also needed improvement. Maruti carried out the required changes, using its own engineering team. In addition, with the help of SMC, it modified the carburettor to improve the fuel efficiency of the car. The result was something the customers liked and there was again a surge in sales. The Omni has continued to be a popular vehicle till now.

This maiden attempt by Maruti to make changes to designs given by SMC, and the success in the market, generated a great deal of confidence among its engineers. They became willing to take on more challenging tasks. This was reflected in Maruti deciding to try and adapt the 800 to meet European specifications, and then getting it homologated for sale in France and other countries. At that point SMC did not have the resources to allocate for this work, and also felt that the emission standards might not be met using a carburettor.

~

Meanwhile, the operating environment in India was getting more difficult. Expenditure on raw materials and components increased substantially. There was a 55 per cent rise in the cost of steel in 1984, while the prices of tyres and other components also rose, as did the import bill thanks to the strengthening of the yen against the dollar, and the weakening of the rupee against all currencies.

The automobile sector was also getting its first whiff of liberalization. It had started around the time of Maruti's nationalization, when the government allowed foreign collaborations for light commercial vehicles. In 1983, the government had approved the tie-ups of Delhi-based DCM with Toyota, and Eicher Goodearth with Mitsubishi, and a year later of Chandigarh-based Swaraj Vehicles with Mazda Motor Corporation and Allwyn, a Andhra Pradesh government-owned company, with Nissan Motors.

In 1985-86, its second year of production, Maruti produced 52,000 vehicles, which was a number higher than the combined production of Hindustan Motors and Premier Automobiles. However, these companies were not sitting idle. Both had started gearing up for competition in 1983 itself. As a first step, they had lobbied against the excise and customs concessions proposed for Maruti on fuel-efficiency norms. The Association of Indian Automobile Industry (AIAM)* made several representations that the concessions should not be restricted to cars below 1000 cc but be given to all fuel-efficient cars (the Fiat and Ambassador had 1100 cc and 1400 cc engines respectively). The government finally conceded the point and extended the benefits to cars above 1000 cc.

In 1983, both Hindustan Motors and Premier Automobiles announced plans for manufacturing fuel-efficient cars with modern body styling.† Hindustan Motors started work on the Hindustan Contessa, collaborating with Vauxhall Motors for the body and Isuzu Motors for the engine. The Contessa had a body larger and heavier than the Ambassador, and Hindustan Motors first introduced it with the same engine as the Ambassador. This was a big mistake, as the car was underpowered, and it was not well accepted. Later, when the much more powerful Isuzu engine was mounted, the company had a hard time overcoming the reputation which the Contessa had acquired. The lesson was that a vehicle should be built right the first time, and make-do solutions do not work. Premier Automobiles, for its part, tied up with Nissan for the NE-118, and increased its licensed capacity from 18,000 cars to 28,600 in 1984. This car was a very old model, and was introduced probably because the investment required was low. The market response was lukewarm. At about the same time, Standard Motors decided to introduce a 2000 cc car from the British firm, Rover. There were great expectations from the car, which was expensive, but it flopped. Here too the car used an old engine, and its performance was not anything like that of the Rover cars in the international market. Indian customers were disappointed,

---

*Now known as the Society of Indian Automobile Industry.

†AIAM Annual Reports, 1983, 1984.

and the message conveyed to manufacturers was that they wanted technology which was up to date and relevant to Indian conditions.

The same message came out loud and clear in the success of the two-wheeler manufacturer, Hero Honda. Bajaj Automobiles Limited had for a long time enjoyed a virtual monopoly in the scooter segment, and its products had a long waiting period. BAL had obtained technology from Vespa in Italy in 1960, and though they brought in other models and variants, the top-selling scooter with a two-stroke engine was still based on the Vespa technology long after the licence expired in 1977. Hero Honda, established in 1984, introduced four-stroke engine motorcycles in 1985, and the market gradually switched from the old technology scooters to the much more fuel efficient and cleaner motorcycles. Hero Honda overtook Bajaj in terms of sales volumes and became the largest two-wheeler company in India. The market had voted against old technology. The fortunes of Bajaj revived only after it introduced a contemporary motorcycle based on technology from Kawasaki. It seemed as if scooters were on the way out, till Honda Scooters Limited introduced scooters with the latest design and technology. Honda scooters have been selling very well.

Early in 1985, the government announced the policy of broadbanding of licences, under which vehicle manufacturers could rework their licences hitherto given for specific products (scooters, light motorcycles, heavy motorcycles, cars, jeeps) to cover an entire category (for example, two-wheelers and four-wheelers) and firms were free to choose the mix of products in each category. This was perhaps the first loosening of the draconian licence system. That year, several manufacturers, hoping to take advantage of broadbanding, sought permission for technical collaborations for new cars, pick-up vans and

LCVs.* A year later, both Hindustan Motors and Premier Automobiles increased their licensed capacities—the former from 30,000 to 50,000 and the latter from 28,600 to 50,000.

~

Even as other companies were gearing up for new products, Maruti launched SMC's four-wheel drive vehicle in December 1985. The vehicle was called the Gypsy, to signify its ability to go anywhere and freely roam around, despite SMC's reservations on the name. In Europe, the word gypsy carried somewhat negative connotations. The Prime Minister, Rajiv Gandhi, came to the factory to give away the keys of the first few vehicles. He himself owned a Gypsy and loved to drive it, often heading off on his own, to the dismay of security personnel.

The Gypsy was the first modern four-wheel drive vehicle in the Indian market. Till then, Indian roads only saw jeeps, which were of World War II vintage, and were manufactured by Mumbai-based Mahindra and Mahindra (M&M). They were noisy and expensive to run, but had a monopoly of sales to the government. They were used by the Army, paramilitary forces, police as well as all the field departments of Central and state governments. Maruti decided to cut into this market.

Among the early successes it had was with the Delhi Police. Ved Marwah was the police commissioner and had been given a mandate to improve the efficiency of the force. He wanted to reduce the response time of the police to any complaint and realized that this could be done only if the police force had faster and more reliable vehicles. The jeeps currently in use were just not suited to the purpose. He got interested in the

*AIAM Annual Report 1985.

Gypsy and came to see me in my office. When he made the proposal for a bulk order of Gypsys, I was naturally thrilled and agreed immediately. He faced some roadblocks in the home ministry, where there was a strong lobby rooting for the jeeps that were already in use. However, he got his way and the ubiquitous Delhi Police Gypsys roaming around the Capital's roads have been a familiar sight since then.

The advantages of the Gypsy over the Jeep were obvious. Nevertheless, Maruti realized that selling the vehicle to governments and displacing M&M would be tough. Thus, it was decided to market the vehicle aggressively and build a strong brand image. The advertisements focussed on its versatility, reliability and performance in all terrains. 'Imagine long drives in wild, bumpy and treacherous conditions being described as comfy', said one advertisement, with a picture of a Gypsy splashing through a water body in a verdant countryside setting. The Gypsy was used by an Army-sponsored expedition and driven from Leh in Ladakh to the northeastern states. Articles were written about the Gypsy and its ability to perform in adverse conditions in the media. The vehicle was entered in the Himalayan car rally, and performed extremely well.

There was a small market for the vehicle from the private sector as well. Construction companies and those offering adventure tourism started to use the Gypsy. Some individuals also bought the Gypsy for travelling to their farms or for use as a sports vehicle. The Gypsys from SMC came with a canvas top and were not air-conditioned. Soon there was a demand for a hardtop as well as air-conditioning. The class of people wanting to use a Gypsy for personal driving were not willing to do so without air-conditioning. While fitting an air-conditioner was not difficult, the effectiveness of cooling in the soft top was inadequate. A hard top was really essential for increasing sales.

Maruti developed vendors for the hard top. These were produced by a hand-moulding process, and production was slow and not of very good quality. Customer acceptability was not very high. SMC did not have technology for a mechanized way of producing a hard top for the Gypsy, and all attempts to develop such a process in India proved unacceptable. This remained one of the reasons why Gypsy sales could not be increased.

Maruti offered the Gypsy to the army, in replacement to the Jeep and the Jonga, a vehicle produced in a government factory in Jabalpur, but using obsolete technology. The Gypsy underwent rigorous testing by user formations in high altitudes, extreme cold and in the desert in summer months. Those using the Gypsy were very happy with it and found performance and reliability superior to the Jeep. The next, and what proved to be a much harder step, was to actually sell and deliver the vehicle to the army, where purchases were all made through a specialized section of the Army Supply Corps.

The first purchase order from the army for 900 canvas-topped Gypsies came in January 1991 and the vehicles were to be delivered before 31 March of that year. Maruti manufactured the vehicles and they were parked for inspection in the factory. Army rules required that each vehicle be inspected by their own inspectors. The inspecting team would check only seven or eight vehicles in a day. It was obviously impossible to complete inspection of 900 vehicles in the time available. The inspection agency would not accept our submission that the vehicles were mass produced, following a well-documented system for quality control, and that sample checking should be adequate. They would also generally not accept Maruti's explanation that what were being pointed out as defects were not really defects.

As was foreseen, the delivery date expired before the bulk of the vehicles had been inspected. Once that happened, inspections stopped. The purchase order had to be revalidated before the remaining vehicles could be inspected. The process of revalidation took another nine to ten months. In the meantime, the vehicles were standing in the open in the factory, braving the elements. The system was not concerned about the consequences.

K. Kumar made several visits to the army headquarters and met officers at various levels, to explain the Maruti-SMC system for ensuring uniformity of quality and adherence to specifications. He pleaded for expediting the process of inspection, but in vain. Kumar and I then met Lt. Gen. M.S. Bhullar, who was director general quality assurance in the army, and pointed out that exposure to the sun and rain would damage the vehicles and neither Maruti nor the army was gaining by rigidly following tortuous government procedures. Quality, I argued, was produced, not inspected and suggested that the army work out some less cumbersome methods of inspection. But the army was not willing to accept this point of view. After this experience, sale of Gypsys to the army came to a virtual stop. However, a new customer was found in the air force. Though part of the same government, and subject to the same rules, we encountered no problems in making sales, or during the inspection process.

It was only several years later that Maruti could evolve a system of making sales to the army. In 1995, the company had taken ISO certification and around 1998, convinced the army to let it go for self-certification. The army inspection then was confined to random checks on 10 or 15 vehicles and could be managed.

~

Meanwhile, there were new problems. The 1986-87 Union Budget increased excise duties on all vehicles from 20 per cent to 25 per cent and the customs duty on components from 45 per cent to 50 per cent. The additional tax burden came on top of the continued strengthening of the dollar and the yen against the rupee—the yen alone by 22 per cent—raising prices of raw materials and components as well as of the controlled prices of steel and power.* As a result, after holding the price line for four years, Maruti had to increase the prices of its cars. The impact of this was felt only the following year. The growth of the automobile market slowed down.

Despite this, 1986-87 was a landmark year for Maruti, not only because of the unveiling of the new 800 cc car. For the first time, it sold more cars—74,511—than other passenger car manufacturers put together, who managed only 51,383 cars. Maruti had clearly won the battle, and it kept increasing its lead thereafter. All the major investments envisaged in the original project were completed and the factory was now set to manufacture its mandated 100,000 vehicles. In 1987, SMC exercised its option to increase its stake in the company to 40 per cent, as stated in the original joint venture agreement. It was, in a sense, an affirmation of the fact that Suzuki had got over its initial reservations about investing large amounts of money in India and in a public sector company. Increasing equity was a vote of confidence in the Indian economy, and the future of Maruti. This year was also significant because the four-year-old Maruti set its ambitious sights on foreign markets. Although the project report had talked about exports—indeed, in the original terms for collaboration there was a 50 per cent export target—nobody really believed this was possible.

~

*AIAM Annual Report 1986, Maruti Udyog Ltd Annual Report, 1986-87.

On the face of it, the idea was bizarre—India was hardly known for exports of sophisticated engineering products those days. But I had two reasons for pushing for exports.

First, of course, was the need to earn foreign exchange. Maruti was attracting brickbats for being a huge foreign exchange guzzler and it was necessary to soften the criticism by earning dollars. Having a special quota for making out-of-turn car allotments for those who could pay in foreign exchange was also driven by the same consideration.

But a far more important reason related to creating a more customer-oriented and quality-conscious work culture in Maruti. I saw exports as a way of benchmarking the company's performance against international standards and exposing it to competition. By then the total dominance of Maruti in the domestic market was established and it was clear that there would be no real domestic competition. The demand-supply gap in the car market had still not been bridged. As a result, dealers were more like distributors than sales agents. The consumers, never having been earlier exposed to international standards of quality and service, did not have high expectations. Maruti was being praised for the quality of its vehicles and customer service. I recognized that we really had a long way to go before we could compare ourselves with international manufacturers, and the danger of complacency setting in at Maruti was very high. I believed that exporting cars to the western world would help Maruti improve its own performance and standards, since we would be receiving feedback and criticism from really competitive markets.

Krishnamurthy, as the non-executive chairman, was not very enthusiastic and cautioned me of the risks attendant on exporting cars. The profits would be small, whereas all the cars that Maruti could produce could be sold much more profitably in the domestic market. Further we could damage our reputation in international markets if we fell below the minimum standards of acceptability. But I felt that the learning experience and the confidence that dealing with global markets would bring would stand the company in good stead in the long term, and be worth the money spent. There was strong support from Dr Kumar and his team, and that helped mc in deciding to take up the challenge.

East Europe (most of the countries in that region then belonged to the erstwhile Soviet Bloc) was a natural target market, for various reasons. The only cars in the countries behind the Iron Curtain then were those made within the Bloc—the Lada, built by AvtoVAZ, a firm based in the erstwhile Soviet Union, and the Trabant, made by an erstwhile East German firm, VEB Sachsenring. These cars were using old technology and were very heavy consumers of petrol. Customers, if given a chance, were bound to prefer a more modern and economical vehicle.

The first step was taken when Dr Peter Medgyessy, who was the deputy prime minister and finance minister of the Republic of Hungary, visited India. Maruti was already a showpiece of the public sector and the government had scheduled a visit by him to the Maruti factory. I showed him around and he was very impressed with the factory and the 800 cc car. He felt that the car would be ideal for Hungary if it could be homologated there and some arrangement for balancing the foreign exchange required to import cars could be worked out.

I held discussions with different ministries to explore how the foreign exchange balancing could be done. India was buying power equipment from Hungary and the trade balance was adverse to India. Exporting cars would help narrow the trade gap. The government approved the idea that the value of cars exported could be set off against the import of power equipment.

Meanwhile Dr Kumar worked at getting homologation approvals. The standards in Hungary were somewhat easier than in western Europe and approvals could be secured without much difficulty. Dr Medgyessy accepted the idea that car imports by Hungary could be made against new orders for power equipment from there. He was really quite keen to introduce the 800 in Hungary as it would save petrol and be a feather in his cap.

The first order of exports came and, in 1986, an agreement was signed with a firm called Mogurt for the export of between 500 and 5,000 cars a year over the next five years. Mogurt would import, sell and service the cars. It was also the firm exporting power equipment to India. Maruti had to import components specific for left-hand drive vehicles from Japan, and also fit seat belts, which Indian cars did not have at that time.

On 24 October 1987—a red letter day for Maruti—the minister of industry, J. Vengala Rao, handed over the keys of a Maruti 800 to Dr Medgyessy at a function held in the compound of the majestic Parliament building in Budapest. I took the deputy prime minister and the industries minister for a short drive in one of the 800 cc cars, with the security policemen holding their breaths. I brought them both back quite safely!

Maruti exported a total of 500 cars to Hungary in the first year, which increased to almost 1,500 in 1990-91 and soared to nearly 4,400 the following year. The cars became very popular. These exports had another very significant fallout. Dr Medgyessy, who rose to become the prime minister, paid an official visit to Japan. He visited the SMC headquarters at Hamamatsu, no doubt because of the success of Maruti cars. There, discussions with Suzuki led to SMC establishing a manufacturing plant in Hungary, in equal partnership with the government of Hungary. Obviously, Suzuki liked the Indian model of a partnership with the government, and replicated it in Hungary. He became the Consul General for Hungary in Japan, perhaps as a reward for making an investment in a car-manufacturing factory in that country. SMC also started to import Hungarian wines, which are of high quality, for sale in Japan.

With cars being sold in Hungary, it was comparatively easier to sell cars in Czechoslovakia and Yugoslavia. Homologation of the cars was required to be done in each of these countries, as standards varied to some extent. Kumar and his team were up to the task and inquiries made from Hungary by officials of these two countries resulted in Maruti getting quick approvals, as the cars were reported to be performing very well. The arrangements were similar, and exports from India had to be balanced by imports from these countries.

We were, however, not going to be satisfied with exporting to the rather insular eastern European markets. Exporting to them gave everyone greater confidence, but we had to enter western Europe. This was a more attractive and really competitive market and the challenge was to succeed in countries in this part of the world. SMC, which had earlier been selling the old model of the 800 cc car in some of those countries, had discontinued sale of this model, and was selling only its bigger cars. This was largely because Japanese cars had a quota in Europe, and it was more profitable to sell big cars rather than small cars. Maruti, therefore, thought there was a good opportunity to sell the 800 cc car to western Europe, provided it was not hit by the quota rules.

When Maruti first mooted the idea, SMC was not supportive. It discouraged Maruti, saying that Indian-made cars were unlikely to be accepted in Europe, that it was too early for Maruti to start thinking of exports to western Europe, and that homologation would be extremely difficult. SMC engineers were fully occupied and would not be able to support homologation of Maruti cars. Perhaps SMC was also worried about its brand image getting tarnished if Indian cars bombed in western Europe.

I was, however, determined to go ahead. The east Europe experience had raised the confidence levels of everyone. In 1989, I asked Kumar and his team to get the 800 homologated in France. He took up the challenge and his teams worked very hard understanding the rules and requirements. SMC, despite its initial reluctance, did help in areas where the Maruti team felt its knowledge was inadequate. The homologation was done at a French institute, UTAC. For the first time, the 800 cc car was subjected to a crash test. Fortunately it passed all tests and the car was certified for sale in France. That was a day of rejoicing.

A. Chardonnet, the SMC dealer in France, was appointed as the dealer for Maruti also. I visited government officials in Paris along with Patrick Chardonnet, the owner of the dealership, and it was decided that the car would be sold under the Maruti name, and 'Suzuki' would not be found written anywhere on the vehicle. The car was to be supplied as an Indian car, so that quota rules for imports from Japan did not apply. Even the various manuals had to be revised to delete all reference to SMC. It was also necessary to ensure that value addition in India met the limit specified in the EU rules, because at that time cars from India could be imported with no duty.

The first Maruti 800 landed in France in 1989, to be sold as the Alto. Chardonnet organized a gala launch at a posh hotel in Paris, with elephants in attendance. A nine-foot pyramid of champagne glasses was put up in the hall. Champagne was poured into the topmost glass from where it trickled down to the rest. In the first year itself, 2,833 cars were exported to France. Many Indians visiting Paris would spot a Maruti car, and duly communicated this to me on return. It gave everyone a great sense of pride and joy. Based on the homologation in France, Maruti's next market in Europe was the Netherlands. The car met with even greater success in that country and the Alto became the largest selling car in that category. Sales were then extended to England, Italy, and Malta.

SMC was particularly doubtful of Maruti's success in Italy, which was seen as a captive market of Fiat, and it was well known that Fiat had enormous political power. However, the Indian ambassador, Kuldip Sehdev, was very supportive. While posted in Hungary, he had been fully involved in the success of Maruti in that country. Once again he came out in support of Maruti. With his help and contacts I was confident that there would be no serious issues with the government. Since the 800 was very competitive with the Fiat small cars, being more fuel efficient and lower priced, there was no reason why it should not be able to sell well.

Maruti used SMC's dealer in Italy, Autoexpo, whose owner, Romano Artioli, was obsessed with automobiles. He too was very keen to make a success of the 800. Later one of his ventures was to buy the iconic Bugatti factory, which had been virtually closed down. He revived the company and produced a few cars. However, the venture was not successful, as there were few buyers for this very exotic car, perhaps because of its high price. His wife, meanwhile, opened boutiques where she was selling various lifestyle products under the Bugatti brand name. These boutiques lasted longer than the car venture.

Artioli did a good job and the 800 was selling in large numbers within a year. Italy continued to be a good market for Maruti till 2004, when sales had to be discontinued because the car could not meet the new regulations in Europe relating to emissions and safety. Over 41,000 cars had been sold in Italy till then. When SMC saw that Maruti had managed to get its cars homologated for France and Italy, and that cars were selling well, it changed its attitude and got its dealers in Belgium and the United Kingdom to also start selling Maruti cars.

Maruti was approached by J.A. Gasan for a dealership in Malta. SMC had a dealer in that country, but he did not want to sell Maruti vehicles, because he was not convinced that they would be accepted by the consumers. Under these circumstances, Maruti could appoint Gasan as its dealer for Malta. Besides the car, the Gypsy was also exported and both vehicles sold very well. When the success of Maruti vehicles in Malta was evident, the SMC dealer put pressure to be appointed to sell Maruti vehicles. We could not do so as Gasan was doing a good job and we had a contract with him.

Europe was not the only market that Maruti tapped. Over the next few years it entered all continents, except North America. In 1989, the Gypsy pick-up was homologated for sale in Australia and in several West African countries. In Australia, farmers would load the back of the vehicle with bales of hay, put the car in first gear, get in the back themselves and start pitching hay for the sheep and cattle to feed on, while the vehicle traversed the vast farms without a driver.

The 800 was already a common sight on roads in Bangladesh, Sri Lanka, Nepal, Bhutan and Mauritius, where it had been sold since 1987. In 1992, Maruti made an entry into the South American market, debuting in Chile. Selling cars to South America was not easy, because of the high cost of shipping. However, Maruti could work out an arrangement with Japanese shipping company NYK under which ship carriers, returning empty to Japan after delivering cars to Europe, would load the vehicles meant for Chile and carry them to Japan. There they would be transhipped to vessels going to Chile via the Pacific. This arrangement was much more economical than shipping directly to South America and enabled Maruti to be competitive.

~

Towards the end of the 1980s, the government tried to improve the performance of public sector undertakings by signing memorandums of understanding (MoUs) with them. The intention was to enter into a kind of contract with each PSU, where it would commit to achieving certain targets, and the government would do what was required for those targets to be achieved. Maruti signed the first MoU in 1988 and, continued to do so till it ceased to be a PSU in 1992. We were, by and large, able to achieve the targets committed to the government. The MoU scheme did not really help in bringing about improvements in the management of PSUs, as the fundamental factors which were responsible for the inadequate performance of PSUs could not be resolved in this manner. However, we could use the MOU mechanism to get approval to introduce a productivity-linked incentive scheme for all employees.

~

The product development plan proposed by Maruti in one of the MoUs included a larger three-box sedan car. Maruti had always been interested in such a car and that is why it had seriously considered the Volkswagen Jetta and Golf in 1981 and 1982. However, at the time of the tie-up with SMC, the latter did not have a three-box car in its stable. It was only in 1985 that SMC developed and sold a three-box car in a joint venture established with General Motors in the United States. The car, with a 1.3 litre engine, had both a sedan and a hatchback version and was launched in Japan in 1989.

Maruti decided to manufacture this car, but, instead of investing in facilities to manufacture a 1.3 litre engine, it was decided to use the 1 litre engine. This engine was already being manufactured for the Gypsy and thus no new investments were required for engine production. We had already submitted a proposal to the government for manufacturing this car in 1986 and got the green signal in July 1988. The project to manufacture this car involved an investment of Rs. 97 crore and was to be financed by internal resources. However, to meet the foreign currency requirements, a loan of $40 million was arranged in 1990-91. At that time the foreign exchange reserves of the government were very low and foreign currency could not be allocated to us.

The 970 cc Maruti 1000 hit the roads in November 1990. The system for making bookings for the car was the same as was earlier used for the 800, as it was expected that the demand would be far higher than the supply. The car was exhibited in a number of cities with the press being invited for the previews. The expectation that demand would be high was correct and Maruti got 251,000 bookings when it called for them in November and December 1989. Maruti, however, kept only 25,000 bookings, selected through a computerized draw. The deposits given by the other customers were returned to them. Maruti did not want to keep customers waiting for long periods of time. The cars for the successful allottees were to be delivered over a one-and-a-half-year period from the start of production.

However, the car had one major problem—the pick-up was somewhat inadequate when the car was running with the air-conditioner on and had to go up an incline. To address this issue, and seeing the success of the 1000 cc car, SMC agreed that we could manufacture the 1.3 litre engine and upgrade our car. Maruti had enough funds from its internal resources to finance the required investment. In addition, the Army had suggested that the Gypsy would become much more acceptable if it had a more powerful engine. Thus, it was possible to get reasonable volumes to make manufacturing the 1.3 litre engine a viable proposition.

The 1000 was launched in perhaps the most trying of times for the automobile industry, resulting from a combination of domestic and global economic and political factors. The country was rocked by agitations—the violent protests against job reservations for backward classes implemented by the National Front government on the basis of the B.P. Mandal Commission Report and rath yatra by Bharatiya Janata Party leader L.K. Advani to gather support for the Ayodhya movement. This disrupted the movement of vehicles and the supply of raw materials.

The 1990 Gulf war brought its own set of problems, with the government taking steps to reduce fuel consumption and keep the oil import bill down. These, according to the AIAM, only created a psychology of shortage, leading to long queues at petrol pumps, and increased turnaround time for transport vehicles. This, in turn, adversely affected transport of inputs and of finished products.

Inflation rates had started to climb, being fuelled by the high fiscal deficits that the government had been incurring through lax financial management. Foreign exchange reserves were fast dwindling, because exports had been steadily declining over many years. Indian industry, thanks to decades of protection, was largely unable to export manufactured goods, due to lack of competitiveness. A very serious economic crisis was looming.

The government took a raft of measures to conserve foreign exchange. In November 1990, it abolished certain categories of imports under open general licence (OGL), apart from placing restrictions on letters of credit and remittances as well as import financing. Customs duty was raised twice and touched 80 per cent in December 1990. The combined effect of all this—and several other measures—was to make imports very expensive. Maruti too felt the heat. The release of foreign exchange for the phased manufacturing programme was severely restricted. Maruti had to buy replenishment licences at a premium to fulfil its production targets. The value of the rupee against the dollar also declined sharply, and this pushed up the provisions the company had to make for repayment of outstanding foreign exchange loans. Excise duty was also raised. All these factors pushed up costs by 8-10 per cent, leaving manufacturers with little option but to increase prices. Combined with the increase in fuel prices, this naturally softened the demand for cars.*

Maruti held its own admirably in this adverse scenario; while sales of other vehicles dropped from 70,994 in 1989-90 to 67,408 in 1990-91, Maruti's sales increased from 1,08,440 to 1,10,031. Apart from launching the 1000 cc car, sales also got buoyed by a large order of 1,500 Gypsys from the Army.

~

If 1990 was a difficult year, 1991 was even worse. Despite the fact that car sales had started to decline in 1990 because of price increases necessitated by excise and custom duty hikes, the government again raised excise duty on cars from 52.5 per cent

---

*Annual Report, Association of Indian Automobile Manufacturers, 1990; Annual Report, Maruti Udyog Ltd, 1990-91.

to 66 per cent in July 1991. AIAM calculated the tax component at 120 per cent of the ex-factory price of passenger cars. Between August 1989 and July 1991, the price of the 800 increased 65 per cent, from Rs. 100,680 to Rs. 166,629. Car prices had been revised upward seven times in that period for most models.

Prices of raw materials and components also kept climbing, mainly because of increases in the administered prices of steel and aluminium and power, and strong inflationary trends. The cost of imports also increased, because of a devaluation of the rupee against the dollar by 18 per cent in July 1991, the need to provide margin money by importers and a requirement to buy EXIM scrips for imports. High interest rates and tightening of money supply pushed up the costs of production and also affected demand for car loans, the interest on which increased by about 10 per cent in 1991-92. Reduced depreciation benefits on cars affected car purchases by companies and independent professionals.

Cars sales declined by 7 per cent. While sales of other cars fell by 28 per cent, Maruti clocked a 6 per cent increase in the sales of its cars and increased its market share to 66 per cent. Maruti sales may also have turned negative since the sales of the Omni and the 1000 cc car were declining. However, we cut prices to maintain sales growth. The prices of the Omni, which had been raised by 8 per cent in December 1991, were reduced by 4 per cent in January 1992. Similarly, the price of the 1000 cc car was slashed by 6 per cent in January 1992. The company still managed to make a profit of Rs. 6.61 crore in 1991-92, though it was lower than the previous year's profit of Rs. 8.82 crore.

Maruti's profitability in those difficult days had a lot to do with its robust exports, which grew 367 per cent. But it was to face some hiccups there as well. In 1991, Europe announced more stringent emission norms for cars, to come into effect from 1993. This could well have put a halt to exports to that continent, unless the cars were modified. SMC felt there was no point making efforts to modify the 800, since it was planning to launch a new car in Europe—the Zen (which was also to be sold as the Alto, since the brand name had been established)—in 1993. Maruti, however, argued that stopping exports would not be in its interests, as it had certain export obligations and also got some export-linked concessions.

I asked Kumar to see whether the 800 could be modified to meet the new emission norms. There were some interim regulations and the idea was to get the vehicle homologated so that exports could continue till 1993. However, that proved to be a very difficult task given SMC's reluctance to support what was thought to be a futile effort. For example, Maruti could not get some components as original equipment from Japan. Maruti decided to buy them as spare parts, and fitted them on the vehicles. Kumar's team persisted with their efforts, and Maruti could get the car homologated—successfully—at TUV, an agency in the Netherlands. However, SMC, which was still vehemently opposed to the idea, said it would not stand guarantee for export of the 800 as it was not sure of what modifications Maruti had done. I kept trying to persuade them, but in vain.

Ultimately, Artioli, who was equally keen to keep on importing these vehicles, stepped forward and said he would be personally responsible for their import, and for any damages arising from their performance, and would not ask SMC to bear any costs. It was only after this letter—and some more persuasion from me—that SMC finally agreed that Maruti could export these vehicles to Italy and subsequently to the Netherlands for two more years.

For Maruti, the successful export of the modified car was further testimony to the fact that it had the research and development capability to carry out significant modifications, even though its laboratory was lacking many facilities. One outcome of this incident was that SMC recognized the capabilities of Indian engineers and accepted the need for Maruti to have adequate engineering and development capabilities in India.

~

Things were, however, beginning to change for the Indian economy and for Maruti. July 1991 saw the initiation of the first major liberalization of the Indian economy, which brought delicensing and deregulation in its wake. Following intensive lobbying by the automobile industry, the government reduced the excise duty on cars to 55 per cent, though that was still 18.25 per cent higher than the duty prevailing in February 1990. For Maruti, a new chapter was about to be written, with SMC increasing its stake in the company to 50 per cent. When this happened Maruti no longer remained a government company. A lot of things were going to be transformed, as a result.

5

A BUMPY RIDE

With the opening up of the Indian economy in 1991, a number of sectors were thrown open to foreign direct investment. The government was keen to show that the policy was pulling in serious investors and wanted to showcase some big-ticket investments to the world. I was asked by the Prime Minister's Office to check if SMC was willing to increase its investment in Maruti. I contacted Suzuki and suggested that with the government policy having changed (till then only a maximum of 40 per cent foreign equity was allowed), he consider increasing SMC's stake in Maruti. Suzuki thought over this and decided to approach the government to allow SMC to make additional investments to increase its equity to 50 per cent. He was aware that if the government stake came down to 50 per cent, Maruti would no longer be a public sector undertaking. All the rules and regulations for such undertakings would no longer be applicable. This would give much greater operational freedom to Maruti, and also enable SMC to increase its role in the management of the company, since it would become an equal partner. SMC could in fact have asked for a larger stake, but at that stage Suzuki felt more comfortable being equal partners with the government than a majority owner.

Around the same time I managed to persuade Ford Motors to establish a joint venture company to produce aluminium radiators. Till then this technology was not available in India. Car radiators were all made of copper brass. Maruti had been facing a problem with these radiators, as pinholes would develop in the tubing and the coolant would leak. There were many customer complaints and we had no solution to offer. Ford assured us that aluminium radiators would perform extremely well and there would be no leakage problems. Moreover, a joint venture with Ford would go down well in the United States and Europe. The government supported this project and these two deals were amongst the earliest examples of foreign direct investment in India post-liberalization.

There were some rumblings over SMC's move to increase equity. Krishnamurthy himself was not too happy with the development. Before making the proposal to increase SMC's stake, Suzuki had met him in August 1991 in the Planning Commission, where he was member. Krishnamurthy told Suzuki that he did not support the idea and if the latter was inching towards taking control of the organization, it may not be the right thing to do. He suggested that SMC retain its stake at 40 per cent, get the government to also reduce its stake to 40 per cent from 60 per cent and sell 20 per cent to financial institutions, vendors and dealers so that it was a board-managed company. Krishnamurthy had made this suggestion to Mrs Gandhi soon after Maruti was formed as a way of insulating the company from government interference. He had pointed out that if the Congress government fell and another party came to power, they could use Maruti as an instrument to hurt her. Mrs Gandhi had agreed but the heavy industries ministry had pointed out that this would appear as backdoor privatization and that it could not be done because of certain assurances given in Parliament during nationalization of Sanjay's Maruti. The ministry had suggested this course of action be adopted some other time.

The criticism against Suzuki's move was somewhat muted. Since the government was aggressively wooing foreign investment as a matter of policy, criticizing one particular instance of foreign investment would have been seen as not only going against the new policy, but also as being discriminatory. One of the features of the new policy was to bring in transparency and simplicity for foreign companies to invest in India, and arguing against SMC's investment would give the impression that the claim of transparency was a sham, and investments would only be allowed on a case-to-case basis, as in the past.

Another problem with Krishnamurthy's suggestion for a 40:40:20 equity holding in Maruti was that it would not meet the objective of showing that the new policy for foreign investment was leading to foreign equity in a company increasing beyond 40 per cent, though this limit had been removed, and additional foreign exchange coming into the country. Both these were important policy objectives.

That is perhaps why Krishnamurthy's objection, and suggestion for the structuring of Maruti, even though coming from a member of the Planning Commission, did not really get debated or support from the government. SMC was allowed to increase its equity to 50 per cent. As a result, Maruti ceased to be a PSU and this became the first instance of privatization. Many years later, Krishnamurthy acknowledged that perhaps his opposition to Suzuki going up to 50 per cent was incorrect and the way events turned out the move was for the best.

In December 1991, Suzuki had written to Krishnamurthy telling him that he had, in September 1991, made a formal proposal to the government to increase SMC's equity to 50 per cent, in accordance with the discussions he had held earlier with the government, and seeking Krishnamurthy's help in getting government approval. This was typical of the Japanese way of working. Though Suzuki was aware of Krishnamurthy's views on the matter, he still sought his support. On the same date, he also wrote to P.K. Thungon, then minister of state for heavy industries, seeking an early decision on the proposal. He also raised the issue about the term of the managing director, since my term was expiring around the middle of 1992. Suzuki felt that a sudden change of the top leadership would not be desirable at this critical juncture, especially as Maruti and SMC had worked very well during my stint. If there was still to be a change in the managing director, Suzuki sought full consultation in terms of the joint venture agreement.

On 2 June 1992, four months short of the tenth anniversary of the original SMC–Government of India joint venture agreement, a Subscription and Amendment Agreement was signed and SMC subscribed to an additional 2,204,860 shares, paying Rs. 269 per share. The price was arrived at on the basis of a formula which, till then, had been used by the Controller of Capital Issues (CCI) in determining the price at which private companies made preferential equity issues. SMC was being issued preferential equity, and so the formula seemed appropriate. In deciding the price for the share issue, the opinion of ICICI Securities had also been taken and it was found that the CCI formula would be quite fair and correct. The government approved the price at which shares should be issued to SMC.

Since there was some amount of criticism of the allotment of additional shares to SMC as well as the pricing, I suggested that an additional condition be imposed, namely that if SMC ever sold these 10 per cent shares, the government would have the first right of refusal and the price would be arrived at by the same CCI formula. The government and SMC both accepted this condition. On signing of the agreement, and SMC subscribing to the additional shares, Maruti Udyog Ltd formally ceased to be a government company.

Under the amendment agreement, the post of chairman-cum-managing director, which I had been holding at that time, was split into a non-executive chairman and a full-time managing director. The government and SMC were to nominate the persons who would hold these two posts for five-year periods by rotation. SMC was given the right to nominate the first managing director. Suzuki proposed my name to the government. On 28 August 1992 Surendra Singh, the then secretary, Department of Heavy Industry, wrote to Suzuki that certain complaints had been made against me and these were being checked for their veracity. Action could be taken if they were found to be true. The government thought it necessary to bring this to Suzuki's attention though it was not, the letter said, the 'intention to constrain M/s Suzuki Motor Corporation's choice of a nominee for the post of Managing Director in any way. In accordance with the Agreement, your final choice will be acceptable to the Government.'

The reply from Suzuki, faxed on the same date, was that some of the complaints mentioned had already been discussed and resolved in the Maruti board. It was not possible to make a judgement without having all the facts in hand. Meanwhile, it said, SMC did not intend to make any change in their nomination of me as the managing director. The government accepted this position, and I was appointed to the post, in a shareholders' meeting, for a period of five years, starting from 28 August 1992. At that point, the government did not exercise its right to appoint a chairman. I had been chairman and managing director ever since Krishnamurthy had relinquished the post of non-executive chairman in 1990. Perhaps, the government thought I would adequately handle the job and a chairman could be elected by the board at each meeting.

With Maruti ceasing to be a public sector company, it was freed from the constraints which prevent public sector companies from maximizing their competitive position vis-à-vis private companies. Overall, there was a sense of freedom from stifling government controls and red tape. Maruti used this newfound freedom to strengthen the organization. Salaries of managers were increased, though they were still nowhere near private sector salaries. We had to keep in mind the fact that the government was still a 50 per cent partner, and therefore policy changes and major regulations had to be approved in the board. The government nominees would have found it very difficult to agree to proposals which were very different from what had existed. However, since Maruti was no longer a PSU, the Comptroller and Auditor General would no longer audit our accounts. Hence we could hire private auditors to do our statutory audit. Unnecessary paperwork, meant only to comply with government systems, could be done away with. We were no longer an Instrument of State and hence paperwork needed to show compliance with the Fundamental Rights while taking business decisions could be avoided. There was greater freedom in taking business decisions and awarding contracts. It was no longer necessary to recruit workers only through government-run employment exchanges, or compulsorily follow the policy of job reservations for scheduled castes, scheduled tribes and several other disadvantaged groups (though Maruti, on its own, decided to reserve the same percentage of jobs for scheduled castes and scheduled tribes). The company now went outside the scrutiny of Parliamentary committees established for the public sector, and various laws which applied only to the public sector.

~

Perhaps it was just as well. The difficult times that had begun in 1990 were not over. In fact, 1992-93 began on a pessimistic note. The economy was still in the doldrums, with high inflation and interest rates, constraints on credit, and a difficult balance of payments situation with a weakening rupee. The Maruti management needed to be nimble-footed to cope with the myriad challenges.

Among the first things a newly free management did was to negotiate and sign a four-year wage agreement in April 1993, but with retrospective effect from April 1992. Keeping the workers happy and content had always been part of Maruti's ethos, but this had become more important now, with the company set to launch another new car—the YE2, better known as the Zen.

The Zen was designed by SMC to conform to the new European standards applicable from 1 January 1993. However, this model was to be manufactured not in Japan but in India, and exported from here to Europe (to be sold as the new Alto, replacing the 800) and other countries, through SMC's marketing channels. This was the first acknowledgement of India's potential to become a manufacturing hub for automobile exports. 'The importance of this development,' as I noted in my chairman's address in August 1990, 'lies in the acceptance by a multinational that India can be a viable source for a sophisticated engineering product, and that such a product can be produced at internationally competitive costs.'

Meanwhile, the original ten-year licence agreement came to an end in 1992. SMC wanted to discontinue the 800, since royalty payment would have ended, and replace it with the Zen. This became a point of tussle between Maruti and SMC. I was not willing to give up the 800, which was our bread-and-butter car, as it were. The cost of the upmarket Zen, with a one-litre engine, was significantly higher, and the car could not have catered to the mass entry market, the way the 800 could. A meeting was convened in Hamamatsu where Y. Saito, the executive vice-president of SMC, insisted on discontinuing the 800. I did not agree and tried to explain why this would be against the interests of Maruti. I found that I could not change Saito's views in the matter.

I thought I had no other option but to resign, since I believed that discontinuing the 800 would seriously hurt Maruti. I could not be a party to implementing such a decision. Suzuki then called me into his room, which was adjoining the room where our discussions had been going on. I explained the issue to him and said that since I was not prepared to implement what SMC wanted, it was only proper that I should quit. Suzuki replied, 'Would I have met you if I wanted you to quit?' He agreed that we should continue to manufacture the 800. In order to ensure that SMC would continue to upgrade the 800, we agreed to pay a fixed royalty of Rs. 1,000 per car, against the 2.15 per cent paid till then, which amounted to Rs. 2,210 per car. The 800 continued to sell in large numbers for many years after that and it is only in the late 2000s that its sales declined. The 800 contributed handsomely to our bottom line. I can have the pleasure of saying, with hindsight, that my insistence on continuing the 800 was correct. Suzuki also displayed great faith in my judgement by overruling the views of his own vice-president.

But manufacturing the Zen posed some new problems. Since Maruti wanted to export the Zen in large numbers, it was necessary to reduce the costs of production. Suzuki, during his discussions with government officials, stressed the need to reduce costs if Maruti was to succeed in its export efforts. The European market was very price sensitive for cars in this segment. Both SMC and Maruti requested the government to consider exempting capital goods from the payment of import duties. The government was sympathetic, especially as earning foreign exchange was a very high priority objective. However, a scheme had to be devised to enable this benefit to be given. The scheme could not be specific to Maruti and had to be available to others who would meet the conditions applicable to it.

I had several meetings with the Member, Customs, in the Central Board of Excise and Customs to find a mutually acceptable solution, which we evolved. In November 1993, the government issued an ad hoc exemption order allowing Maruti to import plant and machinery for the Zen project at nil custom duty on taking an obligation to export 140,000 cars over seven years between 1995-96 and 2001-02. This would result in India earning foreign currency which was several times the value of the capital goods to be imported. Later, it was agreed that the scheme would apply to all who imported capital goods in excess of Rs. 100 crore with the condition that they would have to export, over a period of seven years, products equal to five times the value of the capital goods imported. This eventually became the Export Promotion Capital Goods Scheme. The scheme was subsequently modified to make its application wider. It has provided a big incentive to promote the export of more sophisticated and quality manufactured goods.

The European Commission (now the European Union) also had stringent rules of origin (a trade term for specifying a certain level of localization to avoid exports from one country being routed through another which enjoys duty concessions in the importing country). At that time, cars exported from India could enter Europe at concessional duty, provided the value addition in India was 56 per cent. SMC insisted that it would decide which component would be localized, so as to ensure that quality was not compromised. A certain quantity of imports had to be made in any case, because the cars exported to Europe would be left-hand drive. Manufacturing components for such cars, in small volumes, would not have been viable. This made it even more important that the other components made in India should be of very good quality.

Though Maruti had been making continuous efforts since its early years in bringing about an attitudinal change regarding quality among vendors, the results were mixed. There was still an inclination among many vendors to cut corners and not adhere rigidly to the laid-down systems and procedures. This meant that quality from these vendors was not consistently maintained. While Maruti could get around this problem for cars sold in the domestic market by importing a larger number of critical components, this could not be done for the Zen because of the higher localization levels required by the European Union. Maruti once again had to spend a lot of time, effort and resources in upgrading the vendors' processes and training their manpower, and started a vendor upgradation department in 1993. The effort was not wasted. The Zen, when it was exported, was considered one of the best cars in Europe.

A year later, Maruti launched the 1298 cc Esteem. It was in addition to the Maruti 1000, whose sales rapidly declined. It also rolled out a new-look 800, with changes in the headlights and bonnet and wraparound taillights. The robust sales of all of these saw Maruti further increasing its market share to over 76 per cent in the next two years, even as the waiting list continued to be quite long.

Maruti may have managed the external challenges with aplomb, but it was soon to be wracked by internal wrangling, with consequences that would last for several years.

~

Soon after 1992, the question of successor-planning came up. This concept was alien to the public sector but was an integral part of SMC's ethos, as it is of all the better-managed companies in the world. I was to retire in 1997 and my successor had to be trained so that there could be a smooth transition. R.S.S.L.N. Bhaskarudu, who had joined Maruti in 1983 as general manager after working for twenty-one years in BHEL, and had risen to be director on the board, was the seniormost person. He was expecting his succession to be a shoo-in.

However, Suzuki had come to the conclusion that he was not CEO material and did not feel that he could work with him as a partner. In the Japanese system, personal confidence and trust between top management is given far more importance than academic qualifications and seniority. This approach is, of course, quite alien to the public sector and the governmental way of working, where seniority is the main factor in promotions. This cultural difference between Japan and India, and the inability of each partner to understand the thinking of the other, was one of the main reasons why the dispute between the two sides was to later escalate. Suzuki wanted the field for selecting the next CEO to be widened. Since the government was still playing a strong role in the economy, and given the fact that I had come from the IAS, Suzuki thought it might be a good idea to tap the service for the next managing director also. An IAS officer would be able to manage relationship issues with the government better than an outsider. I was asked to look for somebody from the service who could be brought in as director, marketing (just as I had), and then become one of the options for the next managing director.

I asked around and the names of some IAS officers from the Haryana, Punjab and Uttar Pradesh cadres were suggested. However, they declined, because the government rules then required that a service officer would have to resign from the IAS before joining Maruti. The name of Jagdish Khattar, a 1965 batch officer from the Uttar Pradesh cadre (to which I belonged), who was joint secretary in the steel ministry, was then suggested. I had never met Khattar or worked with him before. I made enquiries and the reports about him were very good. We then met. Khattar appeared to have the right credentials, with nearly ten years' experience in the public sector involving stints at the Tea Board of India (he had some innovative marketing strategies to his credit when posted in London), the Uttar Pradesh Cement Corporation and the Uttar Pradesh Road Transport Corporation. I felt he had potential to lead the company and suggested his name to Suzuki, who gave the green signal to his appointment. In 1993, Khattar joined as officer on special duty, marketing. He was sent to Japan for a few months to expose him to the working and management style of SMC.

The Maruti and Suzuki management did not realize it then, but this was to make Maruti's hitherto smooth ride very rough.

~

The beginning of differences between SMC and the Maruti management on one side, and the Ministry of Heavy Industries on the other started, in a small way, in 1994 over the issue of extension of the licence agreement. The licence for the 800 and the Omni had expired in December 1992, and that for the Gypsy in December 1993. At Maruti, we had taken the view that we needed continued support from SMC for these products, so that improvements made in technology and design in Japan could be made available to us. There was also the need for availing training facilities for our workers and engineers, particularly in the R&D area. If the licence agreement was not extended, we would not be able to make improvements in the vehicles on our own and would become like the other car makers, who continued to make decade-old models with no improvements. We were able to get the royalty rates reduced on the grounds that our volumes were much higher than what was envisaged when the original rates of royalty were fixed in 1982. The Maruti board, which included the government directors, approved the proposal to extend the licence agreement in March 1994 and requested the government to approve our proposal in this regard in April 1994.

After some months, when no approval was forthcoming, I discussed this matter with Ashok Chandra, the secretary in the ministry. He told me that since he was going to retire in a few months, he was not willing to take up any issue which had the potential of creating a controversy and would keep the matter pending for his successor to handle. There was very little that I could do to change his mind and I told SMC that they would have to wait till 1995.

Chandra's successor was T.R. Prasad. My initial meetings and discussions with him were very cordial and it seemed that Maruti and the ministry would continue to work together in a cooperative manner. I was wrong. The events which followed show how much difference can take place in government working, merely through a change of individuals who hold top positions.

In May 1995, Congress leader K. Karunakaran became industries minister. Soon after he took charge I had a long meeting with him and briefed him about Maruti, what we had been able to achieve and also the pending issues. At this and some other later interactions there was no indication that he would not trust the Maruti management and that the ministry would become very interventionist. But in the one year that he held that position (the Congress government's term ended in May 1996), Maruti and the ministry were involved in several collisions.

Besides the issue of extension of the licence agreement, another issue on which differences developed between the government, Maruti and SMC was that of financing the Zen project and also on expanding capacity. The need for this had become evident when, in 1992-93, Maruti produced 128,000 units against the installed capacity of 100,000. Demand was growing and there was a long waiting list for the car. But funds proved a problem. Maruti's profit levels at that time were quite low. Profit before tax in 1991-92 was Rs. 35.8 crore and in 1992-93 Rs. 36.6 crore. Internal resources were not going to be adequate to establish another production line, which would be a modernized version of the existing line. As early as December 1992, the board was informed that the proposed expansion programme would involve an investment of close to Rs. 770 crore and that it would be necessary to enlarge the equity base of the company to avoid any distortion in its debt-equity ratio.

The board had then agreed that the company's equity could be raised to Rs. 198 crore and asked me to discuss the matter with the government, SMC as well as financial institutions. The matter had come up at various board meetings after that but the government kept delaying a decision. Meanwhile the amount of equity needed was reduced to Rs. 150 crore. The government needed to find Rs. 75 crore to invest in Maruti.

But this was too soon after the 1991 economic crises and the government was very strictly controlling all expenditure. We were told that the government would not be able to invest this amount. The option to go public was considered, but neither of the parties was willing to accept this route. Suzuki was unfamiliar with the Indian capital markets and was not sure what the consequences would be of having private shareholders in the company, and perhaps outside directors on the board.

The work on expanding capacity and establishing a second plant, at the same site, started about the end of 1992 and was completed in 1994. This plant, which was to produce the Zen, had a rated capacity of 100,000 units, like the first plant. The funds were secured through a loan raised in Japan, as well as some internal resources. With this plant, production rapidly increased to 278,000 in 1995-96, and the need for another plant was obvious. One of the reasons for Maruti being able to keep prices of cars low—and make profits—was the ability to run both these plants at about 140 per cent of the rated capacity. This was achieved by a combination of balancing facilities, innovative practices and full cooperation from the workers.

While the second line was being installed, Maruti was still looking for funds for its investment requirements. After discussions with SMC in October 1993, an option was suggested to the government—SMC would subscribe to the entire Rs. 150 crore, but the government would have the right to buy back Rs. 75 crore worth of equity within a period of three to five years. The terms of the buy-back were to be agreed between the parties, but essentially they would be based on treating the Rs. 75 crore as a loan. This option did not find favour.

In 1995 the proposal to establish the third plant came up. Maruti wanted to locate the new plant within its factory premises in Gurgaon, like the second plant. However, by this time the ministry had decided that it should play an active role in decision making in Maruti. Karunakaran wanted the new plant to be set up in his home state of Kerala, or at least somewhere in the south. The argument was that cars were sold in the south as well and having the second plant there would reduce the cost of transporting cars from Gurgaon. But Maruti did not think that this would be a good business decision for several reasons.

For one, the capital cost of establishing a new plant in the south would be much higher for Maruti, as land would have to be acquired and the factory, along with supporting infrastructure, built on a greenfield site. In Gurgaon, land was already with us and investments on infrastructure would be limited. This included the standby power generating capacity and water treatment plant.

Moreover, it would have meant that all the vendors who had established manufacturing plants near Maruti in Gurgaon would either have to transport the components to the south, or establish another manufacturing plant there. Transporting parts would not only add to cost but also create the need to keep large inventories in the south because of the distance and transportation uncertainties. In Gurgaon, Maruti worked on a just-in-time system with all vendors who were in that area, and inventory costs were very low. If vendors were to establish plants in south India, capital expenditures would be much higher compared to expanding capacity at their existing sites. Economies of scale would be lost by splitting production in two sites, since total volumes of production in India are still low compared to international standards. Management costs and overheads would also increase. As a result, component costs would go up.

Clearly, running two plants 1,500 km apart would be far more costly than having the plants in the same compound. Supervision and management problems multiply with distance. The ministry also did not realize its assumption that transportation costs would reduce was faulty. The two plants would have to make different models, as the dies, tooling and fixtures could not be duplicated. Doing so would have meant a very large investment. As a consequence, the models produced in the south would now need to move to the north. Models being produced in the north would still need to move to the south. There would thus be no savings as far as transportation costs were concerned. In fact, since the north was a larger market than the south, transportation costs would have probably increased.

Despite these issues being pointed out, the ministry did not change its stance. The stalemate on this continued well into July 1996, when a committee consisting of four directors—Kobayashi and I nominated by SMC and Bhaskarudu and Anup Mukherji (a joint secretary in the heavy industries ministry) nominated by the government—was set up to examine this matter and give recommendations. This had been agreed upon at a meeting between Suzuki and the new minister for industry, Murasoli Maran, after a new government had been formed. In the meetings of the committee, Bhaskarudu would not clearly support the arguments for expanding in Gurgaon and Mukherji would keep repeating his view that a plant in the south would be better. The committee finally gave its report in August 1997, pointing out that a new facility at a greenfield site would not only be much more expensive but would also delay start of production by eighteen months. Since Maruti was making good profits, the delay in increasing production would result in losing huge amounts of money, besides creating customer dissatisfaction due to delayed deliveries. In any case, the expansion had already got delayed by over a year.

This case illustrates the impact which an individual in the governmental system can make. The secretary to the ministry could also have taken note of the continued success of Maruti since its inception, and recognized that SMC and the Maruti management were much more qualified to take business decisions relating to the company. In that event he could have left the decision on location of the expansion to the board and attempted to convince the minister that the government should not interfere in such matters. He did no such thing as he himself was also of the view that the plant should be located in the south.

In terms of corporate governance, the role of the ministry in such cases is a matter of some doubt. If the ministry was questioning a decision of the board, in its role as a 50 per cent shareholder, it should have called a formal meeting with the other shareholder to discuss this matter. One shareholder, even if it is a sovereign government, should not veto the views of the board, as a measure of good corporate governance. In this form of governance nobody remains accountable for the consequences of the delay.

In August 1995, Suzuki wrote to the minister about various pending matters. This included the extension of the licence agreement. The secretary had proposed that a committee of six directors, including three from the government side, examine this matter and report to the government. He had also proposed that the extension of the licence agreement be linked to the establishment of gear manufacturing and a R&D centre. The committee of directors had met and unanimously recommended extension of the licence agreement, without any conditions being attached. Yet the matter was being kept pending. Suzuki said in his letter that SMC would not be able to continue to provide assistance to Maruti after August if the licence agreement was not extended. He also wrote about approval of the expansion project and the reports of three merchant bankers on the best way of financing the expansion. He sought early decisions on all the pending matters, which included revision of the remuneration of directors, so that Maruti should remain competitive and not lose out to other companies. Karunakaran was livid when he read this letter. He called me and gave me a dressing down. He felt that the sovereign rights of the government were being questioned. He was unable to separate the role of the government as a shareholder in a commercial company with that of a sovereign government.

The issue of financing expansion had remained a live issue all this time. In May 1995 A.N. Varma, the principal secretary to the Prime Minister, had gone to Tokyo and, along with the Indian ambassador there, Kuldip Sehdev, met Suzuki. Varma clarified that the government was not willing to reduce equity below 50 per cent because of the political background of the project and likely criticism from the media. This put an end to the option of SMC alone subscribing to the equity increase. Karunakaran maintained the position that the government had money to subscribe to the equity increase of Maruti, but the need had to be properly established. The view expressed by the finance department was different.

Meanwhile the debate on debt versus equity continued. While conventional wisdom is that debt is cheaper than equity, at that point of time I was of the view that equity was a better option because it could be raised at a huge premium, if the equity was offered to the public or financial institutions. Maruti commanded about 80 per cent of the market and, on an equity base of Rs. 122 crore, made a profit of Rs. 808 crore in 1996-97. The premium on the equity would, in a sense, be 'free' money, as dividend would be paid only on the face value of the equity.

Many companies that start as closely held companies, and do really well, unlock value by going public. On the other hand, interest rates in those days were in the 14-15 per cent range, and servicing a loan would be far costlier than servicing the comparatively small increase in the equity which would be required. Maruti's finance director, A. Halasyam, who was a government nominee on the board, did not want to go against the government and refrained from taking a definite stance in the matter. Since no consensus could be reached, a study by three financial institutions—Industrial Development Bank of India (IDBI), ICICI and DSP Financial Consultants (Merrill Lynch)—was commissioned. That study upheld my view that equity was a preferable option. It said that Maruti could not afford to fund capital expenditure entirely through debt and recommended a mix of equity and debt.

In July 1996 I had sent a note to the finance secretary showing that if the government and SMC each put Rs. 480 crore into Maruti, as equity plus premium on the equity, this amount would be recovered by the government from the additional income tax which Maruti would pay on higher profits, compared to what the situation would be if expansion was funded by debt. Maruti itself would generate Rs. 1,800 crore more internal cash if the expansion was funded by equity. But nothing happened and finally Maruti had to fund these plans through a mixture of debt and internal resources.

Between 1995 and 1996, several other issues relating to the operations of Maruti and investments also came up. Maruti wanted to upgrade the 800 with a new, improved four-valve engine which SMC had developed. This engine would be more fuel efficient, generate more power and be cleaner. The existing engine had become very old. The government nominees on the board, however, insisted that the company must establish the validity and performance of the new engine before it could be accepted, and that Maruti engineers should go to Japan, study the engine and its performance, and report if it would perform in Indian conditions and be an improvement on the existing engine.

The Maruti management found this approach hard to understand. SMC was Maruti's technology provider, besides being a 50 per cent partner. Till then its products and technology had been accepted without question and had delivered excellent results. Maruti had also followed SMC's advice in adopting the manufacturing processes and the equipments to be used. Engineers had been trained by SMC. The results had always come up to expectations. Why then doubt an engine developed by SMC and whose specifications and performances were given by SMC as being distinctly superior?

The reason was, of course, the concern in the government that if a new engine were to be manufactured, large investments would have to be made in installing the equipment. Funds would be needed and the question of additional equity would come up. The government did not want to dilute its shareholding, but it also did not want to invest more money. Hence the solution was to not make investments even if they were beneficial to the company. Bhaskarudu also did not clearly support the case for accepting the new engine when the matter was discussed in the board.

The modernization of the paint shop was another point of contention. The first paint shop had been commissioned in 1984 and was nearing the end of its useful life. Depreciation was being charged treating the life of the shop as twelve years. The facility was being used in excess of its rated capacity and any breakdown would mean a serious loss of production. Despite Maruti adopting preventive maintenance practices recommended by SMC, the possibility of a breakdown is always higher in old equipment. SMC believed that the paint shop should be upgraded so that the quality of painting could be improved and capacity increased to match the higher capacity utilization of the first plant. This process would be carried out over two to three years in a manner that would ensure that production was not affected. Investments would naturally be required. Bhaskarudu argued that the paint shop could be used without change for some more time.

The government accepted his opinion and not that of SMC. Here again, the view of the government was shaped less by the technical requirement for upgradation and more by the suspicion that SMC was proposing investments only to create a situation which would necessitate additional equity infusion. There had been a breakdown in the trust that had existed till then between the government and SMC, and responses were determined on the basis of distrust.

Another longstanding complaint of the government—SMC not transferring technology for making gears—came to the fore again. These were still being imported from Japan, although the casing had been localized and the gearbox was being assembled in India. Suzuki and I pointed out that the investments required for making gears was very high, running into several hundred crores, and the gears constituted only about 2.8 per cent of the total kit. It was estimated that gear production would not be economical at the existing volumes, since the cost of production would be higher than the landed cost of imported gears. Moreover, money available for investment with Maruti was limited and could be much more profitably used to expand capacity. There was a large unmet demand for cars, as evidenced by the waiting lists, and selling cars generated good profits. It made business sense to use the available funds for expanding production capacity and introducing new models like the Zen and Esteem. Localizing the production of gears would not lead to extra sales and profits, but would probably reduce profits. Thus, the business interests of Maruti dictated that expansion of production should get priority over gear production. However, the government was not convinced by these arguments and periodically there would be criticism about SMC's reluctance to transfer technology to Maruti. Bhaskarudu and Halasyam, who were government directors on the board, did not also lend support to my views.

The argument that producing gears in Maruti would be costlier than importing them became evident when gear production started in 2007. By that time the volume of car production was over 700,000 units a year (more than double that in 1996). Even then the cost of production of gears in Maruti is higher than the landed cost of gears, which has benefited from the lower import duties but gone up due to a weaker rupee. It is expected that by 2010 or so, when Maruti would be producing over a million vehicles, the local cost of production would equal the landed cost of imported gears. The company would have suffered a very heavy loss if the gear plant had been established in 1995. While the intentions of the ministry, namely to increase localization and acquire technology, were good, there was no real understanding of the commercial and business implications of doing so at that point.

The government believed that SMC had been making enormous profits from supplying CKD kits to India. This belief was based on the assumption that over the years SMC would have made a profit which was a fixed percentage of the sale value of parts to India. Since the volume of production was increasing rapidly, the value of imported parts was also increasing, despite the higher localization levels each year. However, the government did not take into account two facts. One, the base price of the kits had remained unchanged. Two, the yen had appreciated strongly against the US dollar and because of SMC and Maruti absorbing 50 per cent of the impact of the change in the yen-dollar exchange rate, the number of yen which SMC was getting from Maruti for the same part had declined sharply. Clearly, the impact of the unchanged price for the kits and the exchange rate change would be a steady loss of profitability. Data provided to show that SMC was getting a much smaller number of yen for a part supplied in 1992, as compared to what it got for the same part in 1984, was ignored. The reality was that for many years before 1992 SMC was losing money on the supply of parts for the 800, Omni and Gypsy.

These events demonstrate the inadequacy of government officers trying to manage business and industry. While those who man senior posts in the ministries are, almost without exception, possessed with high intelligence, have a great sense of duty and believe that they are in a position where they have to promote national interests, few of them have hands-on experience or understanding of technology and what is required to make a business profitable and competitive in the marketplace. The relatively short tenures on posts dealing with commercial decision making prevents building expertise. While they have authority over the decisions made by a public sector board, and can exercise a virtual veto at board meetings, they have no accountability. Usually they get transferred, or retire, before the results of their actions can be evaluated.

Even then, it can be argued that decisions were taken by the boards and not by anyone in the ministry, and that it is the duty of the ministry to fully examine and evaluate proposals emanating from any public sector undertaking. In the case of Maruti, which was no longer a public sector entity after 1992, the delays in expansion of capacity or introducing a new engine or modernizing the paint shop did not mean that anyone was accountable for the losses suffered as a consequence.

The result was that in 1995 and 1996 most major decisions relating to Maruti were delayed because of the need to convince the ministry, after the board had taken a view on them. But this was not the end of the story. The government does not usually look kindly upon persons who are perceived as 'not cooperating' with what the incumbent minister or secretary wants. When the CBI filed criminal cases against me, after its director had been summoned by the Assurance Committee chaired by S. Jaipal Reddy, the government found this to be an opportunity to try and remove me from the post of managing director. There was a long history to this.

In the early 1990s, a petition had been submitted by some MPs alleging various wrongdoings by me as the managing director. The heavy industries ministry had asked for my comments, which I had provided. Most of the matters were those on which the board had taken a decision. These allegations had also been sent to SMC when it had nominated me as managing director and Suzuki had also replied that he did not find any wrongdoing. The government had accepted me as the managing director in 1992, despite these allegations.

There was a background to this petition. In 1986, an MP had wanted his firm to be given part of the contract for moving CKD kits from Kandla to Delhi and the minister of state for heavy industries had wanted him to be accommodated. This contract had already been awarded in 1984, and Maruti was of the view that splitting the transportation contract would not be in the company's interests. Therefore, Maruti had not been able to accept the request. This MP was one of the signatories to the petition. At that time, I had also been informed that much of the 'information' on the basis of which the petition had been prepared had possibly been supplied by a senior officer in Maruti who had been asked to resign because he was harassing a female employee working with him, and had also acquired a reputation of doubtful integrity. This type of situation developing is not unusual in public sector companies, and is one of the reasons why senior officers are reluctant to take disciplinary action against errant officers.

One of the MPs who had signed the petition was the late Chandrashekhar, who had briefly been the Prime Minister in 1990-91. I met him later to clarify the matters in the petition and he told me that he had signed because an MP had informed him that wrong things were being done in Maruti and he had not gone into the evidence or merits of the allegations. Since the petition was from MPs, it was referred to the Central Bureau of Investigation (CBI), for making preliminary inquiries.

Soon after the petition was submitted three Parliamentary questions were asked about the progress of the enquiries. The government had replied that the various allegations were being looked into. The Assurance Committee of the Rajya Sabha treated the reply given by the government as assurances and periodically sought progress reports. The heavy industries ministry had been seeking more time. Nothing much happened till the end of 1994. Things changed in 1995, especially after differences developed between the government and the Maruti management and the issues received media publicity. The Assurance Committee now asked the government to show more urgency in making the enquiries and also asked why the ministry had not filled the post of chairman. This led to the ministry nominating Prasad as chairman in January 1996, exercising the option that it was given in 1992 but had not used. The decision was obviously taken to convey a message that I no longer had the confidence of the ministry, and that the government would be taking an active role in managing the company. The confrontation between SMC and the government had come into the open.

In January 1996, the Assurance Committee asked the director, CBI, and a representative from the department of company affairs (DCA) to appear before it. The DCA representative was asked to process my removal as managing director, using the Companies Act. The director, CBI, told the committee that two cases had already been filed against me and some more would be filed shortly. In fact, only one more was filed.

In the context of the hearings before the Assurance Committee, Prasad also wrote to SMC, but Suzuki refused to remove me. In a detailed reply, he wrote:

> Maruti is a private company, equally shared by the Government of India and Suzuki Motor Corporation and appointment of the Board of Directors and their positions in the corporate organization are determined after agreement between both shareholders. The Managing Director is to be elected alternately from the Board Members nominated by both shareholders. In reality, it was common understanding that election of the Managing Director of Maruti was virtually conducted in accordance with the agreement of the representatives of both shareholders. Based on such agreement, Prime Minister H.E. Mr Narasimha Rao, representing the Government of India and myself representing the Suzuki Motor Corporation agreed to elect Mr R.C. Bhargava as Managing Director in June 1992. A Managing Director who is elected should not be relieved at

> the sole discretion of either party or your sole judgement, without having mutual consent of both shareholders.

The DCA took advice from the law ministry as to whether I could be removed under Section 388(B) of the Companies Act. The law ministry, in turn, sought the views of the then Attorney-General, Milon Banerjee, who said that I could not be removed on the basis of unproven charges. The heavy industries ministry announced that I would not be removed. This view was apparently not acceptable to the Assurance Committee, and the ministry was asked to reconsider the matter.

The industry ministry again referred the matter to the law ministry. The Attorney-General had changed and the new incumbent, Ashok Desai, advised that the DCA could file a petition for my removal under Section 388(B) as there were 'circumstances suggesting' that the business of the company had not been conducted on sound business principles. This was despite the fact that Maruti had been increasing its market share and profits every year and in 1995-96 the profit had jumped to Rs. 652 crore from Rs. 263 crore in the previous year. The Attorney-General did not specify in what way the business of Maruti was not being conducted properly. He did not think it fit to consider the views of the board or the other equal partner in the company. Nor did he go into the evidence. The judicial decisions which came later in the proceedings before the Company Law Board (CLB) and the special judges hearing the CBI cases showed that the allegations were without substance. Following the Attorney-General's advice, the DCA made a reference to the Company Law Board.

SMC decided that it should become a party to the proceedings and the CLB allowed its request. Even earlier, Suzuki had written to the Prime Minister requesting the enquiries to be closed as he was of the view that the allegations had no merit and that the board had looked at several of them. He also opposed my removal before the CLB. Several hearings were held and ultimately the CLB gave a judgement on 15 December 1997 which was completely in my favour. In its order, the CLB noted that the government had been in control of the company during the entire period when the alleged wrongdoing was taking place. Why, it asked, did the government not take action when the various transactions came to its notice then? What was the reason for the delay in filing this petition till a few months before I was due to retire? It specifically mentioned the Kandla transportation case and said that the government itself had enquired into it. Why 'stale cases, some of which had been enquired into departmentally or otherwise, have been reopened by initiating criminal cases and starting a case under Section 388B by the instant application after a lapse of five to thirteen years?' The CLB stated that the government had not explained why the CBI enquiries were initiated after such a long delay. Despite these strong words from the CLB, the CBI filed a revision in the Delhi High Court after the Kandla case was dismissed by the special judge.

Soon after the January 1996 hearing of the Assurance Committee, the chairman announced to the press that the committee had recommended that I be removed from my post of managing director. I had been judged guilty by the committee without being given a chance to be heard and without any evidence being examined. The press gave wide publicity to the so-called charges and I had no way of putting across my point of view or seeking a fair hearing. The exoneration by the CLB and the courts came many years later and received scant attention. The CBI itself came to the conclusion that there was no evidence to prosecute me in respect of several of the allegations which were before the Assurance Committee and on the basis of which my removal from the board was recommended. These allegations included unduly favouring the late Lalit Suri, by awarding Subros Ltd (a company started by him and his brother Ramesh Suri in 1985 as a joint venture between the Suri Brothers, Denso Corporation and SMC for the manufacture of automobile air-conditioning systems) a one-time contract for the purchase of 10,000 air-conditioners and giving an advance to Subros. Enquiries showed that I had done nothing wrong. Another allegation was about appointing Suri as a dealer in Ghaziabad, going against the decision of the board (in which Krishnamurthy was also named). The fact was that no dealers, including Suri, were appointed except after selection by the board.

The enquiries by the CBI into the over one dozen allegations contained in the petition led to two charge sheets being filed in January 1994, while a third relating to the Kandla transport contract was filed in December 1996. The first case related to the sale of twelve cars under the manufacturer's quota at pre-budget prices in 1991. It was alleged that the twelve people who got the car were unduly favoured, that excise duty was evaded and that the company suffered a huge loss. Initially, the CBI did not even name me in the first information report, but the general manager in charge of marketing and sales and two of his subordinates were named. I did not at first take the case seriously as not only was it evident that the entire transaction had been done according to the prescribed procedure and no loss was caused to anyone, but it seemed funny that a company selling over a 100,000 cars a year should be accused of wrongdoing in respect of twelve cars. The additional director of CBI had called me and I had conveyed my view that there was nothing wrong in the entire transaction. I followed this up with a letter detailing each transaction and arguing that there was no violation of any rule or procedure and the sales were correctly made. I also explained how there was no evasion of excise (the department of excise did not claim that any excise was evaded) and the company did not suffer any loss.

The CBI officer apparently did not like my attitude or the explanation. I suddenly found that I had become an accused in the charge sheet, even though I had not been named in the FIR. The general manager, D.S. Gupta, who was named in the FIR, and was directly responsible for sales, was given a clean chit. In his statement before the CBI he did not strongly put forward the position that nothing wrong had been done by his subordinates.

The CBI filed a charge sheet against the two junior officers and me. I was not charged with having committed any substantive offence but only accused of conspiring with the two junior officers named in the FIR. No allegation was made that any of the accused, including me, derived any benefit from any of the recipients of the cars. The CBI evidence showed that the recipients were not even known to us, most of them being NRIs. The CBI charge sheet did not allege that I and the other officers had any motive to commit this crime.

I did not take the case very seriously because it was very clear that the sales had been made in a perfectly regular manner. It seems that our lawyer also thought that this was a frivolous case and would be closed by the judge. He did not prepare his arguments well and the result was that the CBI special judge framed charges against all three of us. The two junior officers filed a revision in the Delhi High Court for quashing the charges. The hearings took a long time, but ultimately the judge quashed the charges holding that there was no evidence whatsoever to send the case to trial and doing so would be a miscarriage of justice and a waste of judicial time. We were all discharged. The CBI did not file any revision in this case.

In the second case Krishnamurthy and I were charged with conspiracy and abuse of position in the matter of awarding a contract to Chennai-based Hydraulics Ltd to supply shock absorbers to Maruti. We were also accused of favouring Hydraulics while fixing the prices for the shock absorbers and determining the share of their business with Maruti. Again, the CBI did not allege that I derived any financial or any other form of gain from Hydraulics. The CBI also ignored the fact that the process followed in this case in respect of all the impugned transactions was identical to the processes followed for well over 250 Maruti vendors. It also overlooked the fact that only a very few matters relating to dealings with vendors came to me for approval, most matters being decided at lower levels. What did come to me were proposals approved by a committee of officers from different departments and in no case had I ever changed the recommendations in favour of the vendor. It took the special court seven years to discharge this case without framing charges, because it was held that no evidence existed to show that any criminal act had been committed. Again, the CBI did not file a revision petition.

The third case related to a contract for the transport of CKD kits from Kandla port. That contract had been awarded after Krishnamurthy had given his approval and the whole transaction had been discussed and approved in the board and had resulted in saving a large amount of money for Maruti. The CAG had also looked into the transaction and dropped it from his report because he found nothing wrong in it. The minister of state for heavy industries had in 1986 decided to conduct a departmental enquiry into this contract and other allegations against me. The enquiry, carried out by three senior officers of the ministry, could not establish any wrongdoing in respect of any of the allegations. However, the enquiry concluded 'that the sanctity of the tendering process was not followed'. The officers conducting the enquiry failed to record that the contract had been approved by the board or had saved money.

My two-year term as managing director had ended in 1987 and the extension was kept pending till the departmental enquiry report was examined, though I continued to work in that capacity without a formal extension. After a few months, the appointments committee of the Cabinet approved a further term of five years till 1992. This showed that at the highest level the government was satisfied that none of the allegations had any validity. One can only guess at the reasons for this enquiry. As it happened, there were differences over various issues between me and the minister of state.

Besides charge-sheeting Mathur and me in this case, the CBI also included V.K. Dewan, who was the senior manager of shipping and transport and directly responsible for this area of business when the contract was given. When the charge sheet was filed, he was serving as the CEO of a public sector undertaking. The government refused permission for his prosecution on the grounds that this was a normal business transaction and no criminality was involved. Soon thereafter he was also promoted to an even larger and more important PSU. Despite all these facts, the CBI went ahead with the charge sheet against Mathur and me. After many years, the special court discharged both of us without framing charges, holding that no evidence existed of any criminal acts by either of us. The CBI then decided to file a revision in the Delhi High Court, where the case has been pending for some years.

~

Meanwhile, the government wanted to assert its authority in the affairs of Maruti, and this could be best done in the board.

This required that all the government-nominated directors, including the four who were executive directors and had full-time responsibilities, should follow the ministry line. The first matter where this came to a test was the issue of a new four-valve engine for the 800.

Khattar and Kumar, who were directors, were told, in writing, to vote according to the government directives. They were also summoned to meet Karunakaran, who told them that as they were government nominees, they would have to do what the government wanted. Both of them were of the view that the new engine should be introduced and the course of action being suggested by the government would only delay matters and cause loss to Maruti. Bhaskarudu and Halasyam, on the other hand, preferred to follow the government line. Halasyam was a finance man with little understanding of technology, and decided he should go along with the government since he was its nominee. Bhaskarudu took the same line. He was keen that the government should nominate him for the post of managing director.

In the board meeting, Prasad, as chairman, told the government directors that they must vote according to his directions. I protested and said that directors have a fiduciary duty to the company and must act according to what they think is in its best interests. A shareholder should not tell a director how to function in the boardroom. After the board meeting I even made a reference to the DCA seeking a clarification on the issue of whether a director should act in the interests of the company or do what a shareholder asks him to do. The response from the DCA did not give any clear answer to my question. However, even before the matter could be decided in the board, both Khattar and Kumar were removed as directors in June 1996.This was obviously because Prasad thought they might vote against the government. Though Karunakaran had, according to press reports, approved the removal of these two directors in January 1996, the orders were not issued till the late Murasoli Maran became minister in June 1996 in the new United Front government.

My belief is that Karunakaran realized the unfairness of the order of removal and did not really want to implement it. They were replaced by two officials of the heavy industries ministry—Anup Mukherji and Dr E.A.S Sarma, the additional secretary and the financial advisor. Perhaps an additional reason for removing Khattar was that if he was not a director, his chances of becoming managing director were effectively scuttled. There was little that could be done. Khattar and Kumar were nominees of the government—one of the two shareholders in the company and entitled to nominate half the board members—and could be withdrawn any time.

I had met Maran one evening at Tamil Nadu Bhavan in New Delhi, where he was staying, soon after he took over as the industry minister. We discussed Maruti's performance, about which Maran seemed very pleased, and its future direction. This included expansion of capacity, export of cars, and modernization of the facilities. Maran appeared to be genuinely interested in the growth of Maruti and I came away with the impression that we would have a good working relationship.

However, things began to go wrong. I am certain that this was the result of Maran being briefed that SMC was trying to take over control of Maruti by proposing investments which were not really necessary so that there would be a need to increase the equity investment in Maruti. Since the government was not inclined to invest more money in Maruti but SMC was willing to do so, it would mean that SMC's share of equity would increase to beyond 50 per cent.

Maran was perhaps told that I was helping SMC in achieving this objective, was disregarding national interest and both Khattar and Kumar were also siding with SMC and not toeing the government line. Such an understanding of the motives of SMC and my alleged role would understandably result in the minister wanting to protect 'national' interests and view proposals from the Maruti management with a degree of suspicion. The insistence on expanding production in Gurgaon, instead of establishing a plant in the south, may also have been used to create a bias against me, Kumar and Khattar, who were all from the north. It is otherwise hard to understand why Maran's attitude changed so fast and why he did not discuss any of these issues with me directly.

A point of no return was reached when Suzuki wrote a letter to Maran, pointing out that decisions on a large number of important issues were being delayed and that SMC would find it difficult to give further support to Maruti in such a situation. That riled Maran and he summoned me. He was very worked up and said Suzuki was forgetting that he was dealing with a sovereign country. He threatened to throw SMC out of Maruti. I apologized on behalf of Suzuki for any offence caused and tried to explain that Suzuki's intentions were only to ensure the progress of Maruti. Maran asked me to convey his feelings to Suzuki, which I did. Later, Suzuki did write a very conciliatory letter to Maran, pointing out that it was not his intention to challenge the government's sovereignty, but only to promote Maruti. But the damage had been done. The next two years proved to be the most acrimonious in the history of Maruti-government relations.

6

BACK ON TRACK

The tension between the two equal partners in Maruti could not have come at a worse time. India's automobile policy was in the process of being overhauled and Maruti was likely to get some serious competition.

In 1994, almost forty years after its protectionist policies saw the exit of foreign automobile makers from India, the government delicensed car production. This meant that anyone could establish a factory for manufacturing cars, without seeking government permission. Foreign companies were also allowed to invest 100 per cent equity in a car manufacturing company in India. However, if a new manufacturer was proposing to import capital goods, or components for manufacturing cars, he had to sign an MoU with the Directorate General of Foreign Trade committing to balance the foreign exchange cost of such imports with the value of equity brought in and exports from India. These exports could be any goods or commodity and not necessarily cars or automobile components.

Foreign car manufacturers had been watching, with some degree of envy, the success enjoyed by SMC in India. The large deposits collected by Maruti from customers waiting for cars, the almost 20 per cent growth of sales every year and the high profits being made by the company were not available anywhere in the world at that time. The automobile component industry had also developed and made manufacturing in India much easier and more economical. Thus delicensing was seen as an opportunity to invest in a growing and profitable market. Many companies lost no time in tying up with Indian firms to start automobile ventures. South Korean auto major Daewoo Motors tied up with DCM, whose venture with Toyota to manufacture light commercial vehicles was doing badly. Toyota wanted to exit and Daewoo presented the opportunity to them to do so. The DCM-Daewoo joint venture converted the light commercial vehicle factory into one for making cars. The Cielo was launched in 1995, followed by the Matiz in 1999. The cars did quite well till Daewoo's troubles in Korea led to the Indian operations closing down.

French firm Peugeot tied up with Premier Automobiles in 1994 to make Peugeot cars. This project was really doomed to failure from the start because of a number of mistakes made. Many of those who invested in this project lost their money. General Motors found a partner in Hindustan Motors. However, it was decided not to use Hindustan Motor's facilities in Kolkata but establish a brand new manufacturing site near Baroda in Gujarat. General Motors wanted to create a different work culture and this new plant was used to manufacture Opel cars. Honda Motors formed a joint venture with Delhi-based Siel (Shriram Industrial Enterprises Ltd, a spin-off from the DCM group) in 1995. Honda had known the group earlier through its very successful joint venture with them to make portable generating sets. The late Lala Charat Ram also had very good contacts and relationships with the Japanese. The project has flourished and Honda cars are doing reasonably well in India. The following year, Ford tied up with Mumbai-based commercial vehicles manufacturer Mahindra and Mahindra, while Hyundai Motor Corporation chose to set up a wholly owned subsidiary in 1996.

However, several problems were encountered in operationalizing the policy. Initially there was a big issue in determining what constituted a CKD kit and a SKD kit. For purposes of custom duties, a SKD kit attracted the much higher duty which was levied on an imported fully built car, while a CKD kit had a comparatively lower duty. This led to many disputes and legal proceedings between the car companies and the customs department. Some manufacturers were suspected of bringing in components which would constitute a SKD kit, but beating the system by importing those parts through two different ports! Companies were also not able to meet their export commitments.

After some time, as the foreign exchange balances of the government rose, the policy was liberalized. In November 1997, during Maran's tenure, a new policy was announced. Companies would have to invest a minimum of $50 million over a four-year period and the venture would have to become foreign exchange neutral within seven years. They would have to localize 50 per cent of production within three years of starting production and 70 per cent within seven years. Apart from cars, they would be allowed to export components and ancillaries and would get a moratorium of two years for meeting their export commitments. The policy was far more liberal compared to the PMP requirements of the pre-liberalization era.

Meanwhile, despite the difficult relations with the government, and the introduction of some competition, Maruti continued to make steady progress. Domestic sales increased by 22 per cent in 1996-97 over 1995-96 and the market share went to 79.6 per cent from 76.4 per cent in 1995-96. The bulk of this growth came from the smaller cars. In the bigger car segment, Maruti's market share dropped by almost half, from 65.8 per cent in 1995-96 to 38.2 per cent in 1996-97, as the number of players in the car market increased. However, the volume of sales did not decline. In 1997-98, the year I retired, Maruti again increased sales by 4.2 per cent and market share reached 82.7 per cent. This was the highest level ever reached and after that a slow but steady decline started. To an extent this was due to competition, but the disputes with the government and their impact also played a part.

~

Other issues were hanging fire. One related to the renewal of the licence agreement for the Maruti 800 and the Omni which had expired in November 1992, and for the Gypsy in December 1993. The government was reluctant to approve extension of the licences, arguing that technology had already been transferred to India and there was no need to pay any further royalty on these products. On the other hand, the management of Maruti realized that it did not have the same capabilities as SMC to make improvements and changes in the vehicles, and these would have to come from Japan. These models were no longer in production in Japan, and SMC would not work on making improvements on them unless they were paid to do so. Thus, paying a royalty was essential, as otherwise the vehicles would remain without any improvements or changes. That would be something similar to what happened to the Ambassador and the

Premier Padmini after the collaboration with their foreign partners expired. SMC had already expressed its desire to discontinue the 800 since the royalty was ending. I had negotiated a lower royalty, but the approval to this was being delayed in the government.

It took a great deal of effort to persuade the government to understand the value of keeping SMC working on making improvements, and it was pointed out that the royalty would now be less than half. Finally, the board passed a resolution, in September 1995, with the concurrence of the government directors, agreeing to the renewal of the agreement. The royalties on the 800, Omni and Gypsy would be what had earlier been agreed upon between SMC and the Maruti team and would be paid with effect from the dates on which the earlier royalties had ended.

In February 1997, there was a change of guard at the ministry. Prasad was transferred as secretary in the newly created Department of Industrial Policy and Promotion and was replaced as secretary, heavy industries, as well as chairman of Maruti, by Prabir Sengupta. But that did not make any difference to the face-off between SMC and the government. Perhaps Sengupta felt that any change of policy regarding SMC or moderation of the government's attitude might result in his being accused of having been 'influenced' by SMC. It was much safer to continue to act as if the ministry was protecting national interests by not accepting SMC's proposals about making further investments and improvements in Maruti, or on how to fund these investments, or consulting SMC on whom to appoint as the next managing director.

The flashpoint came when, at a board meeting on 27 August 1997, the government nominated Bhaskarudu as managing director to succeed me, as my five-year term ended that day.

Suzuki objected on the grounds that SMC had not been consulted and made it very clear that Bhaskarudu was not acceptable. The government argued that consultation was not necessary, since it was its turn to nominate the managing director under the 1992 agreement. Suzuki did not agree and suggested that Maruti remain without a managing director till the next annual general meeting (AGM), with a committee of directors running the company, an idea that Sengupta and Mukherji rejected outright. The question of a vote was raised. Both parties had an equal number of directors but Sengupta, as the chairman, had a casting vote in the event of a tie. SMC decided not to press for a vote as it thought it would lose. Bhaskarudu was approved by the board as the next managing director. It is an interesting thought as to what would have happened if a vote had been taken. Bhaskarudu could not have voted as he was interested in the resolution. In that event, SMC directors could have defeated the resolution. This would have created a stalemate and a situation which would have been hard to resolve.

The government had wanted to hold the AGM on the same day. This was possible if all the shareholders agreed to waive the statutory notice. SMC refused to do so. Thus the AGM had to be held later after following the legal procedure.

What had particularly riled Suzuki was the fact that SMC had been writing to the government for months, asking for consultations on the next managing director, but the government had not responded. Instead, it had acted unilaterally in naming Bhaskarudu on the day when my term ended. The meaning was clear. The government did not think that its partner in the project should be consulted regarding the managing director. It ignored the fact that in 1992 SMC had written to the government that it was nominating me as managing director, and the government had also written back mentioning the complaints against me but saying that it would accept whoever Suzuki finally decided to nominate.

The already bitter battle turned acrimonious, with Suzuki questioning Bhaskarudu's credentials to be the managing director. In a statement issued on 9 September, he lamented that 'it is extremely regrettable that the Indian government notified us of the appointment of a person who Suzuki believes is not suitable for the post of managing director of a joint company'. He went on to add that 'the appointments of top management should be discussed and agreed between partners of the joint venture at least two months in advance'.

SMC decided to take the legal route and filed a writ in the Delhi High Court asking for Bhaskarudu's appointment to be quashed and a stay on the AGM, or at least prohibiting the AGM from ratifying the board's decision on the managing director. The high court asked the two partners to sort out the problems, but when they could not, it dismissed SMC's petition on the morning of the AGM, holding that the parties should go for arbitration as provided in the agreement between them.

Consequent to Bhaskarudu becoming the managing director, SMC claimed the post of chairman, arguing that the five-year term of the government nominee had ended. The government did not agree, saying that it had appointed a chairman only in 1996 and the five-year term would count from that date. It did not accept the reasoning that not appointing the chairman in 1992, when it could have, was its own decision, and that SMC had not prevented it from doing so. Consequently, SMC's right to appoint the chairman after five years should not be compromised due to the government's own inaction, the company argued. The result was that from 28 August 1997 both the chairman and the managing director became government nominees. At that stage, logic and fair play were lost in the heat of passion. This was clearly against the spirit, if not also the letter, of the joint venture agreement signed when both partners acquired an equal number of shares in Maruti.

Meanwhile Suzuki was examining its other legal options. The conclusion reached was that filing an arbitration proceeding, in accordance with the joint venture agreement, would be the best bet. The arbitration would be carried out in Paris. SMC sought legal opinion both in India and abroad. In India, eminent lawyer Soli Sorabjee gave an opinion that the government should have consulted SMC before appointing Bhaskarudu. That was also the view taken by a former Chief Justice of India, P.N. Bhagwati. An arbitration petition was filed and SMC hired Amarchand Mangaldas as its solicitors. No separate legal action was taken on the matter of who should nominate the chairman.

With a case pending at the International Council for Arbitration (ICA), relations between the government and SMC were hardly cordial. By then very bitter words had been exchanged, with Maran saying SMC was free to exit from Maruti and that a number of foreign firms would be quite willing to step in. In fact there was a great deal of speculation as to why the government had taken such a hard stance against SMC, despite the runaway success of the project. The public sector had received a much-needed boost from the performance and reputation of Maruti. The government had been using it as a showpiece to flaunt the modernization of Indian industry, and to show that India could produce high quality engineering products, and attain productivity and costs levels which had enabled its cars to sell in Europe. Why risk all this by entering into a dispute with SMC?

The government could not have been unaware that it did not have the know-how or the technology to run an automobile plant, where there was a need to periodically develop and introduce new models. The industry had been delicensed and competition was growing. Without help from SMC, Maruti could not possibly compete with the international manufacturers who were in India. The late Lalit Suri, a leading businessman and hotelier, who was quite close to the government, told me that this approach had been adopted because Daewoo had offered to buy SMC's stake if it became available with the Japanese company exiting the project. The government was quite happy with this prospect. It possibly believed that Daewoo would be an adequate replacement for SMC. I pointed out that going along with Daewoo would mean shutting down the Maruti plant for twelve to eighteen months, since the factory would have to be modified to produce Daewoo cars. Manufacture of products licensed by Suzuki could not have continued. All the vendors would also need time to change their tooling to make parts for Daewoo cars, and the parts would have to be homologated, which itself would be a time-consuming exercise. Investments made for Maruti cars would have to be scrapped and would be a costly business.

I also asked Suri to check out Daewoo's creditworthiness, since it was already a highly leveraged company and my understanding was that it was financially quite weak. Would Daewoo really have the financial ability to do what it was apparently promising to do? Suri reverted to me a few days later, admitting that Daewoo's creditworthiness was indeed very low and banking on it replacing SMC was likely to be risky. The Daewoo idea died out after that. Three years later, Daewoo was officially bankrupt.

The immediate fallout of the dispute was on Maruti's fledgling research and development (R&D) programme. After 1992, SMC had been seeking an extension in the licence agreement for the 800 and then for the Omni and the Gypsy. The government, however, argued that SMC was making very little contribution to the technology for the vehicles, that there was no need for any further royalty to be paid. Differing views on this, and the new engine, resulted in the government proposing that Maruti's own R&D should make the company self-sufficient in engineering capability. The question was, how. Kumar had earlier submitted a detailed note on the subject to the board, which suggested sending Maruti engineers to Japan where they would work in SMC's design and development office for two years, after which they would return and start similar work in India. Maruti decided to send thirty-five to forty engineers in batches of five to seven a year. It also committed to the government that it would have the capability to complete the first minor change of a car by 2003 and a full body change by 2007-08. The first batch of two engineers left for Japan in 1994-95 and another batch went in 1996.

After the showdown over the managing director, a furious SMC said that the agreement for R&D training was over and that it would not take any more trainees. The facility which had been extended by SMC was in any case outside the scope of the joint venture agreement but SMC had agreed to Maruti's request as a means of strengthening the company. Between 1994-95 and 1996, Maruti had spent close to Rs. 50 crore on training of manpower and establishment of R&D facilities. Maruti engineers started going back to SMC after the dispute was settled and now SMC is actively working to establish a full-fledged design and engineering capability in Maruti. The dispute between the partners set back this process by at least five years. When the Ministry of Heavy Industries was trying to assert its 'sovereign rights' over SMC in the management of Maruti, the loss which the company would suffer in the long term, due to lack of technology transfer and delay in building internal capabilities was not given adequate consideration. Bhaskarudu was happy becoming the managing director even if it meant losing the support and cooperation of SMC. He should have realized the need to also keep Suzuki on his side.

Meanwhile, the chairman and chief executive officer of General Motors, John F. Smith, on a visit to India in November 1997, offered to mediate between the government and SMC. General Motors was then a 20 per cent equity holder in Suzuki Japan. However, nothing came of this effort. That very month, the United Front government fell and fresh elections were announced for February-March 1998. In December 1997 Sengupta had been transferred as secretary in the Ministry of Petroleum and Natural Gas (though he continued as Maruti chairman) and was replaced by P. Shankar. For SMC, this was a window of opportunity, as the minister would also change if a new political formation came to power. Keeping an eye on the future, they kept in touch with Shankar, who was an officer who understood the futileness of the dispute and the harm it was causing to the growth of Maruti and the automobile industry in India.

On 23 March 1998, another coalition, this time headed by the Bharatiya Janata Party (BJP), assumed office. The late Sikandar Bakht of the BJP became the new industry minister. There was now the possibility of a more pragmatic and business-like view being taken. However, SMC had to tread carefully, since known multinational-baiters, including George Fernandes, were part of the government, and the BJP also had a strong swadeshi brigade. SMC directors Y. Saito and J. Sugimori met Shankar to build a rapport with the new set-up in the industry ministry and see if the arbitration case could be settled outside the ICA.

Simultaneously there were several good Samaritan efforts being made. One of them was by Tarun Das, who was director general of the Confederation of Indian Industry (CII). He pointed out to the government how the dispute, and the long-drawn tension, was affecting investor sentiment. The new government realized this, as well as the fact that running a car manufacturing project was neither its business nor within its competence. It therefore decided to resolve the issue, and soon after taking over, Bakht told the minister of state for industry, Sukhbir Singh Badal, and Shankar, to negotiate with SMC.

SMC, on its part, also opened up other channels to the BJP, inviting member of Parliament Shatrughan Sinha to Hamamatsu for celebrations relating to fifty years of Indian independence. SMC's representative in India, N. Kawahara, remained in touch not only with Sinha but also the late Pramod Mahajan, party general secretary, who was then political advisor to the Prime Minister. The approach was to convey SMC's deep interest in India and the Maruti project, and try and explain how the dispute was causing harm to all the parties. SMC reiterated that it had never sought to challenge the sovereign rights of the State but did need to protect its own business interests and those of Maruti. The government was sympathetic and understood the possible reasons as to why relations between the government and SMC had suddenly soured, despite Maruti performing so well.

Even as the discussions were going on, a completely unexpected strategic-political development took place and worked in SMC's favour. On 11 and 13 May 1998, India conducted a series of nuclear tests, inviting sanctions from across the world. The sanctions imposed by Japan, with its strong anti-nuclear sentiment, were among the strongest. Ending the face-off with SMC was one way of earning brownie points with the Japanese government.

Meanwhile, time was running out. The ICA was to deliver its

verdict on 20 June. SMC was confident it had a strong case but still favoured an out-of-court settlement. After all, scoring a legal victory over the partner—especially when the partner was the government of a country—could hardly make for future good business or working relationships. In the first week of that month, three top SMC executives—Sugimori, Y. Saito and K. Saito—flew to India, amid strict secrecy, to put the finishing touches to a compromise agreement on the basis of which the arbitration proceedings could be withdrawn.

On 8 June 1998, Bakht announced in Parliament that the government and SMC had worked out a compromise. SMC would withdraw its case in the ICA and would appoint Y. Saito as chairman till 2002, while the government would withdraw Sengupta. Bhaskarudu, whose term, in normal circumstances, would have ended in August 2002, would step down in December 1999. Khattar, SMC's original choice for the post, would take over then. Khattar was brought back to the board as joint managing director from 1 July 1998, with the understanding that he would be designated second managing director exactly a year later. The agreement also said that the Maruti board would devise appropriate administrative measures to enhance the effective control of the company, including the formation of two board sub-committees for purchase and marketing in order to strengthen its competitiveness.

The announcement caused a furore in Parliament, with the opposition terming the compromise a sell-out by the government, the most stinging attacks coming from former industry ministers Karunakaran and Maran and from Jaipal Reddy, who had been the chairman of the Assurances Committee of the Rajya Sabha. Two points particularly incensed them. One was that both the posts of chairman and managing director were being filled by SMC's nominees. Secondly, they felt the new agreement gave SMC control over day-to-day management of the company through clause 6.3. The clause read:

> The experience and expertise of Suzuki shall be recognized and respected with respect to the technology and management of Maruti, which includes important decisions on day-to-day management as well as decisions on management policies.

This, it was argued, went further than the 1992 agreement which said SMC's concurrence would be sought on key decisions. There was a demand for an inquiry by a joint parliamentary committee into the whole affair. The government was clear in its mind that what it was doing was in the best interests of India. It stood firm and did not concede to any of the demands of the opposition. Subsequent events relating to the growth of Maruti and its contribution to the further development of the Indian automobile industry, as well as exports, prove that the decision to settle the dispute, give management control to SMC and list the company at a later date, were really the best in the national interests. If the approach towards the management of Maruti and the attitude to SMC, adopted in 1995 by Prasad and Karunakaran and continued by Maran and Sengupta, had not been changed, Maruti would have possibly become like most of the PSUs.

That crisis had blown over. It was now time to move ahead and recover lost ground.

~

The economy was slowing down, with growth slipping to 4.3 per cent in 1997-98. The automobile industry, including the commercial vehicle and two-wheeler segments, could not remain unscathed—growth came down to 1.6 per cent. Within that, the passenger car segment did slightly better, but even here growth was subdued at 4 per cent. Maruti had managed an 8 per cent growth in sales, despite a depressed market, and increased its market share to 82.9 per cent. But that dominant position was about to be challenged, with a host of new entrants driving into the arena. Hyundai's Santro and Daewoo's Matiz were both due to hit the roads later in the year, while General Motors' Corsa was expected to be launched in 1999. As it happened, both the Matiz and the Corsa got delayed; the Matiz was launched in 1999 and Corsa in 2000.

The two-year stand-off had resulted in the project for changing the body shell of the 800—by developing engineering capabilities in Maruti—being shelved. The need for making this change was obvious—the shape of the car had remained the same since 1986 and market feedback indicated that customers wanted a change.

Meanwhile, the two production lines in Maruti, with a nominal installed capacity of 240,000 units a year, were actually working close to 140 per cent of that capacity. There was a need to install additional capacity. Work on a third line had started in 1998, after large delays caused by the dispute regarding its location, and this plant was commissioned in Gurgaon in 1999.

The outlook for passenger cars had started to worsen in 1998, with the overall market shrinking by 5 per cent. Not only was the economy going through a slowdown, customers also postponed purchase decisions, waiting to assess the new cars that had been announced and would be rolled out shortly. Maruti could not buck the industry trend; its sales dropped 5 per cent in 1998-99. This was the first time since its inception that sales had declined, and it was not a very auspicious start to the term of the new managing director.

The company's immediate priority was to recover lost ground. On 1 July 1998, less than a month after the new agreement between the government and SMC was concluded, Kumar (who was brought back to the board on 22 June, a few days short of two years since he was removed) was in Hamamatsu to discuss the new models and cars that should be launched, necessary if Maruti were not to lose market share and successfully face increasing competition.

The bigger immediate challenge was to meet the Euro-I (also called Bharat Stage I) norms by June 1999, because cars which did not comply could not be sold in areas where this norm was made applicable. Pollution levels in Delhi were increasing and the Delhi-based Centre for Science and Environment (CSE), headed by Sunita Narain, had been focussing on automobile emissions, particularly on how diesel vehicles were creating unacceptable levels of pollution. The Supreme Court had taken cognizance of this problem and had appointed a committee under former bureaucrat Bhure Lal to study how to deal with the problem. Khattar and Sunita Narain were members of the committee. At that time, the main diesel car in the market was Tata Motors' Indica. There was a strong belief in Tata Motors that the CSE was attacking diesel cars at Khattar's behest. It seemed to me that Tata Motors was possibly underestimating the integrity of Sunita Narain, and overestimating Khattar's influence over her. Nevertheless this adversely affected relations between Maruti and Tata Motors.

Meanwhile, the government had indicated that Euro 1 norms would be applied in Delhi and some other metro cities in 2001. However, the Supreme Court wanted to know why the norms could not be made applicable in Delhi from an earlier date. I have been informed that no consultations were held with Maruti, and possibly Hindustan Motors and Premier Automobiles, by the Association of Indian Automobile Manufacturers. Since petrol cars were expected to need multi-point fuel injection (MPFI) systems to meet these norms, which no car manufacturer was ready with, it was unlikely that these three companies would have agreed to the date being advanced. However, the association, possibly with the approval of the president, V.M. Raval, conveyed to the Court that Euro 1 norms could be applied in Delhi from 1999. The only cars that were likely to meet these norms were the diesel ones, for which these were comparatively lax. As a result of the association's reply, the Court ordered that Euro 1 would apply to car sales in Delhi from June 1999, two years ahead of what the government had indicated. In other metro cities, the norms were applied two years later.

Premier Automobiles and Hindustan Motors had to stop the sale of their petrol cars in Delhi. The diesel Ambassador, however, could meet the norms, and continued to sell. The efforts made earlier by Maruti to enable the 800 to meet European emission norms in 1991 came in handy now. Contrary to accepted technical thinking, it managed to modify the carburettor of the 800 to meet the Euro-I norms and continued to sell the car in Delhi. SMC was unhappy about the 800 being sold with a carburettor, and refused to be associated with the effort to comply with Euro-I. SMC engineers carried out emission checks on many occasions to determine whether we were really meeting the standards. The work done by Kumar was sound and no fault could be found. Even the Automobile Research Association of India (ARAI) would carry out six-monthly checks. Maruti cars passed every time. This was a real feather in the cap of our engineers. Maruti had also developed fuel injection systems for the Zen and the Esteem. Consequently, Maruti could maintain its sale volumes in Delhi. Sales of the carburettor version of the 800 continued till 2005, when the MPFI system was introduced.

In June 1999, six months before Bhaskarudu's tenure was to end in December, the government appointed him a member of the Public Enterprises Selection Board (PESB). He moved to his new assignment in August. The government apparently realized the futility of having a lame-duck managing director, and recognized the need to have one who would have an incentive for reviving the fortunes of the company. Khattar was now in full charge and had to fulfil the expectations of both shareholders. The government had taken a big political risk by agreeing to give SMC de facto control over Maruti at that point, and to give de jure control when SMC acquired a majority equity holding in a few years' time. To be able to justify this, Maruti needed to prosper and the government needed to gain handsomely from the sale of its equity holding.

Work got under way at a hectic pace on launching new cars, without which Maruti could not hope to regain its market share. This started what came to be dubbed as Maruti's second automobile revolution. Maruti launched new vehicles—the Baleno and the Wagon-R, the latter targeted at the Hyundai Santro, which had become very popular by then. The Baleno never sold in any large numbers, but did fulfil the objective of giving Maruti a presence in the large car segment. Variants of existing cars followed and Maruti was soon fighting its way back into the reckoning. In 1999-2000, Maruti clocked an all-time high in its history—it sold 3.85 lakh cars, an increase of 24.2 per cent over the previous year. The automobile industry as a whole also logged good sales growth, 48.6 per cent over the previous year. Indeed, 1999-2000 was a landmark year for Maruti. It became the largest Asian car company outside of Japan and South Korea, rolling out 400,000 cars. It was the first Indian automobile company to do so and also to get ISO 14001 certification for its environmental management.

Maruti was getting to see some good news after a long time. But it barely got a chance to revel in it.

~

On 23 March 2000, the Maruti Udyog Employees Union served a sixteen-point charter of demands mainly relating to revision of the incentive scheme. While discussions were going on between the union and the management on these, the company was preparing for the launch of the Alto. This was a small car, meant eventually to replace the 800 as the entry-level car. The union was not in a mood to arrive at a reasonable settlement. It had got used to being pampered during the time of Bhaskarudu, and had enjoyed considerable power, due to its political links with the Left and the role it felt it had played in ensuring that Bhaskarudu, and not Khattar, became the managing director in 1997. Its leadership, unfortunately, believed that the role of the union was to create confrontations with the management. Hence these discussions were not making any real progress, and it wanted to display its strength and force the management to bow to its demands. The union leadership also probably felt that it would not remain as powerful under Khattar and wanted to establish its importance. In order to do so, and to create pressure, the workers started a relay hunger strike in September, which escalated into go-slow and led to a dharna and a gherao of the canteen in October 2000. The management, rightly, took the view that a productivity incentive scheme did not require concurrence of the union, and consultations were adequate. Accordingly, on 11 October, a productivity performance and profitability-linked incentive scheme was notified.

Meanwhile, finding that the management was not accepting its demands regarding the incentive scheme, the union had been orchestrating a staggered two-hours tool-down strike, moving from department to department, bringing production down to a mere 299 vehicles a day. This could not be tolerated. A day after notifying the new incentive scheme, the management suspended nearly eighty workers and declared that from the next day, only those workers who signed a good conduct undertaking would be allowed into the factory. Those who did not would be considered to be on illegal strike. A stand-off followed, which lasted for three months, ending on 9 January 2001, when the union called off the strike and agreed to accept the 11 October incentive package.

Did this strike mean that the efforts made from 1983 to create a new work culture had failed? Could it be interpreted to mean that workers and managements could never work in cooperation, with the common objective of furthering the growth of the company? Would the union and management again become adversaries? I believe that the validity of the approach towards educating the workers and management winning their trust remains as important as ever. This strike happened because the union, and its leadership, got involved in the power struggle for appointment to the post of managing director.

Having just come out of a three-month strike, the management had to walk a tight rope. The union had been made to back down, but there was little to gain by rubbing in the point. Real progress required the cooperation of the workers. Without their active support and involvement there could not be real improvements in productivity or substantial reductions in cost. Fortunately, the new union leadership remembered that in the past they had benefited enormously by cooperating with the management, which led to the prosperity of the company as well as all workers. They saw that what had happened was an aberration caused by the ambitions of essentially one or two leaders, and a management which had encouraged them. The strike had caused both workers and the company to lose, and the future prosperity of the workers could only be assured if Maruti once again attained its dominant market position. Since the management was once again extending the hand of cooperation the workers also decided that full cooperation would be the best option for them.

There were sighs of relief, but the crisis had taken its toll on the company. As it is, the two years of problems with the government had left it unprepared to take on the newer cars that had hit the market. Overall car sales were down and in June 2000, three months before the strike, Maruti was holding a stock of close to 17,000 unsold cars. With dealers also putting pressure, because of high inventory holding costs, the company had little choice but to cut prices of its entry-level models in end-June. The three-month strike left Maruti unable to make up for the price cuts through increased sales. At the end of 2000-2001, Maruti had sold only 3.35 lakh vehicles, a 12 per cent drop over the previous year. That was not all. For the first time in its history of eighteen years, the company posted a loss of Rs. 269.4 crore, a huge fall from the previous year's profit of Rs. 330 crore. This was a blow to the pride of the company and galvanized SMC, the management and the workers into restoring high standards of performance.

In order to reduce costs, a large number of activities were rationalized, and the company had to deal with the problem of surplus manpower that was created as a result. It was agreed that this would be done by offering a handsome voluntary retirement scheme. This saw 19 per cent of employees leaving the company. While there was a large initial outflow of money in the form of compensation, it helped to improve productivity and reduce recurring costs.

In 2002, Maruti took up Challenge 30, a project which required that the supply chain department reduce costs of all components by 30 per cent over the next three years. To achieve this, vendors had to be made more efficient and productive, with higher local content in their products, so that lower prices could be negotiated. A very detailed programme was worked out, with the macro target broken up into monthly goals—by department, division and individuals—which were monitored every month and results reported to Japan. After I joined the board in 2003, I was involved in this monitoring along with T. Kobayashi, the joint managing director. At the end of three years, in 2005, the target of 30 per cent had been exceeded by a couple of points. A further challenge, again to reduce costs by 30 per cent, was taken up for the period 2005-08, and this too was achieved, though it was a much harder task.

At the same time as Challenge 30 was started, the production department took up Challenge 50, which required a 50 per cent increase in in-house productivity over the same three-year period. The result was an achievement of just under 50 per cent. For 2005-08 the goal was set at 20 per cent improvement in productivity and this target was met.

The sales and marketing department undertook Challenge 60, which required increasing the market share to 60 per cent. The success on this front was not so good and the market share plateaued at 55 per cent. Even after 2005, the market share has remained around 54 per cent.

By then, the Indian market was exposed to the products of a large number of international manufacturers, who had established operations in India. All of them were anxious to gain market share and had introduced models in all segments, except the entry-level A1 segment. Customers, who till only a few years back had very limited options, now had problems of choice. Many of them, who were perfectly happy with the performance of their Maruti cars, decided to buy some other car only because they wanted to experience change. SMC realized that the market had changed: it would no longer be possible to satisfy customers by offering high quality products at low prices. The customer also wanted, like users abroad, the pleasure of changing models every few years. It was now necessary to address this aspect, even though this would necessarily mean higher costs of production. Facelifts, minor changes and full model changes became part of the scope of discussion in the product development committee meetings, and the role of the engineering division substantially increased. It was clear that this work would have to be increasingly done in India, because manpower resources in Japan were limited.

Competition in the marketplace also made it harder for the dealers to generate profits. Waiting lists had disappeared, and dealers could no longer enjoy the luxury of getting paid in advance, and, therefore, not needing working capital. They now had to keep adequate inventory of all models, as customers were not willing to wait for delivery and would buy another make if a Maruti dealer quoted a long waiting period. Often a customer would talk with different dealers, negotiating the best price. As a result, margins provided by Maruti to dealers started to erode. Maruti also decided that as a policy, dealers should employ sales persons to generate business and not rely on brokers to bring customers, or hope that customers would just walk in. The dependence on brokers was considered to be highly risky in a competitive market, as these persons were driven only by money and could be wooed away by a competitor offering a higher commission. Lastly, Maruti was also expanding the dealership network, to provide better customer convenience, as well as higher availability of managerial resources and working capital, and this led to some fall in the sale volume of many dealers. It thus became necessary to find other ways of enhancing dealer profitability.

A study was done by a leading consultancy firm, A.T. Kearney, and based on its recommendations, Maruti added a number of new activities designed to open sources of income for dealers. These included selling insurance and finance, giving extended warranties and opening outlets for the sale of used cars. Maruti itself established subsidiary companies to support these activities.

All this paid off. At the end of 2001-02, Maruti was back in the black, with a profit of Rs. 104.5 crore, despite the fact that the automobile industry continued to be sluggish. Maruti itself logged a mere 1 per cent sales growth, with sales of the 800 and the Omni actually declining by 3 per cent.

But by that time, Maruti was preparing to embark on another phase of its life.

~

In February 2001, the government decided that Maruti should be listed and that the government would gradually disinvest its equity in Maruti. A team, which included the secretaries of the Ministry of Disinvestment and the Department of Heavy Industry, as well as the managing director and chief executive officer of ICICI, K.V. Kamath, were deputed to negotiate with SMC and finalize the modalities of the government's exit from Maruti. After a month of negotiations, it was decided that the disinvestment would happen in two stages—first a rights issue by Maruti, with the government renouncing its rights shares to SMC, and then a two-step sale of part of the government stake through an initial public offer (IPO). The remaining government equity would be sold by 2007, and as long as the government had at least 10 per cent equity it would continue to have a seat on the board. SMC was to pay a control premium to the government—the price of getting management control over the company—which would come when SMC's equity increased to over 50 per cent.

Negotiations then began over valuation of Maruti shares, the pricing of the rights issue and the control premium that SMC was to pay. This was not an easy task given the measure of distrust that had crept in between the two sides, as a result of the developments of 1996-98. With three consultancy firms appointed to value the company—KPMG, Ernst & Young and S.B. Billimoria—giving three different valuations, an average was worked out—Rs. 3,280. It was decided that the size of the rights issue would be Rs. 400 crore.

The negotiations over the control premium caused some friction. SMC initially offered Rs. 170 crore. The government felt this was too low, especially since SMC had not paid any control premium in 1992. The government argued that SMC would now get total control over management, whereas in 1992 it was only sharing management with the government. The secretary, heavy industries, who was aware that I was advising SMC, spoke to me and said that the government would be willing to accept a control premium of Rs. 1,000 crore. I had conveyed this to Suzuki in Japan. Long-drawn-out bargaining finally resulted in the control premium being raised to Rs. 286 crore at first and then being finalized at Rs. 1,000 crore. SMC was also initially not willing to underwrite the public issue by the government of its shares, but was later persuaded to do so.

On 30 May 2002, following the rights issue which brought down the government's stake to 45.4 per cent, SMC took complete control of the steering wheel at Maruti.

This was followed in 2003 by Maruti's first public issue, with the government offloading 27.5 per cent of its stake in the company. The Rs. 100 face value of the equity was considered too high and it was decided to keep the face value at Rs. 5. The floor price of Rs. 115 was mentioned in the red herring prospectus, and the upper price was set at Rs. 125. It was perhaps not a great time to go to the market, which was a bit bearish. However, that did not seem to matter. The issue was oversubscribed ten times, and the price for the issue was determined to be Rs. 125. Many people thought that this was too high a price. Even the chairman of Life Insurance Corporation, which was a very large investor in the stock market, told Khattar that he would not subscribe at this price. Later, LIC was to buy Maruti shares at a much higher price! The shares, however, opened at Rs. 165 at the time of listing and kept rising. One consequence of the price rise was that many individual shareholders sold their shares as they perhaps thought that the shares could not rise further, and the number of individual shareholders declined over the years. The initial price of the shares also prompted the government to exercise the green-shoe option (where more shares than originally planned can be sold) and it sold another 10 per cent of holding, bringing its stake in the company down to 18.3 per cent.

A last skirmish, though, between SMC and the government was still to happen. Once again, the issue was a new plant.

It was sparked off on 13 September 2004, when Suzuki, at a press conference in Tokyo after a SMC board meeting, announced that the company would invest Rs. 1,524 crore to set up another joint venture with Maruti, called Maruti Suzuki Automobiles India Ltd (MSAIL) to manufacture cars at Manesar. Unfortunately the announcement made was not very clear about the structure of this new company and who would control its management. Nobody in India also thought it necessary to get a clarification and instead there was an uproar, both in government circles and in the stock market, as it was assumed that SMC would control this new company, and compete with Maruti through the Manesar plant. As a consequence, Maruti would get stepmotherly treatment in getting technology and new models. The profits and market share of Maruti would drop.

This led to panic selling of Maruti shares by investors. Maruti share prices fell 10 per cent in one day and the company lost close to Rs. 300 crore in market capitalization over two trading sessions. The government was livid. For one, such matters should have been discussed in the Maruti board, of which the government was still a part. Besides, government regulations at that time required that a foreign partner of an existing joint venture must get a no-objection certificate from the Indian partner if it was to set up a wholly owned subsidiary in the same line of business. The government feared the value of its remaining shares would erode, not exactly a welcome development at the time as the government still had to sell its remaining 18.3 per cent stake. Heavy industries minister Santosh Mohan Dev charged SMC with keeping the government in the dark and ministry officials wrote to the Foreign Investment Promotion Board asking it not to clear SMC applications relating to this venture. Nakanishi, who was then the chairman, and Khattar rushed to the ministry to explain that Maruti would be a majority owner of MSAIL, which would be a subsidiary controlled by Maruti. The incident showed the importance of very clear and complete information being disclosed, at the very first opportunity, in such sensitive matters. While clarifications do lead to normalcy, in the interim period much damage is possible. The government accepted the explanation and the matter was resolved amicably. The stock market duly corrected share values.

There was a history to the establishment of MSAIL. The Gurgaon site had been fully developed with the establishment of three manufacturing plants. There was no scope for any further development here. A new site was needed for future expansion and Manesar was selected. Khattar was successful in negotiating with the Haryana government to purchase 600 acres of land there, on very reasonable terms. The intention was to establish the next production facility there, along with an R&D centre having a full-fledged test track, and also keep some land for vendors. SMC wanted this plant to be very similar to the plant in Kosai, Japan, so that there could be a high level of automation, and the best SMC practices could be established here from the start. Suzuki did not want this plant to become an extension of the Gurgaon plant, which had been built over twenty years and had much more manual operations. He wanted the plants at Gurgaon and Manesar to compete with each other in areas like productivity and quality, with each being a benchmark for the other. At the same time, it was always the intention that in areas like human resource management, supply chain and sales and marketing, the two plants should work as one. For this reason, at the stage of planning the project, he wanted the Manesar plant to be a SMC subsidiary and not a Maruti subsidiary.

Many of the Japanese executives who were in India were not convinced that this would necessarily be a good idea, but since Suzuki had already made up his mind, they did not try and persuade him to change it. When they found that I was of the same opinion as them, they asked me to discuss this issue with Suzuki. I did so and explained the political consequences of having a separate company and the possibility of an adverse government reaction. I had argued with Suzuki that since Maruti was also now a SMC subsidiary, the objectives of the Gurgaon and Manesar plants competing to attain better productivity, lower costs and higher quality could be as well achieved by keeping the Manesar plant as a Maruti subsidiary. Suzuki immediately realized the political implications of having a separate company. Without further argument he agreed that the Manesar company would be a Maruti subsidiary, with Maruti holding the majority equity. Despite this decision, there was a subsequent communication failure.

The subsidiary company (MSAIL) was established, with Suzuki having 30 per cent equity and Maruti investing 70 per cent. Since SMC owned 54 per cent of Maruti, this meant that its financial interest in MSAIL would be to the extent of 67.8 per cent. Investments for establishing another manufacturing line in Manesar were soon approved. Equipment orders were placed and a foreign exchange loan was finalized to pay for the equipment.

Meanwhile, with the help of a consulting company, the system for getting the two companies to coordinate their working was studied. As already planned, the two companies were to have common supply chain development including vendors, common sales and marketing including dealers, while Maruti would manage the human resource aspect. However, during discussions with the consultant, many tricky issues, including those of transfer pricing and taxation, arose and after a great deal of thinking, it was concluded that a solution which would not result in tax litigation on a large scale would not be possible. There were also issues of corporate governance and maintaining arms-length operations, since Maruti was a listed company and the shareholding of SMC was different in the two companies.

The senior Japanese managers in India and Khattar all agreed that having separate companies was not a good idea. It was once again left to me to have another discussion with Suzuki and explain the complications involved in the arrangements, and the risk of expensive litigation. Once again, Suzuki was very receptive and agreed to change the earlier decision to have MSAIL as a separate subsidiary. Maruti and MSAIL were to be merged, but the Gurgaon and Manesar plants would be separate profit centres for internal control purposes. Each would still serve as a benchmark for the other in terms of key production parameters.

On the same day as the MSAIL announcement Suzuki made another announcement that SMC would invest Rs. 427 crore in Suzuki Metal India Limited, and rename this company as Suzuki Powertrain India Limited. The company was till then primarily making aluminium castings for engine blocks and cylinder heads. It was now intended to include the manufacture of petrol and diesel engines as well as transmission gears for Maruti vehicles. The equity holding of SMC in Suzuki Metals initially was 51 per cent, the rest being with Maruti. It was now intended that Suzuki would hold 70 per cent equity and Maruti 30 per cent. Read with the initial interpretation of the MSAIL structuring, this announcement too did not go down too well, but when the correct position was understood, the move was welcomed. The government had for a very long time been wanting gears to be manufactured in India.

Over the next three years, the government sold off its stake in two tranches. It sold 8 per cent in January 2006. On 10 May 2007, the government sold its remaining 10.27 per cent stake in Maruti, about twenty-six years after it had established a 100 per cent owned company in February 1981. Four months later, Maruti Udyog Ltd was rechristened Maruti Suzuki India Ltd.

By then the modernization of the automobile industry—one of the objectives of taking over the assets of Maruti Limited—had been well and truly achieved. Maruti was the largest car manufacturer in the country, with twelve vehicles across different categories of the automobile sector, barring commercial vehicles. And it remained the leader, with 55.8 per cent market share.

7

PREPARING THE VENDORS

The first 192 cars to roll out of the factory in December 1983 were almost entirely Japanese cars, with only the tyres and the batteries being Indian, supplies coming from Chennai-based MRF and Kolkata-based Chloride India (later renamed Exide Industries) respectively. The indigenization percentage was a mere 2.7666 per cent and it stayed at less than 10 per cent till March 1984.

The December 1983 deadline of starting production and sale of cars necessitated starting production with imported SKD kits. SMC said this could be possible only if painted body shells, along with virtually all of the other components of a car, were imported. Where these components were required to be assembled using fixtures and special tooling like the door, the engine or the transmission system, they were imported as sub-assemblies. There was no time to install the welding and paint shops, without which the body panels could not be assembled. A similar position existed regarding the other major assemblies.

An advantage of following this approach was that the workers could learn how to assemble and test the cars, before upstream activities were undertaken. The step-by-step approach to doing complicated tasks, we found as we went along, was typical of the Japanese way. It helped to reduce mistakes and underutilization of capacities.

The use of local components was dictated by their availability—or rather the lack of it. We had to make special efforts with Chloride India and MRF so that there could be some Indian components in the first cars. In any case, the procedure for the acceptance of locally made components for use in SMC was quite elaborate and time-consuming. Any significant use of Indian components in the first cars to be produced could only have been possible if some acceptable components were already being produced in India. This was not the case.

In the project report prepared for approval of investment by the government, Maruti had to indicate the extent to which each vehicle would be localized every year. This was the phased manufacturing programme (PMP), which applied to all foreign technical collaboration agreements. The purpose was to ensure that technology was transferred and absorbed in India, and also to limit the outflow of scarce foreign currency. The government believed that once the components were manufactured in India, technology transfer would have taken place, and the capacity to make further improvements and design better components would automatically develop. This did not happen for many reasons, including the lack of incentive for manufacturers to develop such capabilities. This and other policies regarding the inflow of technology and prevention of competition led to virtually all products, originally produced with the then current foreign technology, gradually becoming obsolete and India never developing, till the 1990s, the ability to export manufactured products. The Directorate-General of Technical Development (DGTD), responsible for technology development, failed to understand that Indian companies operating in a non-competitive environment had no commercial need to create engineering and design capabilities.

In the automobile sector, when a vendor entered into a licence agreement with a foreign manufacturer to produce a component, the agreement rarely included any provision to develop R&D and design capabilities in India. This was the general practice prevailing across other industries till then. One reason was that foreign companies were very reluctant to part with their core intellectual property, unless they had a controlling interest in the Indian company. Another was the fact that vendors, in the early years of Maruti, did not want to increase their investment costs, or licence fee costs, which would have been required if they were to establish a proper design and engineering centre. Vendors who had to make simple components, which did not require know-how from abroad, were also not keen at that time to spend money on any elaborate design facilities. In addition, the volume of production of components and the turnover were at levels that did not make investments in development capabilities viable.

Thus the technology transfer as a result of the PMP was largely limited to creating the ability to manufacture specific components. However, the localization programme did serve the purpose of saving foreign currency and insulating products from the effects of currency fluctuations. This itself was of considerable benefit.

The DGTD was responsible for the implementation of the PMP, and reviewed the localization efforts of all those who had foreign collaborations which required import of components.

The finance ministry would only issue an import licence and release foreign exchange on the basis of what was recommended by the DGTD. Failure to meet PMP targets could result in production levels having to be reduced so that the total foreign exchange released was kept within the limits determined by the government.

Maruti had committed to achieving 95 per cent indigenization in five years. An indicative list of components to be localized each year had been prepared in consultation with SMC, and was based on considerations of availability of technology and ease of local manufacture, among other things. The company had discussions every year with the DGTD to determine the local content for the following year and to get the necessary import licences. Since Maruti had a long waiting list of customers, and had committed both to them and the government that a production volume of 100,000 units a year would be achieved in the fifth year, the fulfilment of localization targets became a high priority, as otherwise shortage of foreign currency released by the government would have led to curtailment of production volumes.

Though the Maruti localization programme was driven mainly by the need to conserve scarce foreign exchange, the lower wage and manufacturing costs in India also provided compelling logic for increasing indigenization levels. In addition, high import content would make exports—which was always an objective of the Maruti project—difficult. In fact, localization protected Maruti from the impact of the considerable depreciation of the rupee, and it could maintain competitive price levels, allowing the 800 to become among the lowest cost cars in the world. Over time, as volumes of production of this car increased, and the rupee depreciated, the price of most locally made components became lower than the FOB price of the same components.

The PMP was often severely criticized and blamed for the poor quality and high prices of Indian products. Import substitution, in most cases, resulted in vendors supplying high cost and poor quality components. One of the reasons was that the production volumes were small. Thus, in the case of the two cars being earlier manufactured in India, the combined volume was barely 40,000 after thirty years of going into production. This volume was usually split between two or more suppliers for each part. This was too small for vendors to adopt good manufacturing systems and buy high quality tooling. All the overhead costs, including management salaries, had to be recovered from the limited production volumes. When volumes increase, the fixed costs do not increase in proportion and cost of production declines. Quality and cost are really related to volumes being above a minimum threshold level. That is why the volume of production for Maruti was fixed at 100,000 units a year. The customers of the components—the automobile companies—also did not demand high quality as this was not necessary for selling their products and making profits. The original equipment manufacturers (OEMs) did not consider getting involved with improving vendor production systems as part of their responsibility. They accepted whatever was available, and could tell the few customers who complained about quality that the fault was of the vendors, and the PMP system, since they could not import better parts.

Maruti offered much higher volumes to vendors, promising a production of 100,000 units a year. The involvement of SMC with Maruti, and the adoption of Japanese standards of quality, also meant that there was a demand for quality components and no vendor component could be accepted unless it met a minimum standard. Thus, two of the essential conditions for better quality and lower costs were met. The Maruti experience of working with vendors showed that if vendor development was undertaken in a systematic way, the environment was positive, and vendors were educated and motivated to improve, they would do so. The problems and limitations of vendors had to be understood and dealt with in a pragmatic manner. With hindsight, the PMP resulted in Maruti avoiding the huge extra costs that would have had to be paid if import content had been higher, because of the yen appreciating from 230 to the dollar to around 100. The four light commercial vehicle projects, all with Japanese collaborations, which were started around the same time as Maruti, ran into severe cost problems due to yen appreciation.

Maruti, however, had to face an uphill task in developing the vendor base. The state of India's component industry in the early 1980s was pathetic and is summed up in this observation by Krishnamurthy in Maruti's first annual report:

> It has been plagued with low levels of demand which do not permit the use of modern technologies, poor quality of inputs, inadequate infrastructural support and lack of incentive for bringing about improvements in product quality and customer service.

Besides the low volume of component production, which made it virtually impossible to produce good quality at a reasonable price, another reason for the poor health of the component industry was the stagnation in the car industry, both in terms of volume as well as technology. The absence of competition, and the low priority accorded to cars in the economic policy of the government, led to the absence of any incentive and opportunity for the industry to upgrade quality and technology. For almost the entire period after 1950, the supply of cars was less than the demand, with long waiting periods. In this situation, the

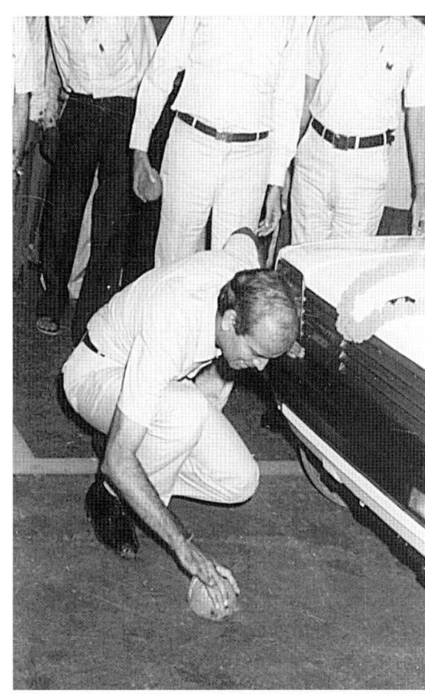

Production of Maruti 800, India's first people's car, being flagged off, October 1983

It began with this: the first Maruti 800

Indira Gandhi being shown the model of the Maruti plant in Gurgaon, at the release of the first car, 14 December 1983

Indira Gandhi handing over the keys to Maruti's first customer, Harpal Singh, an employee of Indian Airlines

Rajiv Gandhi visits the Maruti plant in Gurgaon for the launch of the four-wheel drive Gypsy, December 1985

O. Suzuki, CEO of Suzuki Motor Corporation, on his visit to the Gurgaon Joint Venture Complex in 1988

The one millionth car from Maruti being handed over to Mother Teresa

The managing director, Maruti Suzuki India Limited, receiving the Economic Times Award for Corporate Performance in 1991, from Dr Manmohan Singh, who was finance minister at the time

Maruti's 24-hour mobile service facility is launched, May 1996

The Maruti Initial Public Offer is launched at the Bombay Stock Exchange in 2003, to resounding success

The five millionth car rolls out, April 2005

Maruti ranked No. 1 in the JD Power Consumer Satisfaction Index, for the ninth consecutive year, October 2008

At the celebrations marking a highly successful twenty-five years of Maruti, 14 December 2008

Moving with the times: Launch of the A-Star, November 2008 (above); Launch of the Ritz, May 2009 (below)

manufacturers had little concern for providing quality cars to their customers (they, on their part, would argue that the highly regulated Indian business environment hampered them at every stage). Since the production volume was limited by the licence conditions, there was no real incentive to reduce costs and improve quality so as to grow the market and get a bigger market share. Enough profit, including the cash premium at the point of sale, could be made even otherwise.

The poor quality of original equipment (the parts used in the original car) meant a thriving market for spare parts, the shoddy quality of which ensured a steady demand of replacement pieces. There were enough stories about automobile manufacturers themselves, or their relatives, having majority or full stake in component manufacturing companies and making their profits from selling spare parts at high prices. The absence of competition was a blessing for those in the manufacturing business.

All this was going to change with the coming of Maruti. The company was bringing in a modern product that required components that could not be produced without upgrading the manufacturing processes, as well as the materials used. The testing procedures, before a component was accepted for use, were stringent and SMC would not compromise on quality standards. The objective of modernizing the automobile industry could not, in any case, have been achieved if the component industry were not modernized.

~

Maruti recognized the huge challenge before it, as hundreds of suppliers had to be persuaded to not only upgrade technology and manufacturing processes but also change their attitude to quality and meeting obligations and commitments. Most vendors did not think that a small delay in meeting their supply schedules, or some shortfall in quantities, was a significant matter. They were quite accustomed to changing the source of supply of their inputs and did not realize that this could impact on quality. Many vendors would change their manufacturing process in some area, thinking it would not matter. Maruti had to make them realize that the key to quality lay in consistently, without any deviation, following the approved procedure for manufacture, including the source of supply of inputs and the approved manufacturing process. If any change was to be made anywhere, it had to be first approved by Maruti. The task before Maruti was made harder by the time constraints imposed by the PMP. There was no luxury of a slow and steady process of improvement in quality, if the multiple objectives of meeting PMP targets, maintaining high quality and rapidly increasing volumes were to be achieved.

The problem of developing good vendors was compounded by the fact that in 1982 there were few people in India who would have taken a bet, at almost any odds, on the success of Maruti, or the company achieving a production volume of anywhere near 100,000 units within five years. Maruti was seen as a political project. It was in the public sector, whose overall record of meeting targets and commitments was quite poor. Maruti was to make a low priority product, and the management had no experience at all of this industry. Not surprisingly, the industry was highly sceptical about Maruti achieving its targets, both in terms of time and numbers.

'Maruti is a public sector undertaking. What safeguards do we have if we make investments believing Maruti, and the demand doesn't materialize?' was one question that was always thrown at Maruti executives. Vendors were worried about who would compensate them for any losses and how they could get any redress from a public sector undertaking. When Surinder Kapur, chairman and managing director of Sona Koyo Steering, decided to go into a joint venture with Maruti and Koyo Seiko to manufacture steering systems in 1986, people thought him a fool for taking a government company as his partner and warned him that he would face a lot of problems. Other partners of Maruti in part joint ventures faced a similar reaction from their well-wishers.

Another factor working in the mind of potential vendors was the belief that SMC, like other Japanese companies, would not readily accept Indian-made parts, or help the localization process, as they would prefer to export these from Japan. This belief was not really borne out by experience, as there were no examples of Japanese companies having invested in India and failing to implement the PMP. Those who expressed doubts about the Japanese not supporting local production were perhaps looking at the localization levels in some of the south Asian countries. These were low and it was assumed that it was the reluctance of the Japanese to localize which was preventing higher local production. However, the circumstances in these countries and India were not the same, particularly in terms of the level of industrial development and the quality of engineers and managers. In those days India was far ahead of most south Asian countries. Nevertheless, it was quite a task for the Maruti management to dispel this apprehension. At all levels vendors were repeatedly assured that if they made components of the quality required, Maruti would buy from them. Most components would be tested and homologated in India by Indian engineers, and vendors should have confidence in their adopting a very objective approach.

The highly enthusiastic response to Maruti products was

reflected in the large bookings received in 1983. This made people reconsider the market potential for Maruti cars. During 1984-85, the first full year of operations, Maruti exceeded its production target of 20,000 units. As 1985-86 progressed, it was apparent that the target of 40,000 units would also be exceeded. This dispelled doubts about the ability of Maruti to achieve the declared production targets. Maruti had already started to increase production facilities from the initial 40,000 units to 100,000 units. At that point, vendors, as many others, changed their attitude and realized that Maruti might not fail, and could even dominate the car market in India. There was a sudden rush of people wanting to be vendors and make investments.

Japanese component makers were as sceptical about the prospects of Maruti as the Indian vendors, and were accordingly quite reluctant to even enter into licence agreements with Indian companies. However, seeing the progress achieved till 1985-86, they too changed their approach and became quite willing to form joint ventures and give technology to Indian companies. At that time, the maximum foreign investment allowed was 40 per cent and so the question of Japanese part makers setting up their own subsidiaries in India did not arise.

There were a number of serious constraints in implementing the localization programme. Maruti was a government company, and thus was an 'Instrument of State' in terms of the Constitution. Unlike a private company, Maruti could not just select a manufacturer, even if we were convinced that it was the best, and place orders to produce a component. Nor could Maruti divide business between vendors without following some reasonable system. Consequently, the processes that Maruti had to follow took much longer and required much more paperwork.

A second obstacle was the policy of small-scale sector reservations, under which the government reserved a large number of products, including automobile components, for manufacture by this sector. Small-scale industries were defined in terms of the investment made in buildings and machinery. The prescribed ceiling of investment stipulated at that time was far too low for many of the components to be manufactured with the appropriate technology and in the quantities required. Quality could not be built into the processes because the correct equipment could not be bought within the ceiling, and SMC would not approve components that were not manufactured according to the correct process and which would thus not meet the quality and performance standards.

Continuous efforts, drawing upon scarce managerial resources, had to be deployed to persuade officers in the DGTD and the industries ministry to de-reserve specific components. It had to be demonstrated that project costs would necessarily be far higher than the limits prescribed for a small-scale unit, if the volumes and the quality required for Maruti were to be produced. Fortunately, officials in the ministry were very receptive and acted quickly to de-reserve critical components so that Maruti could meet the PMP targets. Undoubtedly this liberalization of policy contributed significantly to the modernization of the component industry and the growth of automobile manufacturing in India.

At that time, the Indian automobile manufacturers produced close to 50 per cent of the components of a vehicle in-house. This meant that besides the critical components like the engine, many other components were also made by the vehicle manufacturer. The problems of quality and reliability of supplies from vendors probably made them opt for 'make' rather than 'buy'. SMC, and Japanese manufacturers in general, followed a different policy. In-house production of components was limited to only those that were critical for performance or appearance, like the engine, gearbox and outer body panels. All other components were outsourced to vendors. This reduced investment costs, and thus risk, for the vehicle manufacturer. It also reduced cost of manufacturing components, as vendors could supply to more than one manufacturer, attain higher volumes and derive benefits of scale. Further, the vendors, having larger volumes and turnover, could establish research and development (R&D) facilities and develop components for new models by themselves. This reduced the time taken to develop new models and also the cost to be incurred by the vehicle manufacturer.

This policy worked well in Japan as vendors there made it a point of honour to not let down their customers in terms of quality or meeting their delivery obligations. Maruti decided to follow the same policy. Thus the dependence on vendors was to be to the extent of about 75 per cent of the value of all components, excluding steel, paints and similar items. Given the state of vendors in India in 1983, this was perhaps a huge risk, as besides developing the technological capability for manufacturing parts, vendors also had to develop a new attitude towards their obligations to Maruti. SMC was of the definite opinion that this was the correct route to follow for the long term, and that Maruti's management must recognize the scope and importance of the task and make sure that it was done. SMC's views were perhaps also shaped by the need to keep the investment in Maruti to as low a level as possible, so that the risk was minimized.

At the time when the agreements with SMC were signed there was not a single component of the Suzuki car which was available in India. The battery prescribed by SMC was with a polyurethane case, against the traditional hard rubber batteries being made in India. The tyres were smaller than those being used in cars in India then, and also had higher specifications. These were the first to be developed, and became available in time for start of production.

The challenge before Maruti—the most serious one, according to Krishnamurthy's note in the first annual report—was to devise a vendor development policy which would not only comply with the PMP, but also provide components of the right quality, quantity and at the right price and time. To that end, Maruti decided that the company's approach to vendors would be quite different from the prevailing practice. The relationship between automobile manufacturers and vendors in those days was almost a subservient one. Baba Kalyani, chairman and managing director of Pune-based Bharat Forge, remembers that automobile manufacturers treated component makers as people necessary to the system but not necessarily contributing to it. Component makers were not treated with respect, and were not expected to question any decision or practice of the vehicle manufacturer.

The Maruti management decided to treat vendors as important partners, jointly working to create a modern automobile industry. It was quite obvious that Maruti could not achieve its PMP commitments or production targets without vendors fulfilling their obligations. With such a high proportion of the car coming from vendors, the quality and cost of products would be largely determined by the quality and cost of the parts supplied by the vendors. We did not think that blaming vendors or government policy for sub-standard quality was an acceptable option. In any case, SMC would not agree to this, as its international image for quality and performance would be sullied. It was, thus, in Maruti's and SMC's interest to do everything possible to enable vendors to meet targets of quality, cost and reliability of production.

Vendors had to be told about this new approach. At first they were sceptical about whether Maruti really meant what it was saying. The concept of a transparent and interactive relationship with their customer was quite novel. They were unused to getting solid support from the vehicle manufacturers and had to fend for themselves. I explained the logic behind our policy, and the fundamental interdependence of Maruti on its vendors and vice versa. I told them that the more Maruti could sell, the higher would be the supply of parts from each vendor, and consequently their profits would grow. However, Maruti could only sell more if the parts supplied met all the specifications and were produced at the lowest possible cost. The customers would buy more if they could get high quality cars at affordable prices. Consequently, both Maruti and vendors had to take a long-term view of how to build higher and sustainable demand.

On the other hand, if Maruti did not grow, the vendors would also have no opportunities for growth. This would happen if the customers did not like the cars and there were quality problems. Thus, the vendors had to understand that their growth and profitability depended on the growth and profitability of Maruti. There was almost total interdependency between Maruti and its vendors, and both had to work as partners, supporting each other in every possible way. This included Maruti implementing a pricing system that was fair and enabled vendors to make reasonable profits, as a vendor would lose interest if he did not make profits.

There was considerable risk in adopting this approach, as Maruti was a public sector company. In the government system, a public servant who helps a private party to make profits is viewed with suspicion. If Maruti executives helped vendors in ways which enhanced their growth and profitability, motives could be attributed. That is why the vendor policy was approved in 1982 by the board and why Maruti decisions regarding pricing of components, sharing of business between vendors and other issues were all committee decisions. However, as seen earlier, all these precautions did not prevent the CBI filing a case for 'abuse of position' against Krishnamurthy and me in respect of a contract awarded to a vendor.

An important component of the vendor policy was building a long-term relationship with them. Under the public sector procurement policy then prevailing, a public sector undertaking was required to invite quotations for supply of components every one or two years, and award the contract to the lowest bidder. The Maruti management realized that this system would be highly detrimental to the company's interests. Vendors, uncertain about future business, would have no incentive to make the required capital investments, as a large part of these investments would be specific to manufacturing parts which could be used only on Maruti vehicles. Most of the equipment and tooling installed could not be used for production of parts for other vehicles. Even if some equipment could be used for another manufacturer, the production capacity that needed to be installed for Maruti would be much higher than the demand from another manufacturer, and hence there would be idle capacity if business from Maruti did not continue. In such circumstances, vendors were unlikely to make the required investments.

Further, if a vendor was uncertain of the future of his business—which would be the case if tenders were invited every two years—he would consider that making investments to improve productivity and quality were too risky, and unlikely to result in profits. This would have adverse effects in the long term. He would also not invest in R&D. The lowest bidder system generally encouraged cost reduction by compromising on quality.

Maruti wanted its suppliers to invest in appropriate quality of capital goods, high quality tooling, and right operating procedures and realized that in order to do this, the vendors would need an assurance of long-term business. The board approved this approach. A vendor would be dropped only if he proved incapable of improvement and meeting Maruti standards.

In any such long-term arrangement, the system of price determination is a critical factor for success. Maruti decided that as a rule, prices of components would be negotiated every year. The initial price level would be fixed on an analysis of the costs of production. The vendor was required to present a break-up of costs and Maruti engineers did their own homework on estimating the likely production cost of each component. The landed cost of the CKD parts (which included shipping, customs duty and clearance costs) was another guide to price fixation. A locally made part was expected to have a lower cost than the landed cost of that part. This was not always possible at the time of start of production, but Maruti engineers had to ensure that with increasing volumes and localization, costs came below the landed cost. Prices were fixed, by negotiation, taking all these factors into account. Prices were then renegotiated annually on the basis of increases in manufacturing costs relating to labour and materials and also reduction in costs because of better productivity, lower rejections and higher volumes of production. Provision was made for variations in statutory duties or foreign exchange rates. 'Such an arrangement,' the board note said, 'would give to vendors the assurance that subject to their good performance, their growth and profitability at reasonable levels would be certain.'

Maruti also decided not to have multiple vendors for each component, the norm in the industry at that time. One reason for multiple vendors was the reservation policy, which prompted one manufacturer to establish a number of companies to make the same component, so that each company remained within the definition of a small-scale unit. In case the production was combined in a single unit, the investment would exceed the ceiling for a small-scale unit, thus depriving it of the various benefits it would have got. The incentive structure prescribed for promoting small industries worked against the concept of economies of scale and professional management. Another reason for multiple vendors was to reduce the risk of failing to obtain adequate supply of components. A large number of suppliers, the Maruti strategy paper said, would make it difficult to ensure that the same part, supplied by different vendors, had the same high quality, and would also hamper vendor management. In addition, multiple vendors would make it much harder to attain economies of scale, and would not be in the interest of either Maruti or the vendors.

Keeping all this in mind, Maruti decided to have two suppliers for each component. Two suppliers were considered essential to reduce risk of interruption of supplies.

The policy also provided that more than two suppliers could be considered for low technology items, where maintaining quality would not be a problem, but in no case was the number to exceed three. Though the strategy paper noted the risks involved in having just a single supplier, it suggested that this could be considered in cases where substantial economies of scale could be achieved and if the price was attractive enough for Maruti to take the risk. This was done for some components like rear axle assemblies. In the initial one and a half years, however, Maruti decided to have only one supplier for each component, since the volumes required would be small. A second supplier would be brought in when production crossed 3,500 vehicles a month. This, it was argued, would help the first vendor achieve a reasonable level of production and give time to the second vendor to establish itself.

~

The vendor development work started almost immediately after the agreements were signed with SMC in October 1982. Initial appointment of vendors was a critical task, not only from the point of view of the ability of the vendor to meet requirements in the future, but also to ensure that there was no violation of Constitutional requirements and to safeguard against possible charges of favouritism that could lead to vigilance inquiries. Thus Maruti decided to follow a stringent and transparent vendor selection process. A Vendor Committee, which comprised the executive in charge of vendor development, the chief engineer and the head of finance, was appointed for this purpose.

Advertisements were issued in newspapers inviting potential vendors to visit the factory, see the components to be localized and to submit expressions of interest. This took care of the requirement of giving everyone an equal opportunity to compete for the business. Maruti had imported a few CKD kits from Japan and displayed all the components in the factory premises. The components to be developed were divided into two categories—those in which vendors had the manufacturing technology but had to meet the specifications given by SMC (like tyres, shock absorbers, bulbs), and those which not only had to meet SMC specifications but where new technology would be required. The components were further subdivided according to the year when they were expected to be localized. The decision on this had been taken in consultation with SMC, based on the degree of difficulty of manufacturing, the expected time required for bringing in the technology and the investment required.

Interested parties had to submit full information about themselves, including what facilities they had, their experience in manufacturing and management set-up. Maruti engineers then did a preliminary screening and those who appeared to be suitable were shortlisted. A group of engineers then visited the factories of the applicants to verify the information given and also to judge their capabilities. The need to visit the factories and see production facilities was in line with the Japanese practice that the best decisions were taken after seeing the real situation with one's own eyes. On this basis, vendors were registered with Maruti, and a decision taken as to what component could be manufactured by each one of them.

Usually three vendors were shortlisted for each part. It was expected that not all of them would succeed in meeting the Maruti requirements and so some margin had to be kept. Of course, in many cases three potential vendors just did not exist. Drawings and sample parts were then supplied and the vendors were required to manufacture a few pieces and make an offer to Maruti, indicating the time schedule for commercial production and the price at that time. All this work was done at the level of engineers, under the supervision of the heads of vendor development and engineering, and helped by Japanese experts.

When the vendor, after going through the process, submitted prototypes, the engineering department tested them and, if they were approved and it appeared that the vendor could become a commercial supplier of the part, the Vendor Committee held price negotiations. Once these were successfully concluded, the committee made a specific recommendation to the managing director for approving the selection of the vendor and the proposed price. On receiving this approval, a letter of intent (LoI) was issued to the vendor, who was then required to give a larger lot of supplies, which had to be produced following the prescribed production process for mass production.

A second round of testing followed, which involved fitting the component on the car and running the vehicle for 20,000 km on a test track. Shock absorbers and other safety-related components were tested for 40,000 km and over more taxing road conditions. Several parts could be undergoing testing at one time on a single car. The parts were periodically inspected for wear and tear during the testing, and at the end to see if they measured up to the required reliability standards. This was a completely new practice in India and this testing process often resulted in parts having to be modified because wear and tear in Indian conditions was different from what was anticipated, based on the experience in Japan. The process of testing components did result in making the localization slower and often caused much frustration to the vendor. However, everybody conceded that one of the reasons why Maruti vehicles soon acquired a reputation for reliability and quality was this testing process.

Vendors were not happy having to wait to start commercial supplies till the testing was complete, but SMC was very clear that there could be no short cuts in this respect. SMC did not want to risk its reputation for making reliable, value-for-money products to be jeopardized by even 0.5 per cent component failures. In addition to road testing, the parts were also tried for fitment on the assembly line. This was to ensure that once local parts were accepted for use, there should be absolutely no slowing down of the assembly lines and, consequently, loss of productivity levels because the workers were having problems fitting local parts. This was again an example of how meticulous the Japanese were in ensuring that once a decision was taken, its implementation should proceed very smoothly. Only if a part cleared all these tests did the vendor get a production order. The share of business was decided by the vendor department from time to time, based on price and performance.

Another difficult decision in respect of each part was to decide when it should be deleted from the CKD kit. The contents of a CKD kit had to be decided and orders placed with SMC five months before the month in which the imported parts would be used on the Maruti production lines. This was the time required for SMC to place orders with its vendors, for the vendors to manufacture and supply the parts, and for SMC to ship them to Gurgaon. Maruti had to anticipate which parts, and in what quantities a vendor would be able to produce six months in advance, in order to decide to delete those parts from the import list. Given the somewhat disorganized state of many vendors, this was no easy task, and often created situations of crisis, as many vendors failed to meet their commitments.

Amid all the scepticism, there were some component manufacturers who recognized that Maruti was the harbinger of a generational leap for the industry. From operating on the basis of low volumes and high margins, they now had the opportunity to shift to a system of high volumes with comparatively thin margins. From relying largely on unskilled labour, they had to employ a larger number of skilled workers, given that not only was a lot of design and engineering work involved, but the manufacturing process required use of more sophisticated equipment and adherence to systems.

In the early 1980s, Bharat Forge was a small company with total sales of less than Rs. 20 crore, supplying to Tata Motors, Ashok Leyland, Hindustan Motors and Premier Automobiles. But it was an aggressive company and Kalyani decided to piggyback on the opportunity provided by Maruti to change itself. It set up new facilities for its supplies to Maruti, including a new brake plant in Jalgaon, apart from new manufacturing equipment and technology for its forging business. For example, it changed forging technology from the traditional use of hammers to forging presses. Over the years it has grown rapidly, exporting a substantial part of its production. It has adopted the inorganic route to growth and acquired a number of forging companies in Europe. It now has a turnover in excess of a billion dollars and operates in six countries.

In order to make sure that vendors did not become complacent, Maruti decided to introduce a vendor-rating system to evaluate companies on quality, number of rejections, timeliness of delivery and general attitude to business. They were also assessed periodically on steps being taken to improve productivity, upgrade technology and reduce costs of production. The vendor ratings were used to determine the share of business between vendors supplying the same component. When new models were introduced, and the parts to be developed became more sophisticated, the vendor chosen to produce that part was selected on the basis of his performance record.

Maruti also changed the system of making payments to vendors. The supply contract with component manufacturers contained the usual provision of thirty-day credit for the buyer. However, after a few years of operation, Maruti offered to make payments in fifteen days, with a 0.5 per cent discount for early payment. The vendors were delighted, as most of their customers rarely paid them even within thirty days, and they were constantly facing cash flow problems. Working capital could not be easily obtained from banks, and interest rates were high. Money from private moneylenders was very expensive. So, getting paid in fifteen days, and by a manufacturer who was buying a large part of their output, was a boon.

As a result, they started to give Maruti priority over other customers in making supplies whenever they had any manufacturing problems and output was curtailed. Another change made was that vendors were not allowed to come inside the Maruti office for receiving payments. This was partly to avoid loss of productivity in the office, which would result from a large number of visitors, and partly to avoid possibilities of any unhealthy practices developing in the process of vendors receiving payment.

As the possibilities of Maruti beating the odds and becoming a success story increased, many people wanted to invest in component manufacturing and become suppliers to Maruti. It did not matter if they had no experience of any kind of manufacturing. Most of them did not know what they should manufacture. People would often approach me for help to enter into a licence agreement with a Japanese component manufacturer, or request that they be allotted some component which they could manufacture. Many of them suggested that it should be a component which could be also sold in large numbers in the spare part market. It was believed that spare part sales generated much larger profits. They were disappointed to learn that Maruti's policy was to not to allow vendors to sell spare parts in the marketplace. I also advised them that Japanese component manufacturers were unlikely to form partnerships with companies or persons who had no manufacturing experience.

Some thought that political connections could be a substitute for experience, because Maruti was a public sector company. Mathur recalls one politician approaching him in his office at the factory and saying that he had ten acres of land next to the Maruti factory and a few crores of rupees. 'You tell me what I should produce.' Mathur replied that he would not be able to offer any suggestions and that he could see the components displayed, choose what he wanted to manufacture, get the technology and return with a sample. 'Come back then and we'll discuss it.' The politician went into a monologue about how close he was to Mrs Gandhi and that she had sent him. As Mathur listened patiently, the man said, 'I want you to know that I got Mr Krishnamurthy his job.'

That gave Mathur an opening. He said, 'Saab, since he is beholden to you, why don't you go and ask him? In my case, Mr Krishnamurthy gave me my job. So if he asks me to do something I'll do it efficiently. But you will have to speak to him first.' The man left quietly. The next morning, on the way to the weekly project review meeting, Mathur told Krishnamurthy, 'Sir, yesterday I was privileged to meet the person who gave you your job,' and recounted the incident. Krishnamurthy laughed and said he would take care of the matter. The politician never reverted. The message went out to the Maruti management—no compromises.

The management understood that it would be very difficult to ensure quality and performance if a vendor was aware that his connections were powerful enough to influence the management and get him a product to manufacture. The situation would be very similar to a vendor being a close relative of the promoter of a private car company.

~

As the process of localizing components progressed, more and more vendors became part of the Maruti family of suppliers. All of them had to make changes in their production systems and increase their manufacturing capacities, as the volumes required by Maruti were not only higher than what they had been used to, but increased every year by significant amounts. Most of the vendors were those who were already car component manufacturers, like the TVS group, Bharat Forge, Hydraulics India, tyre and battery makers and so on. Some others were established companies, but had never worked with the automobile industry. One example was Goodlass Nerolac, a paint company which had been catering only to the domestic finishes market. This company decided to foray into automotive finishes and set up a plant exclusively for Maruti after entering into a joint venture with Kansai Paints of Japan. This partnership worked well and the joint venture was a success.

There were a slew of small companies and first-generation entrepreneurs who were ambitious and willing to work hard and learn the business. Maruti provided immense growth opportunities for such people. Arvind Dham, an architect with a course in construction management, started Amtek Auto in 1985 to supply connecting rod assemblies to Maruti. He has since made it to the *Forbes* annual list of billionaires. Amtek Auto is now part of the Amtek Group, whose manufacturing activities include forging, aluminium casting and machining.

Rico Auto was another company, established in 1984 by Arvind Kapoor, which started making high-pressure aluminium castings and ferro castings in 1986 for both Maruti and Hero Honda. It now has international operations and a turnover nearing $300 million. The Shakti Group in Chennai first became dealers for Maruti. When Maruti had problems in getting adequate supply of brake drums, M. Manickam, the CEO of the group, expressed a desire to get into this business. Maruti agreed, as the group appeared very professional. The job was very well done and I asked Manickam to develop steering knuckles, a key safety component, which other vendors were unwilling to develop, as each knuckle had to be X-rayed for defects. A large investment was required for this. Manickam agreed to get the required technology. Shakti not only became the main supplier to Maruti, but also started exporting this part. I would often urge Manickam to expand casting capacity, and also start machining components as much greater value was added by doing this. The Shakti group developed excellent expertise and has now acquired large casting companies in Europe.

Maruti acted virtually as a midwife to a large number of vendors, handholding them at every stage. Maruti was often involved in helping them find the right collaborator, aiding with joint venture agreements and getting approvals and licences, arranging financial assistance and negotiating with financial institutions for providing working capital, persuading state governments to allot land, giving short-term advances for them to pay customs duties and importing tooling, and sending Maruti engineers to help them with their production systems.

One of the major requirements of the vendors was to get the appropriate technology for making components that could meet Maruti's specifications and performance standards. Clearly, the most suitable partner would be a vendor supplying similar parts to SMC, or at least another Japanese vendor familiar with the requirements of Japanese car makers. Maruti was flooded with requests from Indian manufacturers to help them in getting such collaborations. Component manufacturers in Japan, as well as SMC, were inundated with proposals from a large number of Indian companies, and did not know how to make a choice. They did not have the resources to visit all the applicants and study their capabilities. They wanted Maruti's help in identifying a suitable partner.

The problem was that as a public sector entity, Maruti could not directly get involved in promoting collaborations between private companies in India and Japan. Any such action could be called into question by the CBI and the vigilance authorities.

Explanations would have to be given as to why a particular party was selected and it could be alleged that this was for some consideration. In addition, those who were not selected could go to court and Maruti would need to convince the judge of the reasons why these companies were rejected. This would have been an enormously time-consuming process, besides creating risk for those involved. On the other hand, time was of the essence in arranging collaborations if the localization targets were to be met. Delays would hurt us more than anyone else. Unfortunately, the system did not recognize this.

Difficult as the problem appeared to be, the solution also lay within the system, which essentially required that the right process should be followed on paper. So Maruti decided to set down on paper its inability to get involved in arranging collaborations between Indian and Japanese companies and informed all concerned accordingly. Informally, however, Maruti engineers and the vendor department would evaluate the applicants seeking collaborations, and decide a shortlist of those who appeared to be the most suitable. The local SMC experts would be involved in this process. The top management would be kept informed. This list, with the reasons for selection, would be conveyed orally either directly or through SMC, whose help was often taken to introduce Indian vendors to Japanese companies. The Japanese company was always asked to check out the companies being suggested before finalizing any agreements.

As a result, close to forty joint ventures and technical agreements between Indian and Japanese component manufacturers were signed in a short period of time, and this greatly facilitated the process of localization. There were no allegations of any wrongdoing in this process. Among the more successful joint ventures were those of Kalyani Brakes, part of the Kalyani Group, to which Bharat Forge also belonged, with

Nabco, a Japanese leader in the brake business. Another major success was the Noida-based Motherson Auto, which started as a supplier of wiring harnesses, entered into multiple collaboration agreements and joint ventures and is now known as Motherson Sumi, incorporating the name of their partner, Sumitomo Wiring Systems.

Mathur and the late Dr R.D. Deshpande, who was the first head of engineering, were in charge of developing Maruti vendors. They had their task cut out for them. Mathur describes it graphically: 'Ensuring that the production line was not disrupted was like feeding a shark which eats round the clock. We were buying 1,200 or 1,300 components. Even if we had a crisis on one component every three years, it was still a crisis every day for us.' The crisis could take the form of a quality problem, disruption of production due to shortage of raw materials or imported sub-components, labour unrest or disruption in the transportation system due to a number of reasons.

In all foreign collaborations, the government was keen that the technical agreement should cover not just know-how for manufacturing and testing, but also know why—why products are designed the way they are and the underlying technology behind the design. The reason was to facilitate absorption of technology and create the ability for further improvements, so that further extensions of licence agreements should not be required. This was clearly not possible for the components which SMC bought from its vendors, since it was the vendors who had the intellectual property rights. However, for the localization of components, it was necessary to give complete and detailed drawings of the components and SMC was in a position to supply these to Maruti.

The drawings that came from Japan, however, posed a huge problem. When the vendor started to use the drawings to manufacture components, in many cases the product produced differed from the sample supplied by SMC. Maruti's engineering department was very unhappy, being used to the western system, where drawings were sacrosanct, and could not understand why the component produced according to the drawing did not match the sample which came from SMC. When the matter was taken up with SMC, the explanation was that components were being improved and modified constantly, and it was not considered essential to spend scarce and expensive engineering man-hours to modify the drawings all the time. Drawings thus often became out of date. It was suggested that the sample products should be taken as the reference. Maruti then starting updating the drawings from the samples before passing them on to the vendors. In addition, it gave the vendors five sets of components and kept five sets, so that checking would be easier.

~

In 1985, Maruti was faced with the problem of vapour locks on the fuel pump, which pumps petrol from the fuel tank to the carburettor. A common problem in the Ambassador and the Premier Padmini was that in summer, or when going up to the mountains, a vapour lock would develop in the fuel pump and bring the car to a stop. As this was due to overheating, the solution was to put a moist cloth over the fuel pump and keep wetting it with cold water after every thirty minutes. Since a fuel pump was a comparatively simple item, Maruti took up its localization early and the localized pump was first used in 1985.

That year, Delhi had one of the hottest summers in history and the same vapour lock problem occurred in a few cars when the temperature crossed 45 degrees centigrade. This was a big blow to our pride even though the number of cases was not large, being confined to seven or eight out of every 1,000 cars sold in Delhi. The matter was also raised in Parliament and that added further urgency to finding a solution. As a first step, Maruti flew in 30,000 pumps from Japan, which threw the foreign exchange budget out of gear because even the airfare was paid in foreign exchange. This was nevertheless considered necessary, to ensure that the problem was immediately resolved. The pumps which were developing vapour locks were replaced free of cost. The customers were happy, as they had not expected such quick and effective a remedy. Perhaps this was the first instance of a 'recall' in India. The rest of the imported pumps were used on the production line. The engineers in Maruti compared the imported pump with the one that had been localized, and it was found that the localized pump had a small dimensional variation in one component. Once this part was corrected, the problem disappeared.

On one occasion, Chennai-based Wheels India, which was using imported steel to manufacture wheel rims, had made a mistake in its application for an import licence. The imported material was held up at the port and could not be cleared. Consequently, production was delayed and the pipeline ran dry because trucks took ten to fifteen days to reach Delhi from Chennai. The only solution to keep the lines running was to airlift the wheels from Chennai, till the normal delivery cycle by trucks was restored. The costs were borne by Wheels India.

Logistics posed another headache. The largest quantity of tyres was supplied by MRF and Dunlop, whose plants were in Tamil Nadu. Tyres were bulky and required large space for storage. With production levels at near 800 vehicles a day, 4,000 tyres were required daily. One week's inventory meant 28,000 tyres, posing a storage nightmare. If kept in the open, water would accumulate inside them when it rained. On the other hand, the covered space required for storage would be huge.

The maximum inventory was required during the rainy season, when transportation disruptions were most likely to occur, but this was the time when storage in the open would create difficulties. Thus it was very hard to determine the correct inventory level in the factory, and at times there would be shortage of tyres. Cars were then produced without the spare wheel being fitted with a tyre. The tyre was fitted later when new stocks arrived.

The rear axles too came by truck from Chennai. This was one of the few cases where Maruti had a single supplier. Trucks would break down or be stranded by floods during the monsoons. Or else, they would be held up for days at octroi posts on practically every state border. Truck drivers were not trained to keep Maruti, or even their own management, informed of what was happening. Though they were supposed to call from every major town on the route, few did this. There were a large number of thefts in Madhya Pradesh, with entire trucks getting hijacked. During the 1984 anti-Sikh riots following Mrs Gandhi's assassination, several Sikh drivers disappeared and there was no way of knowing whether they were hiding to save themselves or had been killed. On such occasions the rear axles had to be transported by train, with someone accompanying them, to ensure they reached the factory in forty-eight hours and production lines could be kept running.

Maintaining full production and preventing stoppage of assembly lines was a priority objective with Maruti. It was realized that the single most critical factor in maintaining production would be the supply of components according to schedule. Thus, the weekly management committee meetings identified components where the inventory was becoming critical, or where there could be problems with a vendor maintaining adequate level of supplies. This detailed and frequent monitoring by top management of the supply chain was effective as, over the years, Maruti not only met but also exceeded its production targets. The credit for this also goes to the young officers in the purchase and vendor departments, who worked as if they were personally responsible for meeting production targets. The fact that purchase of components, inventory and consumption had been computerized also made it possible to do monitoring more effectively. However, there were many instances where the level of a component shown by the computer differed from the physical stock. There were a number of reasons why this happened and it became necessary to train those in charge of the store to not only rely on the computer data but to also cross-check with the physical situation.

~

Despite all the efforts made, there were shortfalls in the indigenization programme. In the directors' report in Maruti's first annual report, Krishnamurthy noted that 'despite the best efforts of the company, considerable difficulties have been encountered in obtaining quality products and in accordance with the schedules promised by the vendors'. Some of these were well-established companies which took 'longer than promised in developing acceptable samples' and were not able to keep up with Maruti's production requirements. Consequently, Maruti had to fall back on emergency imports and even fly domestically manufactured components that should normally have been transported by trucks.

Even the process of flying in components was not as simple as one would think. Due to security reasons, there was a cooling period of twenty-four hours before cargo would be cleared for acceptance by airlines. People from the purchase department would wait at the airport so that the minute this period ended, they could take charge of the components and get them loaded.

In Delhi, the items were unloaded and transferred directly to the assembly line, regardless of the time of day. As a result of all these problems, more parts had to be imported and the indigenization programme had to be revised downward. The target of 31.5 per cent indigenization up to March 1985 was brought down to 23 per cent.

The lament about vendor failures was repeated the following year in the chairman's address to the board of directors. Krishnamurthy noted that soon after the introduction of the 800, the company had started rolling out 5,000 vehicles a month and needed the component manufacturers to match their pace of supplies with Maruti's consumption. 'However, most of the component manufacturers have not been able to respond to this need in the short period of time available during which Maruti has built up its production volume.'

Maruti then decided to get even more involved with its vendors, forming joint ventures to manufacture components that were critical to the quality of the vehicles, or were bulky to transport, or required high technology and large investments, or where the economies of scale dictated a single source.* In Japan, SMC also had an equity stake in several of its component suppliers. The idea of forming joint ventures emanated from the experience of SMC, which was keen that this be speedily implemented. SMC decided that, in addition to Maruti, it would also subscribe to the equity in those joint ventures where technology from Japan was required.

Having a stake in the companies enabled Maruti to be involved in all aspects of the establishment of the production facilities and the processes for manufacture. The establishment of these joint ventures greatly helped in achieving the PMP targets, besides reducing the problems relating to quality and stability of supplies.

*Chairman's address by V. Krishnamurthy, 30 August 1985.

Initially, five joint ventures were formed. These were to manufacture seats (Bharat Seats), glass (Indian Auto Safety Glass),* sheet metal parts (Mark Auto),† plastic mouldings (Machino Plastics) and steering components (Sona Steering Systems)‡ and accounted for 24 per cent of the value of the car. Three of the joint ventures—Bharat Seats, Machino Plastics and Mark Auto—were located within the Maruti factory complex, while Asahi Glass and Sona Steering took land nearby. Their close proximity to the Maruti factory was necessitated by the need for supervision of parts relating to safety (steering systems) and to cut down the cost of transporting bulky or fragile parts like seats, plastic mouldings and glass. Later, to bring in an element of competition and as a fallback arrangement, three more joint ventures were set up—Sona Car Seats (renamed Krishna Maruti) for seats in 1993, and Jay Bharat Maruti and Caparo Maruti for sheet metal components in 1988 and 1994 respectively.†‡

---

*Incorporated in 1984, it changed its name first to Asahi India Safety Glass in 1986 and later to Asahi India Glass in 2002.

†Mark Auto was taken over by Krishna Maruti, another joint venture in which Maruti participated, in 2005 and renamed Sat Krishan Hanuman (SKH) Metals.

‡It was renamed Sona Koyo Steering Systems in 1998.

†‡Apart from Maruti, the other joint venture partners in each of these firms were: B.M. Labroo and Associates Indo-Asahi Glass Co. and Asahi Glass Co. of Japan in the case of Asahi Glass; Rohit Relan & Associates and SMC in Bharat Seats; K.M. Talwar and Rattan Kapur & Associates in Mark Auto; Machino Techno, M.D. Jindal and SMC in Machino Plastics; Surinder Kapur & Associates and Koyo Seiko in Sona Steering; S.K. Arya in Jay Bharat Maruti; Caparo Group Ltd and M.D. Jindal in Caparo Maruti; Kapur & Associates and SMC in Krishna Maruti.

Sona Steering had Koyo Seiko of Japan as a partner, in addition to Maruti and Suzuki. Getting Koyo to invest wasn't easy. Kapur, who was then managing Bharat Gears (a company owned by his father-in-law and Apollo Tyres chairman, the late Raunaq Singh) had been talking to Koyo Seiko even as he was seeking a partnership with Maruti. Mitsubishi, Nissan, Mazda and Toyota were all geared up to enter the Indian light commercial vehicle market and he knew business opportunities were set to boom. However, Koyo Seiko had earlier burnt its fingers in India, with a failed joint venture with the Andhra Pradesh government, and it took a great deal of persuasion on Kapur's part to get them to agree to partner with him. Perhaps the fact that Maruti and SMC would also be equity partners helped to create the necessary confidence in Koyo.

Asahi India was promoted by B.M. Labroo, who was then working with United Breweries. He had found a collaborator for manufacturing windshields from Europe and negotiations with that company were at a fairly advanced stage. Meanwhile, Asahi Glass of Japan had also shown interest in coming to India and SMC discussed with me how this could be facilitated. One option was that Labroo should partner them and not the European company. I suggested to Labroo that he should consider this option also as there would be an advantage in having a partner who had the confidence of SMC. At that point having two makers of windshields would probably have made both projects unviable. Labroo also realized that if Asahi Glass came into India with another Indian partner he would be at a disadvantage and he opted to partner with them.

The equity stake that Maruti took in these companies varied. In Sona Steering, Maruti had only 10 per cent equity. On the other hand, Mark Auto was a 50-50 joint venture. The others fell in-between these limits. A shareholders agreement was signed in each case, which defined the roles and responsibilities of both parties. The management control was with Maruti's partner, as the company did not want to get involved in the day-to-day management of so many companies. If Maruti had assumed control over the joint ventures, there would soon have been demands from the employees that they should have the same terms and conditions as Maruti employees. In addition, Maruti would have had to find human and other resources for managing each one of these companies. All this would have diverted attention from the main task of building Maruti, and the objective of having vendors would have got defeated.

On the other hand, since Maruti was represented on the boards of these companies, it could effectively influence management decisions and policies. In the initial period, Maruti engineers were very closely involved in all decisions relating to establishment of the projects. To give comfort to the partner, it was provided that for the first seven years or so, pricing would be on a cost plus basis, with an assured return on equity. Maruti had the right to go into the details of all costs of manufacture and procurement of materials.

Many years later, we realized that in forming these joint ventures, Maruti actually violated the Government of India Rules of Business, since public sector companies could not subscribe to the equity of private companies without Cabinet approval. Nobody—not even the government representatives on the board of Maruti—was apparently aware of this requirement, as it was never raised by anyone at any stage of the establishment of these joint ventures. It is hard to predict how much time would have been taken to procure government approval for establishing each of these companies, if the correct position of the rules was known at that time and formal proposals for forming so many joint venture had been moved. Whether the proposals would even have found favour also remains a matter of conjecture. In this case, at least, ignorance helped in localization of 24 per cent of the car, and development of some very good automobile component-manufacturing companies.

Since Maruti was determined to play an active role in ensuring that these projects were successful, and met all the schedules prescribed for them, it was necessary to have an organization to ensure effective implementation. A separate department was formed and Dr Krishan Kumar was brought in from the Indian Railways to head it. He was a very experienced engineer, and took to his task with great sincerity. Like Mathur and Deshpande, he, too, had a tough time persuading the joint venture partners to work in a professional manner. Though the administrative control of the companies was with the respective promoters, Kumar, with the help of three or four assistants, was acting as a facilitator for everything—from helping them with the technical agreements and equipment to finding contractors and architects and finalizing the layout of the factories, ordering raw materials and monitoring supplies. Kumar also had to accompany the promoters to Hamamatsu in Japan to meet SMC executives to discuss project details.

The companies had to take approvals from DGTD for all imports of capital goods and other materials. Import licences were issued only after the DGTD made a positive recommendation. Kumar had to visit Udyog Bhavan with the partners to get these clearances. That led to DGTD officials asking him why he was accompanying them, since he was a public sector employee, and helping a private entrepreneur was not the role of a public servant. Kumar had to point out that it was Maruti's commitment to DGTD on localization that would be jeopardized if these companies faced any problems, leading to delays in localizing components. Moreover, penalties would be imposed on Maruti, and not the vendors, if localization targets were not met. This was a new viewpoint for these government employees, because normally public sector employees are more concerned about ensuring that correct procedures are followed rather than getting involved in achieving results, if it meant adopting practices which were unconventional and also risky for the individuals concerned.

Joint ventures, in the initial years, sometimes ran into financial difficulties. The procedures followed by the public sector banks for approving applications for long-term loans as well as working capital limits were both slow and rigid. A delay in getting approvals could hold up project implementation, and consequently Maruti's production plans. Thus Kumar, though a senior deputy general manager, would personally visit banks and persuade officials there to expedite decisions. The intervention of a senior public sector manager helped in giving bank officials the confidence to cut some red tape. In other cases, Maruti itself would give short-term loans to joint ventures to help them.

Barring Kapur, who was familiar with the auto components industry, given his stewardship of Mumbai-based Bharat Gears, the other joint venture partners had no experience of this sector. However, they were people with good business experience, but in the way traditional proprietorship companies functioned. This meant that decision making was centralized in the owner, who rarely trusted any professional. Not only did he alone take financial decisions, but usually all cheques were also personally signed by him. Decisions were based more on gut feel than on any analysis of data. Account keeping was usually designed to minimize payment of income tax, and generation of some cash for meeting various expenses of the owner.

One of the tasks that Maruti faced was to bring about an

attitudinal change among the joint venture partners. Maruti required them to follow systems and work in a totally professional manner, delegating power to professional managers and adopting transparent accounting practices. While some learnt very fast, others took time. At that time, in line with other industrialists and businessmen, whose attitudes had been shaped by the licence and control raj, most of the partners had a very short time horizon while taking business decisions. Few businessmen then thought of long-term sustained growth, or how to build companies which could be internationally competitive.

For example, most manufacturers used tools and moulds made in India. Not only were they cheaper, but there was no need to obtain an import licence. The desire to avoid the process of getting an import licence was understandable. However, these toolings were almost invariably of low quality, and it was not possible to get consistent quality of production from them. Till Maruti came on the scene this did not matter, as quality was not something which anyone insisted upon. At the same time, investment levels were kept low, and profits were high. SMC insisted that all tooling for critical parts should first come from Japan so that quality could be high. Later, when production was established, and engineers understood technology, cheaper sources could be explored.

Many of the joint venture partners argued that if they could not use Indian-made tooling, they should be allowed to get cheaper tooling from Taiwan and South Korea. They found it hard to understand that buying tooling from Japan was essential to save time and ensure that components were made available according to the localization schedule. They did not realize that because they themselves did not have the expertise to check the tooling quality, Maruti and SMC engineers would need to go to the manufacturer's works in these countries to inspect the tooling. The checking process would involve the tooling manufacturer producing a pilot lot of components on their machines and shipping the components back to India, for testing in the laboratory and on the assembly lines. Clearance for shipping the tools could be given only when these checks were successful. Manpower resources with SMC and Maruti were limited and delays would be inevitable if this process was followed, and particularly if some defects were found. In addition, the die manufacturer could blame the raw material for quality defects and even question the checking process in India, and this could cause further delays. However, if the first tools came from SMC's vendor in Japan, there would be no need to carry out any detailed checks as the tool would be a replica of what was being used successfully. Experience showed that this policy worked well and in such matters trying to save money on tools would really have been penny wise and pound foolish.

Kumar had to point out to many vendors (other than the joint venture partners) who wanted to persist with the traditional way of using Indian-made tools that they were ignoring the fact that if the components produced were rejected, they would lose all Maruti business, and suffer a total loss of their investment. Further, since the Maruti pricing policy took into account the tooling cost, buying tooling from Japan would not adversely impact on their profitability. In fact, one of the reasons for initially adopting a cost-based pricing system was precisely to ensure that vendors did not cut corners in using raw materials, or the correct equipment and tools for production. This could never have been ensured in a system which required tenders to be floated and parts bought from the lowest bidder. Those who were then involved with policy making in government, and framing policies for public sector buying, perhaps did not fully understand the importance of the various inputs going into the production system in order to achieve high productivity and quality.

But old habits of making a quick buck do not always die out easily. One joint venture partner was found to be asking the supplier of raw materials to inflate prices and give him a cut in cash. He told the supplier that senior management in Maruti wanted this money. Mathur was told this reason for the higher prices for the raw material when he went for price negotiations with the supplier and insisted on a lower price. The same vendor was also found to be using the dies provided by Maruti to supply components to another automobile manufacturer, through a subsidiary company. The profit margin was naturally very high. On being confronted, the vendor apologized profusely, and promised to mend his ways. Maruti had no real option but to let the vendor continue, as there was no other source for that component. But, it should be said to the credit of this vendor that over time he did change and has continued to work well.

Kumar was racing against time to ensure that each joint venture company established manufacturing capabilities as scheduled and also expanded production to keep pace with Maruti. Mathur and Deshpande had to do the same task with other vendors. They, and the teams under them, worked long hours, without any overtime, only because each one of them was very strongly motivated to ensure that Maruti met all the production schedules which had been announced. Their efforts belied the general belief about the lack of result orientation among public sector employees.

The deletion of components manufactured by the joint venture vendors from the CKD list had to go through the same process as components from other vendors, with the same kind of risks. The parts also had to go through the same rigorous testing procedures. Often, there were three to four iterations or rejections before a component was finally accepted. At times this could mean that a part had to be 'reborn', or included in the CKD list again, and sometimes such parts had to be air freighted to keep the production going. The top management did not look kindly at such an event and vendors as well as executives in Maruti made all possible efforts to prevent these occurrences. This acceptance process did add to the cost of the vendors. Usually the bulk of the investment required to manufacture the part would have been made when the sample part was supplied. However, the commercial production of the part could only start after all testing was complete and the part had been deleted from the CKD list. This took a few months. The manufacturing capacity would, on many occasions, not be fully utilized till the imported part inventory with Maruti had been used up.

~

One of the most difficult areas of developing vendors to meet Maruti requirements was in the area of quality. In 1983, when Maruti talked about the need for better quality, the general response was that it would mean higher prices, and it would not be possible to meet the price targets. This was largely because people generally, and most vendors in particular, confused quality with specifications. It was widely assumed, even amongst persons who should have known better, that the higher the specifications the better the quality. Quality was not understood to mean consistent conformity to the laid-down specifications, with variations being within prescribed tolerance limits. High quality also meant that out-of-specification components would be very few, perhaps less than 50 per million. Specifications could vary widely. A tap could be chromium plated or gold plated. The latter would not necessarily be of higher quality if it was not made exactly as per specifications, and did not perform its function of regulating water flow as efficiently as the chromium-plated tap. Also, the more exotic the specification the higher would be the cost. It took time before the difference between quality and specifications began to be understood. Maruti had to repeatedly tell vendors that what the company wanted was very strict and consistent adherence to all the specifications laid down.

All manufacturing companies in India, had—and still have—quality inspection (QI) departments. The idea was that after products had been manufactured, the QI inspectors should ensure that they met with the consumer specifications. If a customer was very strict about quality, 100 per cent of the products would be inspected before shipment. In addition, inspection would also be done for all the components that went into the assembly of the final product. Parts that were rejected during inspection would be sent back for reworking and inspected again. If rectification was not possible, the part would be scrapped.

The Japanese, who were always looking for reduction of costs, had long ago realized that supplying good quality products by inspecting the components at each stage, and also inspecting the finished product, was extremely costly as the parts inspection department had to employ a large number of inspectors. The production process slowed down, leading to lower productivity. Even then, experience showed that it was not possible to ensure that bad products did not slip through the inspection process. There was the additional high cost of rejections and reworking and repairing of the defective parts and products. The whole process of inspection was non-value adding and was required because the production processes did not ensure that defects were not created and workers got the product right the first time. The real answer to producing good quality, therefore, lay in improving the production process to such an extent that inspections would become redundant. Quality had to be built into the processes, and workers trained to implement those processes exactly as prescribed. Each worker had to ensure that he got it right the first time.

This was one of the first lessons learnt from SMC when the production processes were being planned and manpower requirements were being worked out. In turn, Maruti passed on the same message to the vendors. They were told that quality had to be built into the manufacturing process and not sought to be attained through inspections. The prescribed processes had to be followed with total consistency. This required a high degree of discipline. The manufacturing equipment, including the tooling, had to be capable of consistent adherence to the specifications. The system of maintenance had to be adequate to ensure that any deviations due to usage and wear and tear were detected and rectified in time. The procurement of raw materials and bought-outs had to be from sources who would follow the laid-down processes and systems, thereby ensuring consistent quality, and no change in the source of procurement should be made without first getting Maruti approval. To enable vendors to develop the appropriate systems, Maruti insisted that all vendors get ISO certification. Maruti helped the small vendors in doing this by bringing in the cluster concept, under which a group of vendors were taken through the steps required to get certified. Later, the CII and others adopted this system of improving the quality levels of small and medium industries.

It was also explained to vendors that producing good quality components the first time resulted in a reduction of costs. To the extent that rejections or rework could be reduced, production volumes would go up, with no additional cost. This meant higher productivity. There would be consequent savings in costs. To the extent scrap could be reduced or eliminated, there would be a saving of materials and manufacturing costs. The cost of inspection would also come down. It was shown to vendors that under the existing system the cost of quality was really quite high. Many vendors were quick to learn the importance of following processes to improve quality. Undoubtedly, the rapid development of the automobile component industry, and its ability to access the international markets, was a result of the efforts made by Maruti to educate manufacturers on the concept of quality, and the profit which they would generate for themselves if quality levels were improved.

Despite a majority of vendors trying to adhere to the system of rigidly following all the laid-down processes, Maruti kept on experiencing problems because a vendor would change his source of an input, or substitute one material with another, or make some other variation in his process, without first informing Maruti and following the processes laid down for making such changes. Inevitably, quality problems would crop up. Usually such situations arose with vendors who did not themselves learn the manufacturing processes and were also undisciplined in their functioning, as a result of which they were unable to enforce manufacturing discipline in their organizations. While there has been considerable improvement in this respect over the years, much more needs to be done.

Perhaps in 1983, the component manufacturers were not entirely to blame for the attitude towards quality and training workers. A large part of their management time in those highly regulated times was devoted to managing government inspectors and sundry bureaucrats. One supplier, on whom Maruti was putting a lot of pressure to improve since his performance was not up to the mark, agreed to send his works manager to Japan for training. On his return, Mathur asked the man what he had learnt. His answer was a telling comment on the business environment of India in the 1980s. He said there was no correlation between what a works manager did in Japan and what he did in India. 'There they are only concerned with productivity and quality. Here I am caught up with labour inspector, electricity, sales tax. Where do I have the time to go to the shop floor and look at quality?' The explanation certainly had an element of truth in it, but it was not the full truth. Maruti, and many of its vendors, showed that in the same environment, much more could be done to improve quality and productivity.

Maruti had an extremely rigorous checking procedure for accepting vendor parts. Checking was done on a sample basis, and 100 per cent inspection was required if there were defective parts found in the sample. The vendor had to come and segregate the defective parts and take them back for rectification, if that was possible. Keeping production going often became a problem when such segregation was required. The received parts had also to be counted and often errors were detected.

At each vendor conference, vendors were told that the task of inspecting and counting incoming parts by Maruti was really non-value adding, and thus led to higher production costs. This was primarily the responsibility of the vendor and they should do it right the first time. Why could Maruti not trust them to at least count correctly? In Japan, components moved to the lines without any counting or checking. Why could Maruti not emulate the Japanese in this comparatively low technology work? Packing systems were modified to ensure that counting of the parts was easy and virtually automatic. Over time, a large number of vendors have moved to the stage where their certificate of quality and numbers is accepted as they have proven their capability and reliability.

When any vendor's part was rejected due to quality reasons, the system required that the root cause of the problem be correctly identified and correctives applied. The issue was treated as closed only when it was reported that the corrective action was effective. The need to identify the root cause was again a departure from conventional practice. Normally, defective parts, or faults in a product, were rectified and rarely did anyone bother to find the root cause of the problem and amend the system to ensure that the defect did not recur. This practice was not confined only to the vendors. Even within Maruti, engineers drawn largely from public sector companies had the same system of dealing with defects. The Japanese taught them that to get at the real cause it was necessary to ask 'why' anywhere between three to five times. I myself had to frequently ask 'why' many times when any problem was reported, and this helped to inculcate this habit in more employees. I would also periodically ask how many of the ISO or QS systems had been modified in the previous six months. Unless systems were being modified and improved, defects would continue to crop up and continuous improvements in quality could not be made.

In spite of this obsession with quality, the no-tolerance culture took a long time to seep in. Mathur and Deshpande, for example, were frequently fielding '*adjust kar lijiye*' (let it pass) requests. Vendors would admit that their product had a slight problem but promised to set it right the next time round. What the

Maruti materials team had to do was to see why a supplier was not being able to stick to the tolerance levels—was the basic process under control, making this a random occurrence and, therefore, meriting a waiver, or was there some serious flaw in the manufacturing process? Maruti engineers working in the purchase and vendor development departments would spend at least half a day every day on the shop floors of suppliers.

Some of the vendors, especially among the joint ventures (there were one or two that had come in using political clout), even complained to the government that the Maruti management was being very rigid on quality. But the government refused to interfere. Senior executives in charge of vendor development often never came to know about these incidents and hence functioned with supreme confidence.

Others decided to seize the opportunity to change themselves. Kapur sent workers to Japan, in groups of ten or twelve, for six months' training in Koyo Seiko. Sona Steering would invite engineers from Koyo Seiko and also get help from Maruti so that quality levels could improve. Bharat Forge was another group that took full advantage of the exposure to Japanese manufacturing practices. Krishna Maruti invited top-level Japanese experts to help improve systems and educate its employees on how to produce consistent quality.

The biggest difficulty the Maruti management faced was that the vendors would not reveal the real nature of any problem being faced by them but would resort to delaying tactics or plead with Maruti to agree to something that was not acceptable. This happened despite the fact that vendor conferences were organized at regular intervals where Maruti encouraged the suppliers to talk about their problems in an open manner. It took some time for vendors to believe that criticism of Maruti systems would not result in adverse consequences for them. Traditionally, vendors in such conferences just listened and certainly did not say anything remotely critical of the customer. I encouraged vendors to change and become active participants in the meetings. The idea was to jointly look for changes which would bring down the total costs and improve quality and productivity As a result, many good ideas emerged and Maruti made improvements.

At one such conference, vendors said their trucks got held up at the factory for long hours. This was analysed and it was found that the number of unloading points were too few for the number of trucks which were coming to deliver components. Hence they had to queue up for unloading. Maruti then changed the system of loading/unloading components. Many more unloading points were created. Each was designated for identified components. The attempt was to also ensure that the distance moved by the components after unloading, either for storing or going to the assembly line, could be minimized. The results were excellent, and truck turnaround time was substantially reduced as also the internal movement of components.

Once, one of the vendors in Chennai was delaying supplies, giving one excuse or the other. When it continued for a month, a very angry Mathur went down to meet him and demanded an explanation. It was only then that the man confessed that he was waiting for funds from the bank. This was a common problem. Maruti was growing at upwards of 30 per cent a year and working capital flows were not able to keep pace, as the banking sector, not used to this rate of growth, just could not cope. Their processes were far too cumbersome and slow.

Mathur then called up the supplier's bank manager, who said the proposal had been sent from the local branch office to the regional office only two days earlier. It would then have to go to the head office and be considered at a meeting of the board of directors. The board meeting was the following month. Mathur, thanks to Maruti's immense clout, directly called the managing director of the bank and told him that Maruti was buying 80 per cent of the supplier's offtake and that the delay in clearing the loan was disrupting car production schedules. The supplier got his working capital in two days flat.

Maruti also developed a vendor rating system. Vendor performance was evaluated on a number of parameters, the main ones being rejection levels, meeting committed schedules, and price of components. Points were allotted on the basis of performance each month in accordance with a predetermined scheme which was also known to the vendors. The rating of vendors was used to decide the share of business between the suppliers of a particular part. When a new model was introduced, the vendor with a higher rating was given preference for developing parts for that car. If a vendor was unable to improve his performance, Maruti also looked to develop another source and the non-performing vendor was dropped. The transparency of the system ensured virtually no complaints from vendors when Maruti decided share of business or who should develop a new component.

~

Though Kalyani and Kapur insist that Maruti brought a sea change in the way component manufacturers operated or viewed quality, Maruti encountered problems even in 1993 when the Zen was about to be launched. The Zen was to be exported to Europe under the SMC brand as the new Alto, and SMC was anxious that its reputation for quality in Europe should not suffer. This required that local components had to meet stringent quality standards. The car could not use too many imported components as cars imported from India attracted a lower custom duty than those from developed countries, but to be eligible, there had to be at least 56 per cent value added in India.

One of the reasons why a high level of local content became difficult was that the cars sent to Europe were left-hand drive. Thus, all components specific to such cars had to be imported, as local manufacture in small numbers would not have been economical. In addition, there were some specific components required to meet the higher emission norms prevailing in Europe. The 56 per cent value added had to come from the remaining components. This was not an easy task considering the state of the component industry in 1993. Maruti engineers had to work really hard and the local content norms were met. The hard work paid off because the Zen, when it was exported, was considered one of the best cars in Europe.

The dogged perseverance of Maruti and the patience of its team in dealing with the component manufacturers, and the introduction of many new concepts based on the Japanese experience, all had a positive fallout in the long run. When the car industry was opened to the world in 1993, most major car manufacturers decided to come to India because of the strong component industry. India is now recognized as an automobile component manufacturing hub. In the early 1980s, component exports from India were $6 million. Today exports are nearing $4 billion and growing. India is also becoming the small car manufacturer for the world markets because of the low cost and high quality of production here. More importantly, the component industry has gained a reputation for quality, with thirteen Deming Prize winners and forty TPM Excellence awardees.

Despite this, component manufactures still have a long way to go. Quality levels are not consistent across the industry. The practice of excellence has to permeate all the suppliers, including the Tier II and Tier III vendors. The Tier I vendors have to take on this responsibility, with assistance from the car manufacturers. Vendors have also to transition to the next level where, given specifications and performance requirements, they could design and produce components of international quality without seeking help from outside. The industry has not yet been able to build strong design and engineering capacities. However, many companies are appreciating the need for investing in design capabilities. Many foreign companies have also come to the conclusion that having an R&D base in India is likely to be of great benefit. It seems that in the next few years India would be able to design and build cars without seeking any large help from foreign companies. The task of modernizing the automobile industry, given to Maruti in 1981, would then be complete.

8

A NEW CUSTOMER CULTURE

When it was nationalizing Maruti Motors Ltd in 1980, the government had decided that the company should produce and sell 100,000 cars a year. This, according to Arun Nehru, whom Mrs Gandhi had consulted before the decision to take over Maruti, would be the minimum volume necessary to make it a viable project. Indeed, volume was the name of the game in the automobile business. Not only were high volumes required to lower production costs and attain higher quality, but the viability of the sales and after-sales network was also critically dependent on this factor.

The importance of volume was something that Krishnamurthy and I had learnt in our discussions with the consultants from the United Kingdom who had come with us to Europe in 1981. However, there were sceptics galore who, as we were nearing the start of production, warned us that 100,000 units could not be sold in India and it would be unwise to make investments for creating such a huge manufacturing capacity. However, the public response to the three SMC vehicles taken up for initial production, when they were exhibited all over India, convinced us that it would be possible to sell 100,000 units, as there was a large latent demand for cars, provided the product met customer expectations, was rightly priced and was backed by good after-sales service.

Believing that a large demand existed was only the first step. It was necessary to establish a sales and service system which would enable these cars to be sold efficiently, and ensure that the users were able to get high quality after-sales service, as Maruti car users would largely be from the middle class, which was very conscious about getting value for money. I told my marketing and sales team about my own, not very happy, experiences of buying cars and getting them repaired and serviced, and drove home the point that Maruti owners should not feel that the company was doing them a favour by selling a car or servicing it.

The concepts of marketing and consumer satisfaction were almost alien to the automobile industry of that time. With the supply of cars lagging far behind demand neither car manufacturers nor dealers had to bother about marketing the cars or going an extra mile in providing after-sales service. All that the manufacturers needed was a distribution system. Nor did they need to bother very much about modifying cars to suit customer requirements. This was partly due to the conditions of their manufacturing licences (there was little they could change without going back to the government for permission) but probably more because customers did not have any choice and had to accept what they could get.

Maruti was to change all that. Krishnamurthy summed up the new attitude in his chairman's address in July 1987: 'We simply cannot forget that we are *not* (emphasis added) in the business of selling cars. We are selling to our customers a long-term commitment to take care of their needs for transport efficiently and economically.'

The first step had actually been taken in 1981, even as Maruti started scouting around for collaboration partners. The decision, first, to commission the market survey to determine what kind of a car people wanted, and then reversing the heavy industries ministry's decision to manufacture the Renault R-18 and opt for a small car instead, was a first-ever acknowledgement of the importance of the customer in the automobile industry. The fact that a public sector undertaking was adopting a policy of customer-orientation was especially significant, at a time when even most of the private sector cared little for its customers.

This obsession with the customer at a time when Maruti operated in a monopoly—and could have got away with a high-handed attitude—was to become the leitmotif of the company over the years and stand it in good stead twenty-five years later, when the competitive scenario got extremely cut-throat, and helped it keep a 54 per cent market share in a market with fourteen players.

~

The first decision we had to take was whether cars should be sold through Maruti's own sales outlets or through a network of private dealerships, as the rest of the automobile industry did. Some argued that Maruti could earn higher profits if it owned the sales channel. However, both Krishnamurthy and I were convinced that a public sector organization could not successfully implement a service function, which required constant interaction with the public. There were enough examples from the hospitality sector, airlines and railways to prove this. The flexibility that a sales organization required cannot be ensured in a public sector ethos, and decision making is necessarily bureaucratic and slow. Procedures have to be followed strictly and the paperwork has to be perfect to ensure protection from possible vigilance and other enquiries. More importantly, public servants in India are not known for treating the customer as king, or believing that they get their salaries from their customers. Rather, citizens approach government employees as supplicants. There is also very little identification of government employees with the performance of their organizations—an absolute must in a service industry. SMC also agreed with this view and was in favour of privately owned dealerships. So we decided to go along with this.

The dealers were going to be the lynchpin in the whole marketing exercise, since they were the public face of Maruti, and much thought went into developing a sound dealer policy. As a paper on 'Approach to Appointment of Dealers in India' pointed out in 1982:

> . . . this opportunity (the selection of dealers) should be utilized for introducing standards of service to the customer, and an approach to marketing and sales, which are found in highly competitive situations. The possibility of doing this would only be available at the time of selection of dealers, and the finalization of contractual conditions with them.

It was decided that for a sale of 100,000 units a year, dealers would be appointed in sixty cities. Considerable importance was attached to ensuring that dealerships were profitable. The management believed that dealers would follow systems and provide good service if they could make money in a legitimate manner. That would only be possible if their sale volumes were adequate. If the dealers found that the dealerships gave them good profits, they would also be less inclined to indulge in wrong practices, because they would not want to lose the dealership. Calculations were done and it was estimated that in the bigger towns a sale of 2,000 cars a year would enable a dealer to make reasonable profits. Since the volume of production would build up over the next few years, it was logical to activate dealerships in a phased manner. This would ensure that dealers could be given reasonable volumes from the time of starting operations. Thus, the plan was to activate the sixty dealerships over a period of three years.

The task of training dealers and their personnel, as well as establishing well-equipped workshops, also necessitated a phasing of the activation of dealerships. SMC service experts had prescribed the layout of dealer workshops, for different level of sales, and the equipment to be used in them. The Maruti range of vehicles brought in absolutely new technology to the Indian automobile market. Not only would customers be unfamiliar with the new requirements, but so would the mechanics and engineers, unless they were well trained. If customers were not to reject Maruti vehicles, problems that cropped up in cars would have to be addressed promptly and effectively, which only trained personnel could do. Adequate spare parts would also have to be made available, which would have been a bit of a stretch if sales were started simultaneously all over India. Any inadequacy on the after-sales service front, the management realized, would lead to people getting disillusioned, and winning back customer goodwill would not be easy. If, however, Maruti earned a reputation for high quality after-sales service (which it could if its till-then scarce resources were concentrated in a few high-profile locations and not spread too thin), half the marketing battle would have been won. Similar to what Maruti had to do to develop vendors for the parts to be used in the car, manufacturers of workshop equipment, which SMC wanted installed, had also to be developed, as they were not available in India. Establishing training facilities for mechanics also took time, as not only had infrastructure to be created, but the trainers themselves had to be trained. Several engineers were sent to Japan for this purpose.

Sales were initially to be started in the four metros—Delhi, Mumbai, Chennai, Kolkata—and were to be extended to all the state capitals by the end of 1984-1985, the first full year of production, when around 20,000 vehicles were expected to be rolled out. Accordingly, sixteen dealers were activated in the first year, twenty in the second year, and twenty-four in the third year. The first two dealers, Competent Motors (Raj Chopra) and Ganga Automobiles (Ashwini Suri) in Delhi, were inaugurated by Suzuki. While Competent has remained one of the leading dealers in India till now, unfortunately Ganga got into problems and closed down in the mid-1990s. The dealers were allowed to appoint sub-dealers and approve servicing outlets in other towns in their jurisdiction.

~

The criteria used to select dealers were business experience, financial muscle and the availability or ability to own land/ building for the showroom and the workshop at a suitable location. Newspaper advertisements were issued, initially in January 1983, and then periodically depending on when a dealership was to be awarded in a city, inviting applications from interested persons. Along with their applications, the applicants had to furnish a bank guarantee of their ability to invest up to Rs. 50 lakh in the case of metros, Rs. 30 lakh for

Class A cities and Rs. 20 lakh in the case of other towns. In addition, just before deliveries of cars started, dealers had to make a cash deposit of Rs. 5 lakh (which would carry an annual interest of 10 per cent). The investment requirement would become smaller if the dealer had land for a showroom and a workshop.

Though the general sentiment was against appointing people who had been dealers of Hindustan Motors, Premier Automobiles or Mahindra and Mahindra (it was manufacturing jeeps) the board decided that they could be considered if they were the best available applicants and were prepared to give up the existing dealership. There were very good reasons for not allowing a person to be a dealer for another car manufacturer. Firstly, there would be a conflict of interest. Secondly, it could lead to diversion of funds from the dealership business of one manufacturer to that of the other manufacturer. This problem would be present even if different family members were holding the dealerships, as often all family members were part of what is known as a Hindu Undivided Family (HUF). Incomes from businesses done by the different members of the HUF were all pooled and used by all the family members. In such a situation, it could not be ensured that Maruti sales were not adversely affected by what happened in the other dealerships. In a few cases this policy had to be enforced even when a dealer brought strong political pressure to bear to make an exception in his case.

Dealer selection was the only area where the management took political recommendations into account. It was felt that one of the requirements of success of a dealer would be his relationships and influence in the allotted territory. If the candidate met all the other requirements of being a dealer, it would be an advantage if an important political leader, familiar with the territory, felt that the person would make a success of the dealership. At the same time, the management was conscious of the fact that however objectively a dealer was selected, there would be no stopping the rejected candidates going to court and challenging the appointment. Maruti, as a public sector entity, had to follow—and be seen to follow—the principles of equal opportunity for all and no discrimination on any ground. A court could stay the appointment of a dealer till the case was decided and that would immensely harm sales, as there would be no dealer in that territory. Moreover, it would take a great deal of time and effort to convince the courts of the validity of the criteria adopted for selecting a dealer, and there was no guarantee that the courts would be convinced. The selection of a dealer also involved making a judgement of the comparative capabilities of the applicants, and the courts could strike down a subjective judgement on this aspect. In any case, much time and effort of the management would be required if a spate of cases were filed, and we just did not have the resources or the time to handle such a situation.

Accordingly, it was decided that all applications for dealerships would be placed before the board, without any evaluation of the applicants being made on paper. The board would be given an oral presentation of the strengths of each applicant, including recommendations, if any. The board members were expected to apply their minds to the suitability of the applicants and take a collective decision on who should be awarded the dealership. This was seen to be the best way to handle the political input and also to avoid legal challenges. This is the procedure which was followed in awarding all the dealerships till the mid-1990s, when a modified system was introduced.

Selected candidates were issued letters of intent (LoI), which would be converted into contracts after the required infrastructure was created and other conditions had been met. The system worked well. Though there were a few legal challenges to the award of dealerships, mostly in small towns, the courts upheld the decisions, as they were collective board decisions. In April 1983, the first lot of LoIs were issued to twenty dealers in sixteen cities.

Interestingly, one of the applicants for a dealership was a young man from Ludhiana called Sunil Bharti Mittal. He came with his father, Sat Paul Mittal, who was then a Congress MP. SMC had also recommended his name, as he was importing and selling their portable generator sets in India. However, he came somewhat late, as a dealership in his town had already been committed to another person and there was no scope for a second dealer. Years later, Mittal got into the telecommunications business and founded the Bharti group, which has become the largest mobile telecommunications company in India, and has also diversified into other businesses. Mittal is now among the world's richest persons, and acclaimed for his entrepreneurial and management capabilities.

The dealers chosen in the initial years all performed well. However, after some years, with changes in the ministry, the Maruti management and board came under a lot of pressure to accommodate unsuitable persons as dealers. Maruti dealerships were very profitable in those days as there was virtually no competition. The dealer did not have to employ any working capital, and the vehicles commanded a premium. The role of the dealer was virtually that of being a distributor. Naturally, getting a dealership was considered to be a very safe way of making money, and hence became an object of political patronage.

While senior ministers like N.D. Tiwari and the late J. Vengal Rao kept away from making recommendations for dealerships, their junior ministers did not exercise the same self-restraint. The common perception was that public sector companies were controlled by the ministry, and ministers therefore had the right to give directions to the management on various matters. A minister probably felt that he would lose face if he were to tell a political supporter that he was unable to direct the management of a public sector firm to do a small thing like award a dealership. Unfortunately, most of the recommendations made were for people who were totally unable to meet the minimum requirements for a dealership. One person who came with a strong recommendation was a 'social worker' with no assets and no declared source of income. The inability to award a dealership to him made one minister of state very unhappy. Somehow Vengal Rao heard about this matter. He called me and said that under no circumstances was a dealership to be awarded to this person, as it was not a clean case. Some months later, after Vengal Rao had quit his post, the minister of state ordered an enquiry against me in the Kandla transportation case and the extension of my term as managing director was delayed.

Fortunately, not all ministers wanted to use dealerships as an instrument of political patronage. Ajit Singh, who was industries minister from December 1989 to November 1990 during the National Front government, was one of them. He called me one day and said, 'Look, I'm coming under pressure and I don't want to be accused of making money on dealerships. So please find a way out.' He wanted a system that was transparent, one where he could credibly tell applicants that the decision on a dealership was not discretionary.

Maruti decided on a new system. After advertising for a dealership, a list of the three best candidates would be prepared, based on their financial strength, availability of infrastructure, and experience of business. The shortlisted applicant had to be a resident of the city where the dealership was to be given. If any person had strong political recommendations, he still had to meet these conditions, but could be shown some leeway in being included in the shortlist. Thereafter, the shortlisted candidates were required to give sealed bids on how much money they could deposit with Maruti for the award of the dealership. The highest bid would get the dealership. Thus the process was like an auction for the dealership, except that the deposit amount would be refundable and interest would be paid on it. The element of discretion in the award of dealerships was eliminated. The system had flaws, since it did not necessarily lead to the selection of the best person as a dealer. In addition, keeping a large amount of money as a security deposit, which Maruti did not need, reduced the working capital of the dealer, and could potentially hurt sales. However, it seemed to be the only way of avoiding conflicts with the political system and was one of the costs of Maruti being a public sector entity. Ajit Singh was happy with this system and approved it.

This system helped Maruti in the mid-1990s, when another important minister was pushing the case of a person who did not seem suitable. He was put on the shortlist, but came third in the bid and, therefore, could not get the dealership. The minister was very unhappy, but there was little he could do. He did suggest that the system of appointing dealers be changed, and there should be no 'bidding' system, but was advised that such a change would be very difficult to defend and could lead to much political embarrassment.

~

As in the case of vendors, new dealers also had to be familiarized with an entirely new work culture and made to understand that aggressive sales and top-of-the-line after-sales service were an integral part of operating their dealership. The customer would form an opinion about Maruti not only from the product he or she bought, but also the quality of the experience while making a purchase and then maintaining the vehicle. Dealers were repeatedly told that competition would come, and they had to ensure that a Maruti user remained a buyer of Maruti vehicles even when there were other product choices available.

It was, however, not easy to change the mindset of most dealers, when there were long waiting lists of customers wanting to buy vehicles, and the car commanded a large premium. Maruti realized this and tried to get over the problem by introducing systems for all the operations of a dealership and insisting on these being followed. Continuous attempts were made to bring more professionalism into dealer management. Over time, many dealers realized the value of working according to systems in terms of attaining higher sales and profits. In fact, like with vendors, Maruti realized that dealers would only be motivated if they were profitable. Maruti had to ensure that dealers realized that their own growth and profitability was inextricably linked with that of Maruti. The three pillars of the dealer policy were: provide them good growth opportunity, provide good profitability and provide respect. Maruti adopted a partnership approach with the dealers as well, handholding them, teaching them not only on how to deal with customers but also how to manage their businesses to become profitable.

There were clear norms for showrooms—minimum size, décor, and facilities for customers. The intention was to make a visit to the showroom as pleasant an experience as possible. In the early years there were not very many models to be displayed, and potential customers were not very familiar with the products the company was offering. Thus, Maruti wanted all models to be displayed in the showroom to enable customers to see them in an attractive setting. This required good lighting, decoration and adequate space to move around. The showroom staff had to be trained to explain the features of the vehicles and their advantages over those in the market. Since complying with the regulations and local laws involved a lot of paperwork, the attempt was to ensure that this could be done as conveniently and quickly as possible. Dealers were quite happy to invest in showrooms as costs were not very high, and Maruti sales did result in good profits. However, on many occasions I had to caution our sales staff not to go overboard in insisting that dealers make five-star showrooms, and to keep costs and profitability of dealers in mind while persuading them to make investments. Some dealers thought that making the best showroom was an end in itself and would automatically result in high profits. It took some time for them to learn that much more was required to be done to win and retain customers, and make profits.

In 1987, Maruti launched a corporate identity campaign. The signs outside showrooms were standardized and they had to display the Maruti name prominently along with the dealership name, instead of only the latter name being shown as was being done till then. The facilities inside the showroom were also standardized. The idea was that the Maruti brand name should become popular, the customers should recognize a Maruti dealership from far, and the buying experience should be as similar as possible all over India.

As with showrooms, Maruti also provided guidance on how to establish workshops—number of bays, equipment, paint shop layout, storage and handling of spare parts, among other things. Maruti personnel had to approve the workshop site and the layout (the drawings for which were prepared with SMC's help). A standard list of necessary equipment was provided, in accordance with the specifications given by SMC. Some of the equipment—computerized engine diagnostic equipment, wheel alignment systems, and brake tester, to name a few—was a first for dealers in India. Each workshop was required to install two post lifts (on which cars were positioned and raised, enabling mechanics to work on the underbody). Till then, workshops only had pits over which cars would be positioned, and mechanics stood in these pits to check and work on the underbody of the cars.

Workshop practices also needed a major change. Traditionally, each mechanic was a specialist who would do work in his area only. These areas were electrical systems, engines, transmission, suspension and body work. When a car came for service, different 'specialist' mechanics would check and service different parts of a car. In addition, each mechanic had one or two helpers, to do the less skilled work like washing and cleaning parts, fetching tools or oil and tightening nuts and bolts. Most of the employees were underutilized, and never worked anywhere near eight hours in a shift. The specialist mechanics often sat idle when parts were washed and cleaned. It was impossible to ensure that the jobs to be done every day would provide equal work for all the specialist mechanics. On some days there could be more work in one or more of the specialized areas and less in the others. Another major defect in this system was that servicing of cars was held up if some 'specialized' mechanic was not available.

SMC, quite rightly, did not want these practices to continue. Their basic principle was that one mechanic should do all the work required for servicing a car, whether electrical or mechanical, and would have to be trained to handle all systems. Further, he would have to do the entire servicing of a car himself, with no helpers. This system was designed to ensure accountability, as only one person would be responsible for the quality of work done on a car. It would also considerably reduce manpower and improve productivity. Implementing this was not easy. The older and more experienced mechanics were most unlikely to agree to the change. They would think that doing the work of helpers would lower their status. It would also not be easy to train them to learn new skills because of the age factor. It was decided that, by and large, it would be better to train fresh pass-outs from ITIs, and then employ them in the dealerships. Thus a training centre for mechanics was established in the service centre at the Maruti factory. As the sales and service network expanded, regional training centres were established. The young workers from the ITIs were without hang-ups and were quite happy to work in accordance with the new system.

However, it was difficult to bring about an attitudinal change in some aspects of servicing cars. The procedure for servicing the car—the sequencing of each activity, and the time to be taken for it—was laid down in a chart. The time was set out because each mechanic had to service two and a half cars in one shift. The mechanic had to follow this sequencing to the last detail and tick off each item when it was done. This was also to ensure that no activity was missed. Mechanics followed this so long as they were learning. Once they became familiar with the work, they would not follow the right sequence. I would pay attention to checking this when I visited workshops and over time the culture of following the system has been established in the mechanics.

Since after-sales service was considered to be extremely important to ensure customer satisfaction, Maruti followed a strict 'no sales without service' rule and dealerships were activated only after the servicing facility was fully in place and approved by the service department. So great was the emphasis on servicing that a senior manager-level executive from SMC, M. Kawasaki, was posted in the service department to oversee this activity. He remained in India for a long time, and made a huge contribution to the development of the quality and spread of the after-sales network of Maruti. It was his example which led our own engineers to learn to dirty their hands and clothes and do work on the cars themselves.

In 1985 Maruti decided to set up its Maruti Authorized Service Stations (MASS) across the country. These were small service stations run by private individuals and located in cities where the dealer did not have any workshop. The mechanics in these service stations were trained by Maruti, which also provided the minimum required tooling. It was clear that the number of workshops which a dealer could establish would be limited and would not provide service coverage to large parts of India. The object was to bring service facilities nearer to the customers. The workshops which then existed did not have the know-how to service and repair Maruti cars because of the change in technology. Maruti realized that a wide network of service facilities and availability of spare parts were essential to promote both car ownership and to encourage people to travel by car outside their cities of residence. Starting with 117 MASS outlets in 1986-87, the network gradually grew and in 2008 the number stood at close to 2,000. One of the most remembered advertisements is one in which a little boy in a barren mountainous area tells people in a car that there are no hotels and restaurants in that area, but there is a MASS.

Quite apart from the convenience for customers, the combined service network of the dealers and MASS opened up immense job opportunities. The unemployment problem in the 1980s was huge, but the spread of Maruti vehicles and the consequent demand for service and spare parts helped in finding jobs for many young people.

~

Because of the monopoly in the small car market in the early 1980s, the gap between supply and demand and the consequent premium on many of its products, Maruti's top leadership had to wrestle with the phenomenon of black marketing. Having to pay a premium on the list price of products was not something new to Indians in those days of controls and licences. In some cases the government tried to control prices through administrative measures, but the market forces were stronger and only resulted in retailers charging a premium. It also spread corruption among those who were charged with enforcing the administered prices or the rationing of the product. As a result, scooters, cars, cement, steel, coal and even cooking gas were periodically sold in the black market. Dealers could collect a premium on cars in short supply by manipulating the booking list, especially if there was no proper system for making a booking, or nobody monitored the booking system sincerely even if it was prescribed. There were allegations that the cash collected by the dealers was shared by many persons, including the manufacturer.

Krishnamurthy and I wanted to ensure that Maruti and all its personnel were protected from such allegations. Thus the system of computerized delivery lists was evolved. It brought total transparency in the sale process as every customer knew his or her number in the delivery list, and could check the numbers of the persons to whom cars had been delivered. A dealer could not jump the queue by taking money. However, the system did not prevent individuals from making cash profits by booking cars and selling the allotment letter at a profit when the delivery number matured. Booking of Maruti cars, in fact, became an inflation-proof investment avenue.

Maruti tried various measures to check this. It first limited the number of bookings by a single person. People found ways of circumventing this restriction by making bookings in the name of family members, servants and even friends and also by making variations in their initials. An attempt was then made to check the addresses, but even that was not foolproof. Maruti then tried to restrict sales, by specifying that bookings could only be re-sold to blood relatives. Though this was partly effective, it resulted in the company having to do a great deal of policing work, instead of concentrating on improving the sales and after-sales processes.

There was reason to believe that some dealers were also booking cars themselves, but in names which were probably fake. However, there was never any evidence to establish this. One manager of a Delhi-based dealership was found to be charging premium on cars and Maruti got him sacked. He was reinstated some months later, as the dealer pleaded that he was very competent and should be given another chance. Some years later, this dealership had to be terminated.

In 1989-90, another method was tried to curb speculation and sale of allotment letters. Customers were told to deposit with the dealer a fixed deposit receipt (FDR) of Rs. 35,000 in their own name when their allotment was about to mature. This would be transferred in favour of the dealer at the time of delivery. This helped curb premium sales to a limited extent, as the buyer of the allotment letter could not use this FDR. The original allottee would need to buy the car to use the FDR, and then make a sale and get a premium. The new buyer's name would be the second one on the registration book. Those who were buying cars at a premium preferred to buy the allotment letters, as theirs would then be the first name on the registration book, instead of the second.

In 1990-91, the system changed again, with customers being told to pay to Maruti, through the dealer, the full 'C' form price (on which they were to be paid 12 per cent interest), when their allotment number matured. This helped, as the original allottee had to find the full price of the car. The car would be registered in his name. The person buying the car from him would be the second name on the registration book. This system led to a substantial cancellation of bookings, and resulted in a 40 per cent reduction in the waiting period. However, this did not totally end speculation or sale of cars at a premium.

The only effective way of controlling black marketing was to increase production and to reduce the demand-supply gap. Maruti could have increased prices and mopped up the premium but did not do so, primarily because it wanted the car market to deepen and conditions to be created where the two shareholders—SMC and the government—would feel confident about making investments to increase production. In addition, being a government company it did not want to be charged with profiteering—not considered a very respectable activity those days.

Besides having to deal with black marketing, Maruti also had to ensure that dealers did not take advantage of the shortage situation to harass or cut corners to save money at the cost of customers. Old habits die hard, however. Some dealers were found to be short-circuiting the pre-delivery inspection, which they were required to do to ensure that the car was in perfect condition at the time of delivery. Some dealers, still in the old mindset, believed that giving a car to the customer was enough of a favour and spending time and money on pre-delivery inspection was a waste. Defects could be rectified later, and in any case the customer had no option of buying any other product. Maruti had to repeatedly tell dealers that despite it being a seller's market, the policy was to be as customer friendly as possible, and systems and procedures had to be followed strictly. If a dealer was not willing to accept this, Maruti would be constrained to find another dealer. Gradually the message went home, and the quality of pre-delivery service improved.

Another malpractice was that of dealers not paying interest on booking deposits to customers. When some customers complained, I had to ask the Maruti staff to go through their books and ensure that this was done, though this should not really have been its job. Maruti even did random checks with customers to see if interest was correctly paid, as in some cases it was found that the dealer's employee was fudging the records. In a few cases fines were imposed to bring home the importance of complying with the instructions from Maruti. Another common phenomenon in those days was customers, with any contact in Maruti, making requests to ensure that they were given a 'good piece'! This was a hangover of their experience of buying Ambassadors and Premier Padminis. Due to the absence of stringent quality control systems, which SMC brought to India, the quality of individual cars made till then did vary and a 'contact' in either of the two manufacturers did ensure that the car was delivered after proper pre-delivery inspection and that it was better in quality. I often had to explain to important customers that each car produced by Maruti was exactly like another, as the systems were designed to bring this about. The concept of a 'good piece' was inapplicable, as all pieces were made in exactly the same way, using components which were all of the same quality. What could be ensured was proper pre-delivery inspection by the dealer.

There was one exception to this general position. Customers were aware that the local content of cars was increasing, and most people believed that the imported components were superior to the local-made parts. A request was often made that a VIP should be given a car with higher import content. I had to explain that this was also not possible as in the mass production system followed by Maruti it was impossible to custom-make cars. Fortunately most VIPs understood the difference in our manufacturing system from that of Hindustan Motors or Premier Automobiles. I did get to know that some employees, when buying Maruti cars, were getting locally made parts changed with imported parts. This led to our changing the system of sale to our employees, which resulted in their not being able to choose the specific car they would buy. It was randomly allotted from the stockyard.

~

As in the case of the vendors, Maruti was battling a mindset. Special training programmes were organized for the chief executives, managers and sales personnel of the dealers to instil in them the realization that the customer is the person who keeps them in business. Customer satisfaction was, therefore, to be top priority. To that end, Maruti introduced several practices that were completely unheard of in the Indian automobile market.

Dealers, for example, were told to drop customers back to their homes or offices after a car was given for servicing at the workshop. Later, the more progressive dealers started to pick up a car from the customer's residence and deliver it back after servicing. Another new practice, one which really surprised customers, was of a workshop person calling them a few days after a car had been serviced or repaired to check if they were satisfied. A system of tracking customer complaints was introduced, which was gradually refined over the years. As soon as a complaint came, it was given a number and the monitoring mechanism kicked in. The complaint was tracked until the time the customer gave a satisfaction note. It wasn't enough for the dealer or the Maruti staff to say the complaint had been taken care of.

Related to this was working out an index of customer complaints. Ten complaints per 10,000 vehicles was set as a benchmark. Initially, the number of complaints was between 25 and 30, and this was gradually brought down through the complaint tracking and resolution system. Repeat complaints were considered unacceptable and Maruti started a root cause analysis of all complaints, especially those of a repetitive nature, asking five 'whys' and taking steps within the system to ensure that they did not recur. I used to be particularly concerned about customers who wrote to me with complaints.

I used to ask our quality staff for the reasons of the origin of such complaints and also demand similar analysis by our service division as to why such complaints could not be solved by dealers, compelling the customers to approach me. The intention was to find out whether there was a lack of capability or commitment on the part of dealer's staff to resolve customer complaints. In order to go deeper into the matter, a meeting was organized with important dealers from whom such complaints used to originate and they were made aware about the types of grievances being received by my office. Dealers were requested to be more proactive and resolve the customer complaints in a manner as to avoid repeated visits by the customer for the same defect. Some dealers complained about the premature failure of components. A meeting was then organized with vendors, who were apprised of this issue by our quality assurance staff. The vendors were requested to undertake root cause analysis and implement suitable counter measures to prevent recurrence of these defects.

During the weekly management committee meetings, I used to discuss the customer complaints received in my office, to find out why such problems arose and why the processes had not improved over the years to prevent their occurrence. Kobayashi, the joint managing director, then came forward to suggest that he and Kumar would conduct an on-site meeting every Monday with the members from engineering, quality assurance, parts inspection, vendor development, and service and production divisions to discuss the problems experienced in the market and on the production line.

One major advantage of this meeting was that not only the senior management people but also the staff of various divisions, who were more involved with these problems, could attend these discussions. As a result, getting the quality issues resolved quickly became a more focussed effort. Because of the cross-functional nature of the discussion, quick action could be taken by the concerned divisions. Since the meeting was held every Monday the concerned divisions were under pressure to take suitable counter measures by the next meeting. This was also followed by a monthly meeting of various divisions with the joint managing director and director engineering where the warranty failures of the components were discussed. This kind of interaction helped in cutting down the delays which used to arise because of the departmental bias and concern of each division to protect its turf.

It was not only the dealers who had to be educated. Customers also had to be persuaded to accept a different way of doing things. SMC followed a policy of not allowing customers in the workshop area where the cars were actually serviced. Till then it was the usual practice for customers to be near their vehicles during servicing or repairs. They wanted to ensure that work was actually done and that new parts were not removed and replaced by old parts. The trust level in the workshop was low, and not without justification. In some cases, customers also developed an arrangement with the mechanics to come to their homes and service or repair their cars. SMC understood the thinking of customers and their reluctance to leave cars entirely at the mercy of the workshop. Hence, a waiting area for customers was provided, which overlooked the shop floor, from where they could watch their cars being serviced, without coming into contact with the mechanics. The waiting area was comfortable, with air-conditioning, drinking water and refreshments. Later, dealers also provided television sets and DVDs. As time elapsed and customers developed confidence in the workshops, the number of persons who would wait in the workshop and watch their cars kept declining.

When a customer brought a car for servicing, a supervisor would interact with him and record all the items which needed attention. If necessary, the car was taken for a drive to check the complaints. Thereafter, a job card was prepared and an estimate was given to the customer and the delivery time indicated. At times, after the work was started, it was found that some more work needed to be done, involving an increase in costs. Initially dealers would get the additional work done and the customer would be faced with a bill which was much higher than what he expected. This led to complaints. Dealers were told that as a rule they must get the customer's approval, on telephone, if the cost was going to increase significantly. A record of the conversation was required to be kept. A more frequent cause of customer unhappiness was delay in giving delivery of the vehicle. The workshop managers had to be constantly educated on the need to keep to time commitments and to install proper monitoring systems in the workshop to ensure that delays did not occur. If a delay was inevitable, the customer was required to be informed well in advance. In recent times, workshops have started using the bar code system to monitor progress of a car as it is serviced or repaired, and the workshop manager can now control work much better.

~

Despite the fact that Maruti kept drilling the message of customer satisfaction on every possible occasion—in training sessions, at dealer conferences, individual interactions—it did not seem to be getting across. Even as late as July 1985, one and a half years after the car was launched, the Maruti board expressed concern about increasing complaints about the manner of functioning of several dealers. It then decided that it should increase competition between dealers, an idea that had been mooted even in 1982, when the dealer policy was being drawn up. However, it could not be implemented then because there were too few cars to be sold. As volumes increased, it became possible to implement the idea.

When the first dealers were appointed in 1983, they were located in the capital cities of states. They could sell cars to anyone who came to them, but they could not solicit business in a state other than where they were located. Later, when more than one dealer was appointed in a state, there was need to define a territory for each dealer. Initially, these territories were defined in terms of districts of a state. A dealer was expected to develop sales and promote business within his territory. Dealers were not allowed to 'poach' in the territory of another dealer. But Maruti soon realized that there was very little competition from other manufacturers and the restriction on poaching from outside their territories gave dealers a monopoly in their own territories (though there was some competition among them in cities where there was more than one dealer, like Delhi or Mumbai). Even before the process of liberalization started in 1991, Maruti had realized that the customer could only get a better deal if there was competition and he had a choice of dealers from whom he could buy a car.

Accordingly, in July 1985, it was decided that in states with more than one dealer, each would be allowed to treat the entire state as one territory. This meant that dealers could compete with each other within the state and solicit business throughout the state. Dealers could, however, exercise the right to establish new outlets within the territory only after getting the permission of the marketing department. New workshops could also be opened anywhere in the state after getting the approval of the service department. These restrictions were intended to keep control over the way competition developed and also to maintain minimum standards of showrooms and workshops. Recently, Maruti has decided to remove the restriction about getting permission to open a sales outlet or a workshop, provided the investment in them is made from the internal accruals of the dealership. While taking the decision, for purposes of a territory, Punjab, Haryana, Himachal Pradesh and Chandigarh were treated as one state, as were all the north-eastern states and Union Territories. Customers located in a state or Union Territory would be free to buy a car from any dealer in that area.

This certainly did bring about a significant change in the attitude of dealers, though there was still much distance to cover before they could be said to be really customer focussed. In many ways, dealers continued to behave as if they were doing the customer a favour by selling a car. This attitude carried over in the case of some dealers even into the early 1990s, after the economy had been opened up and it was clear that competition was inevitable. An executive officer in marketing and sales, Mayank Pareek, who was then in field sales, was witness to one such incident. Three persons walked into a showroom to check out cars. When the dealer realized that only one of them was the buyer and the other two were merely accompanying him—taking friends or relatives along while making significant buying decisions is a common Indian habit—he ordered them out and told the buyer to stay. Within the company too, incidents would keep occurring which were not compatible with the concept that the customer comes first. The reason in most cases was the desire of personnel to place what they thought was Maruti's best interests before those of a customer. It took time for them to understand that, in the long term, looking after the customer's interest would also best benefit Maruti.

Apart from spurring competition between dealers, the board felt that Maruti should expedite the setting up of a company-run dealership in Delhi, something unheard of in India but which SMC was keen on. This was a change from the initial years, when the idea of company dealerships was not considered to be appropriate. However, by then many manufacturers in Japan had started to have their own dealerships, and this probably led SMC to also want to start a company dealership in Delhi. While the idea was to establish a model dealership and set standards for other dealers, it was also expected that a dealership would be very profitable.

There was delay in implementing this proposal, largely because of the difficulties in getting a suitable site. Being a public sector undertaking, Maruti had to follow government procedures if it wanted to buy land or rent a showroom. Advertising produced no results, partly because property transactions usually involved a large cash component, and Maruti was not in a position to pay cash. No suitable showroom was available on rent. Maruti learnt that the government-owned India Tourism Development Corporation (ITDC) had a large property in Naraina in west Delhi, where it had been running a workshop to maintain its fleet of cars. The workshop was not running well and was making losses. ITDC was willing to consider renting this property to Maruti and closing its own workshop. A transaction with government companies was very 'safe' for both companies and four years after a decision had been taken, Maruti started its dealership, called Maruti Sales and Service Delhi (MSSD).

MSSD not only sold cars from this site but also had a large workshop. The quality of work there was of a high order, and the workshop soon acquired an enviable reputation. Car owners brought their cars to this workshop when the problems were difficult and complex. The workshop was also used to train young service engineers, by requiring them to actually service and repair cars. Business grew and by 1992, this workshop was handling close to 2,000 cars a month, the maximum in any single workshop in Delhi. The sales were, however, not doing so well. An analysis showed this was largely because Maruti was a government company and could not, therefore, do many of the things which private dealers did to keep customers happy and to compete with others. Nevertheless we persisted with the sales operations.

Soon after the operations at Naraina started, the ITDC gave notice that it would not renew the lease and wanted its property back. Efforts to persuade ITDC to change its mind did not appear to be succeeding and Maruti had to reconcile itself to giving up the Naraina premises and finding an alternative.* A showroom, owned by one Inder Singh, was found at Malcha Marg in the Chanakyapuri area, but it had no space for an attached workshop. The workshop in Naraina continued to function, and talks with the ITDC continued. Not totally unexpectedly, the ITDC, which was not exactly a cash-surplus company, did not insist on our closing the workshop, partly because they realized that while they were getting a good rent from Maruti, they were unlikely to run their own workshop at a profit.

The sales operations shifted to the new premises in Malcha Marg in 1987. This was a very central and prestigious location in an area where most embassies and diplomatic residences were located. However, after running operations here for five years, by when competition in sales had intensified, Maruti realized that none of the objectives of establishing a company-run dealership were being achieved. Sales were low and Maruti was not making profits. The main reasons for this were inherent in being a PSU and could not be resolved. I convinced SMC that this concept could not work in India and it was decided to close this outlet in 1992.

Meanwhile, since Maruti was not sure as to how long we could continue with the workshop in Naraina, a search for an alternative site continued. Some time in 1996, we came across a company called J.J. Impex, which was up for sale. It had operations in the Okhla Industrial Area in south Delhi, had a big factory shed and enough adjoining land for it to be converted into a good workshop. The company had run into losses and

*The property, however, is still with Maruti and the workshop continues to function from there.

the promoters had decided to close their operations. Maruti decided to buy the company and the board approved the purchase in July 1997. A new workshop was established here. The name of the company remained unchanged. Later, Sumitomo Corporation of Japan, which was keen to enter into the automobile business, decided to invest in 47.5 per cent of equity in J.J. Impex. Maruti held another 47.5 per cent and the remaining 5 per cent stake was with Maruti Countrywide, a joint venture of Maruti with GE Capital, established to finance the sale of cars. The workshop in Okhla, known as Maruti Service Masters, started functioning in August 1999.

The workshop at Naraina continued to function and became a part of Maruti Service Masters. It was decided that the service activity should be further expanded and new workshops were opened in Chennai and Delhi. The original concept was that these workshops would generate good profits and the company would be able to pay dividends to the investors. This did not happen. When the investors were asked to put in more money for the new workshops, Maruti Countrywide did not agree, and reduced its equity to 1.74 per cent. The divested stake was picked up equally by Maruti and Sumitomo Corporation, Japan, which, in turn, transferred 10 per cent of its stake to Sumitomo Corporation, India.

In 2007, further expansion of J.J. Impex was proposed. Sumitomo did not want to make any further investments as it had, till then, still not received any dividends. In fact, it wanted to sell its equity to Maruti. At this stage, the entire concept of expanding the workshop business was re-examined. It was concluded that there was no real value in Maruti devoting scarce managerial talent in running workshops, which were not making profits, and which activity dealers were doing quite well. Dealer workshops were, on the other hand, their main profit centres. This experience, like that of selling cars, showed the difficulty of a large company entering into businesses which were not core competency areas, and which never could be given the same attention by the management as making and selling cars. It was decided to drop all plans of expansion and limit Maruti Service Masters to only two workshops, primarily to serve as places where training could be imparted and where new practices and systems for improving service could be developed and tested. Sumitomo decided to retain its existing equity.

~

Besides sales and service networks, a customer needed easy availability of genuine spare parts, at reasonable cost, if he was to get real value out of his vehicle. SMC had studied the Indian spare parts market, with some of their specialists spending time in the spare parts market in Kashmiri Gate in Delhi, and also in other cities. Vehicle manufacturers at that time had not developed any system which guaranteed that customers could buy genuine spare parts. The original equipment vendors usually developed their own sales channels for selling spare parts, and these were sold as genuine parts. The vehicle manufacturer also sold some parts through dealers. The spare parts of most vehicles in the market were sold by a retailer, and most of them had signboards saying that they were selling genuine parts. However, customers had no way of ascertaining whether these spare parts conformed to specifications and were of the same quality as the original equipment (OE) parts.

It was not uncommon for the original part supplier to sell 'seconds' in the spare parts market. In most instances, there were no stringent quality checks by the vehicle manufacturer to ensure that what went into the spare parts market was of the same specifications as the original part. What complicated matters was the fact that there were any number of companies who were making and selling spare parts for all types of vehicles, including cars. They did not usually follow the specifications regarding the materials to be used, and did not have any process to check performance or quality. Some of them sold the parts under their own company name, and at prices which were lower than the prices of 'genuine' parts. Others sold the parts as 'genuine parts' in packaging identical to that of the original part supplier. This market for spurious parts was huge. The original part suppliers as well as the association of part manufacturers regularly complained about the spurious market. However, police actions did not make any significant difference to the extent of the spurious market.

Customers realized that they had no way of ensuring that they were buying genuine parts even if they paid the higher price. Many of them decided that it was better to take a chance and buy the lower priced parts. The vehicle manufacturers seemed to have reconciled themselves to this position, as they did not take any actions to develop a system for providing genuine parts to the users of their vehicles, even though they were aware that use of spurious parts was affecting the performance of cars and also the safety of car owners.

SMC decided that Maruti should follow the Japanese system and make sure that customers could obtain genuine parts. A spares part division was part of the original organizational structure. Experts from Japan were posted in Maruti for developing the appropriate systems and a large warehouse was designed and constructed, according to SMC specifications, as part of the original works in the Gurgaon factory. All vendors were told that they would have to supply spare parts to Maruti at prices which would be higher than the original equipment prices, and they would not be allowed to sell Maruti parts in the market.

The idea was that Maruti would sell the spare parts after subjecting them to the same quality checks as were being applied to the original equipment. The sale to dealers would be made in especially designed packing for Maruti Genuine Parts (MGP). Besides using these parts in their workshops, the dealers could also make retail sales to individuals getting their cars serviced or repaired elsewhere. Each dealer was required to have a spare parts store and Maruti helped in educating his personnel about proper management of spare parts. In addition, Maruti decided to appoint one or two spare parts stockists in each state, who were to only sell Maruti parts obtained from the company, and were allowed to open outlets under their name.

Simultaneously, Maruti carried out a sustained customer education campaign explaining the benefits of using genuine parts and telling customers that they could only be sure that a part was genuine if it was bought either from a Maruti dealer or from an outlet of the spare parts dealer. If any other outlet was selling a part, even in the Maruti packing, that should not be considered to be genuine. All dealers were warned that if they were found to be selling spurious parts, they would lose their dealership.

This arrangement worked well with dealers as the gain from selling spurious parts was not worth the risk of losing the dealership. The business of the spare parts stockists also had large potential, and it was expected that they would not want to risk losing it by selling spurious parts. Maruti officials frequently checked the spare part stocks with dealers, and also tallied the workshop usage with the buying of parts from Maruti. When I, as managing director, visited any dealer I made it a point to check the spare parts warehouse for spurious parts.

A major objective of appointing spare parts stockists was to make them the main source of supply of genuine spare parts for the MASS. With the spread of these service stations, a large number of cars were being serviced by them and it was important that genuine parts be used. It was not realistic to expect that these service stations, run by a small staff, would be able to find the time and would make the effort to get parts from the dealer outlets. The stockists were supposed to develop a system of feeding these service stations.

However, after some years it was found that most of the spare parts stockists were not very effective in selling parts to the MASS. In order to reach these workshops, the stockist needed to have a mobile delivery system and also needed to provide credit. When a spare part was in short supply—and this was not an unusual event for many years after Maruti started—the dealers were given preference by Maruti in being given supplies. At the same time, Maruti also introduced an incentive scheme for its dealers, based on the volume of spare parts sold by them. Many dealers adopted a very aggressive attitude and sold spare parts at a discount so as to be able to earn the incentive. They particularly targeted the MASS. Most of the stockists could not compete with them and gradually went out of business. Sale of spare parts, however, continued to climb.

In 2006, Maruti again started appointing separate dealers for the sale of spare parts. Vehicle dealers were barred from selling parts to the MASS in the state where such a dealer was appointed. However, the spare parts dealer was given targets for sale and was to ensure that all MASS were buying genuine parts. This policy was adopted as it was found that the supply of parts to these service stations was not uniformly good all over India. Further, Maruti did not want vehicle dealers to spend too much time in supplying parts to them, as it was leading to unhealthy competition between dealers. A spare parts dealer, whose main business was to supply MASS, could be quite viable as the number of these stations and their consumption of parts was large. The arrangement is working well, and sale of parts has increased.

Initially, vendors were not happy at not being allowed to sell spare parts. Traditionally, spare parts were supposed to generate a large part of the profits of a vendor. However, most vendors were in no position to refuse what Maruti wanted, especially as the parts were being developed according to drawings and samples given by the company. In addition, Maruti was paying a higher price for the spare parts and the vendor was spared the effort of developing a sales channel for these and the risk of collecting money from their dealers—not an easy task at the best of times. In addition, this arrangement reduced the working capital requirement of vendors, always an important benefit. Some vendors argued that they had contracts with their dealers and could not avoid giving them Maruti parts for sale. In such cases, they were allowed to sell to their dealers, but they also had to give the same parts to Maruti for sale to its own dealers. In many cases, issues relating to pricing arose and it took some time and effort to ensure that parts sold through the Maruti channels, or the vendors' channels, were priced the same.

Maruti was successful in gradually changing the spare parts usage culture. More and more customers opted to use genuine spare parts even though they were higher priced. The efficiency of the spare parts division also kept improving with time. It now compares favourably with that of SMC Japan. Most dealer orders are despatched within twenty-four hours, the first-time fill rate is about 98 per cent and the back order position is very small. One consequence of this is that dealers are able to repair and service customer vehicles without any delays. In the earlier years, when parts were not so easily available, some customers would buy parts from the market, which were not genuine, so that there was no delay in the work being done on their vehicles.

At first, when the vendors were still to build adequate manufacturing capacity, the supply of many parts was not enough to meet the demands of the spare parts market. This led to dealers over-indenting for parts in short supply as the despatches were generally in proportion to the pending back order of each dealer. If a vendor increased production and the supply of parts, the dealers would want to cancel their back orders as they did not really need all the parts they had ordered. Management of back orders and inventory was quite a difficult task. One of the parts usually on back order was clutch linings. The manufacturer, C.K. Daikin, would never increase production adequately. Whenever the managing director of the company met me, he would tell me of his plans to expand and I would tell him that what he did was always going to be too little and too late. I was surprised to find, even in 2009, that clutch linings were still in back order!

The prices of the spare parts had to be revised frequently, partly to reflect the lower cost of production of parts that had been localized. Maruti was aware that customers were very conscious of the cost of maintaining their vehicles, and profits on the sale of parts could not be as high as was the case in the western world or even in Japan. Thus, while the spare parts division was a profit centre, Maruti framed its pricing policy in a manner that would promote the sale of vehicles, by instilling in the mind of customers that Maruti cars had the lowest maintenance costs. I was also aware that if genuine spare parts were high priced, it would be comparatively easy for the grey market to develop and many customers would move to using the lower priced parts. In fact, on a few occasions Maruti had to deliberately lower the price of a particular component to prevent non-genuine parts from entering the market. SMC experts accepted my assessment that such a policy would, in the long term, benefit Maruti more than trying to make large profits from spare parts. The results were very satisfactory. While the spare parts operations do contribute a reasonable amount of profits, the widely held belief is that Maruti parts are the lowest priced and Maruti cars the least expensive to maintain.

~

From the outset, Maruti had tried to function as if it were in a competitive environment. The systems introduced in the area of sales and after-sales service were given by SMC, and they were all from the highly competitive Japanese environment. The intention was to make owning and maintaining a car as pleasurable an experience as possible. The Maruti management wanted the company to make buying, operating and maintaining a car a different and much more satisfying experience for customers. Despite the fact that it had to face very little real competition, Maruti was successful in changing the mindset and practices followed by a large percentage of dealers. Many dealers, who in the years of shortage of cars did not understand the relevance of building good relations with customers and winning their loyalty, later realized the value of the systems and processes that Maruti insisted should be followed. Competition increased dramatically from the mid-1990s, and dealers had to adapt or perish. Some dealers actually closed shop, as they could not adjust to the new requirements.

Competition brought more choices and options before prospective buyers of cars. The buying decision was often influenced by an experience with a dealer. Dealers had to constantly think about how to win customers and increasing the convenience level for buying cars was an obvious factor. Buyers could not be expected to travel long distances to collect their cars or take them for servicing and minor repairs. Thus, many more outlets and workshops were required. Customers would also not want to wait for long periods to buy the vehicle of their choice. If the colour or options they wanted were not available, they would go to some other dealer. Thus, dealers needed to expand operations and stock different models and a larger variety of colours. This increased the need for investments and for working capital.

At the same time, with increasing production by competitors, the waiting time for cars disappeared and dealers could not operate on the money paid by customers in advance. Dealers had to arrange their own working capital. Bank borrowings were much cheaper than getting money from private financiers. However, banks would not lend, even to Maruti dealers, unless they had a reasonably satisfactory balance sheet and systems of sale which were acceptable to banks. At dealer conferences, even in the 1980s, I had emphasized the importance of ensuring that all incomes were entered in the balance sheet, and that personal expenditures were not booked as company expenditures. While this would mean paying more income tax, it would also make balance sheets stronger, thus making it possible to obtain credit limits from banks. This would lower financial costs, as borrowing from private sources, which was a common practice, was much more costly. Bank limits would ensure enough working capital, which would lead to an increase in sales. Thus, paying tax was a way of strengthening the dealership and ensuring long-term success.

In the earlier years, only a few dealers took this advice seriously. Gradually more and more dealers realized the long-term benefits of having healthy balance sheets. Further encouragement was provided when Maruti permitted dealers to open new outlets and workshops, provided they did this by making investments from their internal accruals, as shown in the balance sheets.

Maruti started preparing dealers for a competitive market by setting sales targets for vehicles that were no longer in short supply, and hence had no waiting lists. Dealers were told that they had to learn to sell vehicles for which there were no queues. This was an entirely new concept for an industry used to a ration-like environment. Initially, some dealers found it difficult to adjust and would complain that they had been set targets that were too high. However, Maruti insisted that dealers learn how to sell cars instead of just distributing them.

One major change was to gradually wean away dealers from largely making sales to customers who were brought to them by brokers, and instead employing their own salespersons to find customers. SMC had been pointing out the danger of excessive reliance on brokers, who had no loyalty to any car company, and who could start taking customers to a competitor if they found that would help them earn more. The sales force increased over time, with Maruti providing training to them on how to sell cars. Despite high attrition rates in this sales force, the bulk of sales are now made through dealer-employed salespersons.

Over the years, Maruti expanded its sales organization in the field. Till about 2000, India had been divided into five regions, each headed by a regional manager, for purposes of field supervision and dealer development. There are now four zones headed by general-manager-level officers and sixteen regional managers. In addition, a computerized, real-time dealer management system has also been introduced which enables the marketing and sales division to access all data from each dealership. The idea is that with these tools the performance and capabilities of each dealer would be enhanced and there would be a higher level of customer satisfaction.

Till October 1996, Maruti spent very little money on advertisements and on sales promotions. The reputation of Maruti products had spread by word of mouth, as well as through a fairly large exposure in the media through news stories. The Maruti brand was well known, and competition was virtually zero. However, in that month Maruti decided it would run an advertising campaign for the Maruti 800. It was a first. The iconic car had never needed to be advertised, though advertisements had been issued for all the other cars in the Maruti stable. Till then, Maruti had a very small advertising budget of less than Rs. 10 lakh. The advertisement campaign for the 800 pushed the budget up to Rs. 29.6 crore in 1996-97 and it has grown steadily since then. Overall spend on all sales promotion as well as advertising doubled from Rs. 58.2 crore in 1996-97 to Rs. 101.3 crore in 1997-98. In that year the turnover was over Rs. 8,400 crore and thus the amount spent on sales promotion and brand building was just 1.25 per cent.

Yet, when competition actually drove in, Maruti was handicapped by internal wrangling and was ill-prepared to deal with it. It had nothing but its existing models to offer. No new models, or even upgrades of existing models, could be presented to the customers. Maruti was seen as a public sector company which was losing its way and unable to play a leadership role despite its huge market share. Particularly galling was the launch of the Hyundai Santro, positioned as a tallboy car. It was a novelty for the Indian market. SMC had a tallboy in its stable—the Wagon R, which was the largest selling car in Japan in that category—but Maruti could not introduce it till 2000, when

SMC and the government had made peace. Whether the Santro could have become the success it did in India if Maruti had brought in the Wagon R two years earlier will remain an unanswered question.

Of all the foreign companies who have come to India, Hyundai has been by far the most successful. A major reason for this has been its choice of products. Except for Daewoo and Hyundai, all the other foreign car companies decided to manufacture medium-size cars, with engine capacities between 1.3 litres and 2 litres. Despite the success which Maruti had been enjoying with the 1.3 litre Esteem, the market for this range of cars was really quite small. Although this segment grew fast every year, in terms of percentages, the total volume of cars sold remained small. Percentages are deceptive if the base is not considered. With so many manufacturers competing for this volume, none could attain any viable size. This in turn impacted dealer profitability and the ability to provide after-sales service at reasonable costs. The Matiz, and later the Santro, were small cars, in the Zen category, and were well priced and fuel efficient. Their volume of sales grew quite rapidly.

Fortunately, Maruti recovered ground quickly as soon as peace was made between the government and SMC, launching five new cars within a year after December 1999. That created its own set of problems, though. The cars were launched at a high cost, since the import content was high. The vendors could not manage enough localization of parts for five cars in the time available. With Hyundai and Daewoo being very aggressive on pricing and consumer sentiment being down, Maruti could not pass on all the costs to the customers and for the first time in its history, it had to offer discounts on its cars. That became one of the reasons for the company's first-ever loss in 2000-01, one it quickly recovered from.

This recovery was facilitated by SMC deciding to play a much larger role in the management of Maruti. As full-time Indian directors retired, they were not replaced by other Indians. One reason probably was the likely influence of the government in the process of selection. One vacancy was filled by an Indian director and that was not a happy choice. However, the more important reason was that SMC was very worried about the loss incurred by Maruti in 2000-01 and wanted to have a greater say in the management of the company. Khattar, as the managing director, soon remained as the only Indian full-time director, and his primary role was in managing the external environment. Internal management decisions were largely taken by SMC personnel posted in India, with reference to Japan as required.

One consequence of the loss in 2000-01 was the implementation of a very stringent cost-reduction programme. Besides reducing costs and introducing new models, what helped Maruti were the efforts made in earlier years to make dealers realize the importance of being customer friendly in all their actions, which showed results at this critical juncture. That focus continued, with the company extending its network of dealers and service stations. In 2000, it started an initiative to provide service stations every 25 to 30 km on the express highways and by 2001, twelve national highways had been covered. The intention was to give Maruti owners the confidence to use their cars over long distances. It was perhaps a result of all these efforts that Maruti ranked first in the customer satisfaction ranking for India by global marketing information firm J.D. Power Asia Pacific in 2000, a position it has retained till 2008.

~

With increasing competition, the profitability of dealers had started to decline. They now had to hold larger inventory, and use their own funds for this purpose. More money had to be spent on sales promotion and in winning customers. It was quite common for buyers to negotiate with dealers and seek a price reduction or extra freebies when closing a transaction. Manpower costs also increased significantly as the demand for trained and competent persons went up with new dealerships being commissioned. Thus it became necessary to find ways of helping dealers improve their profit levels.

Khattar commissioned consulting firm A.T. Kearney to make recommendations on how to improve dealer profitability, and also create new sources of income for Maruti. As a result of the study, several new initiatives were started in the areas of financing cars, acting as agents for insurance companies and selling pre-owned cars after renovation.

Financing purchase of cars was not a new activity. Dealers had already been involved in using their good offices to secure finance for customers for Maruti vehicles. It was quite usual for customers to ask the dealer whether he could arrange finance for them. Dealers had been happy to oblige and earned a commission. Citibank was the pioneer in introducing financing of cars in India in the early 1990s and had become the market leader. Maruti found that the availability of car finance was one factor responsible for the rapid growth of its sales. It seemed that if Maruti entered this business it would further help promote sales, as dealers could be actively involved in the activity. However, as a PSU, Maruti realized it could not successfully run its own finance company. Political factors could make the business non-viable. The alternative was to form a joint venture.

Citibank was happy with the idea, as a partnership with Maruti would also strengthen its position. A joint venture company was established in 1995 to offer customers finance for buying cars. The joint venture started to use the premises of dealers to offer finance to customers and business did grow. The dealers earned commission from this activity. A little later, another joint venture for the same purpose was formed with GE Capital. Both these joint ventures did well for a few years, but then competition in this field increased and the joint venture partners did not have the same interest in this activity. Gradually private sector banks, and particularly ICICI Bank, took over the leadership in automobile financing. Dealers, however, continued to offer their services to banks for financing activities and earned good money from this activity.

Maruti now expanded its portfolio to cover leasing and fleet management for companies through N2N and also offered extended warranty on cars. It also decided to get into selling insurance. This required Maruti to become the agent for an insurance company. However, since the law required that an agent could sell insurance policies of only one company, Maruti had to establish a subsidiary company for each insurance company which gave Maruti an agency. Eight such companies exist and operate through the dealers. Customers find that buying insurance policies through dealers is very convenient as the settlement of claims is far easier and virtually hassle-free. As a consequence, almost 92 per cent of new cars sold take insurance through the dealers. Similarly, almost 75 per cent of renewal of policies is also done through dealers. This activity generates profit for both Maruti and the dealers.

Maruti had attempted to sell used cars earlier, in 1991, but the effort had not been successful despite Amitabh Bachchan, the iconic film star, inaugurating this business for Competent Motors in Delhi. Sai Service in Mumbai, run by the family of noted politician Suresh Kalmadi, was perhaps the only dealer who made a real success of the second-hand car business. Maruti now decided to do this in a much more organized manner, and started a subsidiary, True Value. The intention was not only to generate incomes for dealers but to also promote sale of new Maruti cars by offering to buy old cars at reasonable prices and selling a new car in exchange. True Value outlets of dealers were gradually opened, as it was not possible to provide trained manpower all at once to all dealers. Evaluators trained by Maruti helped dealers evaluate old cars. This task was carried out in workshops and owners made aware of the price at which they could sell their cars. The idea was to get them thinking of buying a new car. Certain rules were laid down as to the cars which could be bought, renovated and sold as True Value cars. These carried a six-month warranty and gave the buyer assurance about the product. Other cars, which did not fit the definition of what could be a True Value car, were also bought by dealers and sold after doing some renovation, but they were not True Value cars and did not have a Maruti warranty. This used-car business helped dealers make better use of their workshop capacities, increased consumption of spare parts, and helped dealers increase profits. Presently about 40,000 new cars are sold every year under the exchange scheme. At the same time those wanting to sell or buy a used car find that they have a means to do so without running the risk associated with dealing with brokers.

Another activity started by Maruti to increase dealer incomes was to offer accessories for sale by dealers under the brand Maruti Genuine Accessories. This business has also grown and accessory sales are in excess of Rs. 100 crore.

~

Along with all this, a balanced scorecard system was introduced to determine dealer performance. Dealers were evaluated on various parameters, which had different weightages. Depending on the total score, dealers were each year classified as platinum, gold, silver and bronze and suitably rewarded to motivate them. The weaknesses of dealers were highlighted to them and Maruti executives helped in trying to make improvements. Some dealers who failed to measure up to the requirements of the new environment quietly folded up their operations.

Maruti became a listed company in 2003 and SMC acquired management control by virtue of getting 54 per cent equity. The government was committed to a total exit from Maruti by 2007. The operations of Maruti became more closely integrated with those of SMC and it was decided that at least one new model would be launched every year. In May 2005, the Swift was launched and it went on to become a huge success. It was a sporty-looking car and appealed to the younger generation. Other launches followed—the Wagon R that runs on liquefied petroleum gas (LPG), the Zen Estilo, the DZire, and the SX4. The market share of the company remained above 54 per cent despite the increase in the number of competitors.

Maruti became Maruti Suzuki India Limited when the government sold its last shares in the company. SMC decided that small cars for the Indian as well as the global markets should be designed and manufactured in India. The A Star, launched in December 2008, is SMC's small car for the world markets. At the same time Maruti Suzuki is rapidly building research and design capabilities so that in a few years small cars can be designed and engineered in India. With that, and vendors developing engineering capabilities, the modernization of the Indian automobile industry would be complete.

9

THE PEOPLE CHALLENGE

'We may be owned by the government, but we have no intention of running this as a government company.'

Behind this startling statement that opened one of the early circulars Krishnamurthy issued to Maruti's staff was the acknowledgement that the objectives of the company could not be achieved within the existing hidebound public sector culture and work ethic. This was despite the fact that he was recognized as one of the most successful managers in the public sector, having turned around BHEL in the 1970s, making it into a highly profitable company. But it was this very experience that made him aware that BHEL had many weaknesses and could not be said to have attained excellence, if measured against international standards.

In the 1980s, even the Indian private sector, sheltered from competition, was lagging far behind international standards of performance. Over the years, a culture had developed in which the shop-floor workers—who form the bulk of the employees in the manufacturing industry—did not identify their careers and prosperity with the company and its performance. Trade unions had their own agenda and objectives, mostly political, and in conflict with the growth of productivity, better quality and competitiveness of the company. The management's commitment to placing the interests of the company above their personal interests also lacked credibility, leading to distrust and strongly adversarial relations between management and workers. In the absence of visible management commitment to the company, a large section of the supervisors, executives and managers also did not have complete commitment to the company.

The result was that the energies of different segments of employees did not converge in propelling the company forward. Instead, they often cancelled each other out. What India was experiencing in the 1980s was similar to what Japan had faced in the early 1950s. In Japan, however, the government and industry realized the need to work together to usher in a new, highly productive, work culture. In India, the socialist governments did not trust the private sector, decried the profit motive and believed that the public sector and a controlled private sector would usher in industrialization.

Suzuki understood this situation. He had first-hand experience of a similar work culture, in Pakistan, where SMC was making cars in partnership with the government. Production would come to a halt several times a day when the workers broke for prayers. There was little concern for punctuality and discipline. Productivity and quality levels were below his expectations. He thought that things might not be very different in India, though he hoped that given the multi-cultural society in India, it might be possible to introduce a better work culture. So when Krishnamurthy and I had our first detailed meeting with him at Hamamatsu in 1982, and conveyed to him that Maruti should attain the quality and productivity levels of SMC, he agreed to help the company achieve this objective, provided that his advice was followed on all matters. We promised to do so.

The Maruti top management was eager to understand why the Japanese industry had become so highly competitive, despite the fact that most of the raw materials, including energy, had to be imported. At that time, the popular belief in India was that Japan was subsidizing its exports. Nobody believed that costs of production could actually be much lower than in India, or elsewhere. However, as the volume of Japanese exports grew, it became obvious that subsidies on that scale were not feasible.

A visit to Japanese factories highlighted the enormous difference in productivity levels with India. The Japanese had brought about a complete transformation in the relations between a company and its employees, with the workers being as committed to the company's welfare as the management. As a result, every employee was fully involved in enhancing quality and productivity, reducing costs and finding ways to make improvements in all activities. We realized that in fact the costs of production in Japan were very much lower than what all of us believed was possible. While all management books emphasized the importance of human resources in achieving excellence, and most managements paid lip service to this concept, the Japanese had found a way to actually make it happen. We realized that if Maruti were to attain a performance level different from PSUs and even private industry, we would have to follow the Japanese route to excellence. We were also aware that we could set new norms of performance and systems of functioning, since Maruti was starting from scratch and was, therefore, free from the baggage of existing practices.

~

Suzuki made it plain from his very first visit to India that he meant business. The project was discussed in detail, including the manpower needed, particularly in the production areas. Maruti had provided a leave reserve of 15 per cent of the manpower required for different departments. This was the usual practice in the government and PSUs. Private industry also kept a leave reserve. The various kinds of leave entitlements in India added up to much more than 15 per cent, and the leave reserve was to fill the vacancies of those who went on leave. Suzuki did not accept this system, and pointed out that the level of absenteeism in Japan was only about 3 per cent. Employees took their vacations during block closures of the company for preventive maintenance or during the 'golden week' (an eight- to ten-day shutdown across most industries and businesses from the end of April to around 5 May, which coincides with a number of Japanese national holidays). He wanted Maruti to bring down absenteeism to 5 per cent or less. Two preventive maintenance closures would also take place in Maruti and employees could go on holiday then. The need for change, he explained, was not just the cost of employing the extra manpower. The absence of a regular worker would affect both quality and productivity, as the substitute would never be able to achieve the same standards, lacking the training or the experience of the person he was replacing. The leave reserve employees would be rotating, for short periods, between a variety of jobs and so could not be expected to learn to do any job as well as a worker who was doing that job on a regular basis.

Suzuki also proposed much higher norms of machine utilization than what was generally achieved in India. For him, an eight-hour shift meant that the machine had to operate productively for that period of time. He did not accept the practice prevailing in India under which a worker was deemed to have arrived on time for his shift if he entered the factory gate at the time the shift was to begin, or that work should end so that the worker could be at the factory gate when the shift ended. He wanted the worker to be at his workstation, ready to work, when the shift started and leave only when the shift ended. He also wanted the duration of the lunch break—which was not included in the eight hours—to be controlled so that no working time was lost due to workers returning late from lunch. There would be two seven-and-a-half-minute tea breaks during a shift, something unheard of in Indian manufacturing at that time. All factories had ten- to fifteen-minute breaks and even these were often prolonged. Thus, effective working hours (during which the lines and machines should be operating) should, according to Suzuki, be seven hours and forty-five minutes. Managers had to ensure that all components, tooling, etc were available so that production actually took place during the shift duration, and work did not stop due to lack of some input. It was also expected that the two preventive maintenance shutdowns would lead to no breakdowns during the working period. Not surprisingly, the requirements of both men and machines, and consequent investment, came down significantly when production capacity was calculated on this basis.

The achievement of these standards of performance required discipline and a strong sense of punctuality. When Suzuki left India after this visit, he told us that he would send us a gift on his return to Japan. The gift duly arrived. It consisted of several large packages. When they were opened they turned out to be time clocks, which had to be punched by everyone when entering or leaving the shop floor or offices. Even directors had to punch the clock, which would be installed as close to their place of work as possible and not at the factory gate.

Special care had to be taken to ensure that the time clocks were kept in good order and were not tampered with. In many factories where time clocks had been used, employees had found ways of damaging them so that they did not have to clock in. It was also noticed that at times one employee would carry another person's identity card and punch in for him also. It took a combination of policing the time clocks and educating the workers to inculcate the habit of punctuality.

Workers were clearly told what was expected of them at the time they were recruited. They had to reach the factory ten to fifteen minutes before their shift started, change into their uniform, do the mandatory physical exercises—again a first for Indian industry—and be at their respective workstations when the conveyor line started. In offices, too, the administrative and managerial staff had to clock in before the shift started, clean their workplace and make sure that they could start work at 9 a.m. Enforcing this was helped by the fact that Maruti had arranged for buses to pick up employees and bring them to the factory. The timings of the buses that plied on different routes were such that employees reached the factory at least fifteen minutes before the shift started. If an employee was late in reaching his pick-up point, he had to find his own means of reaching the factory and that cost money. Thus there was a built-in incentive to be punctual.

Even though Maruti was starting on a fresh slate, ushering in this work culture posed its own set of problems. Maruti had, as a policy, restricted recruitment from other PSUs, where there was not much emphasis on punctuality, high attendance levels and discipline. However, it could not have a blanket ban and, hence, the initial recruits included persons from other PSUs. They found it difficult to understand and appreciate the work culture Maruti was trying to foster. But it was equally difficult dealing with the other workers, most of whom hailed from villages and agricultural backgrounds and had no work experience, being fresh pass-outs from Industrial Training Institutes (ITIs). The pattern of agricultural work is seasonal and not uniform throughout the year. The concept of starting work at the same time every day, and working for exactly eight hours, was alien to persons from such a background. They were also used to celebrating all festivals, as most of them fell in the lean season for agricultural operations. At harvest time, it was expected that all able-bodied persons would work in the fields. Thus workers in most Indian factories had the habit of going home for festivals and at harvest time. As a result, the attendance level in companies sometime falls to as low as 75 per cent. Achieving an overall attendance of 95 per cent appeared impossible in this scenario. Maruti had to spend much time and effort in educating the workers about why the company was insisting on high attendance, discipline and punctuality, and how, over time, they would benefit if they followed our directions. This process of education was backed by a whole bunch of policies and incentives which rewarded high attendance and punctuality.

For example, unutilized casual leaves could be encashed at the end of the year, while medical leave and earned leave could be accumulated up to 240 days and encashed at the time of retirement. No other PSU had such a policy and absenteeism spiked at the end of the year as employees availed their unutilized casual leave. In addition, Maruti also offered an attendance bonus. Attendance was calculated both for the month and for the year and there were graded rewards for up to 100 per cent attendance, with 95 per cent being the threshold. Those who had high attendance over a three-year period were publicly recognized and awarded certificates at the flag-hoisting ceremony on Independence Day. The attendance record of employees also determined promotions as well as selection for training in Japan. The senior management were expected to set an example in this matter. Thus I, during my sixteen years with Maruti, had an average attendance of nearly 98 per cent.

~

Interaction with the Japanese brought out the fact that workers in Japan had developed full confidence and trust in their managers. They believed that their managers were fully committed to the success of the company. The managers placed the company interests before their own and did not use any asset of the company for their personal benefit, quite unlike the practice in many family-owned companies in India. At the same time, they followed all the rules, polices and practices which were prescribed for the workers, again a departure from most Indian companies where managers had a different set of rules. Finally the workers believed that management was fair and transparent, even though it expected high standards of performance from the employees. They believed that managers would look after their legitimate interests in a reasonable manner.

Krishnamurthy and I realized that a similar situation had to be created in Maruti if the company was to emulate the Japanese levels of quality and productivity. Merely exhorting workers to behave in a certain manner would not be adequate—it had to be backed by the actions and behaviour of the managers, especially the senior management. In most Indian companies, workers believe that the company is run for the benefit of the promoter, that they are paid as little as the management can get away with, and that the promoter has little genuine concern about their welfare. There is not only a class distinction between the workers and the promoters and managers, both also see each other as adversaries.

How could we change this and create a team spirit? Being a PSU, Maruti had no promoters in the private sector sense of the term and Krishnamurthy and I had to play this role. We realized that what we did would establish the culture of the company. As a first step we decided to treat workers and managers in the same manner in as many areas as possible. We also decided that blue-collar workers should be respected for the contribution which they would make in a manufacturing company, and they should not feel that white-collar workers had any advantage over them. We decided to follow the Japanese in having a company uniform, which had a clear role in building teams and downplaying individual differences. Our uniform consisted of the distinctive light grey trouser and blue shirt embossed with the Maruti logo. Everyone from the managing director downwards had to wear the uniform. The uniform was made of the same material, had the same design and the same manufacturer for all employees. Some other companies also prescribed uniforms, but the insistence on wearing them was not very strict, except in the case of the shop-floor workers. Even here, exceptions were allowed. In many cases, the material and design of the uniform was different for workers and managers. The Maruti management realized that the whole purpose of having a uniform would be lost if these mistakes were repeated.

Initially, some of the senior managers, who had come from the government or other PSUs, said that they would be embarrassed going for meetings outside the office or attending functions wearing the uniform. The fact that Krishnamurthy and I used to do so did not cut much ice with them. Krishnamurthy decided to provide them with a changing room, where they could wear suits and then go out. Once back in the factory, or office, they had to change back to the uniform. After some time, the task of changing clothes proved irksome and managers started going out in the uniform. They realized that wearing the uniform did not lower their status at all. As Maruti's success and reputation increased, workers took pride in wearing the uniform, as they wanted to be recognized as Maruti employees. One big step was taken in creating worker identification with the company.

Another important step was a common canteen for all employees, regardless of rank. The food would be the same for all, as would be the plates and cutlery. Everyone would need to stand in a queue for self-service and then sit at a table designed for six persons. There were no separate tables or seating area for managers. The workers were thrilled with this arrangement, not only because it removed the distinction between them and managers, but also because they realized that the quality of food would remain consistently good. The junior engineers and managers were also quite happy to accept this arrangement. However, some of the senior managers were not willing to accept this radical innovation. They found a room, got an air-conditioner installed, brought lunch from home and started eating there. Krishnamurthy soon got to know about it. We decided that strong action was needed. The room was locked and the officers were told that they could either eat in the canteen or do without lunch. They soon started going to the canteen.

There was no real problem in implementing another departure

from general practice—providing common toilets. Most Indian offices had separate toilets for officers and the clerical staff. In factories, there were separate toilets for workers and managers. One consequence of having common toilets was that all the toilets were kept clean, unlike elsewhere where the toilets for workers and clerical staff are usually not well maintained and tend to smell badly.

The arrangement for seating in the office area was also designed to foster this sense of team spirit and oneness. In Japan everyone, including directors, sat in open offices. Suzuki explained that open offices were essential to establish better and easier communication between all the employees. Many bad decisions were taken because of lack of complete information with decision makers. The open office culture made sharing of information and consulting others much easier. There were separate rooms for meetings, confidential discussions and visitors.

We realized that open offices also helped in doing away with the hierarchical culture in Indian workplaces which created distinctions between different employees in an organization. Thus, the clerical staff sat in crowded offices, with no arrangements for cooling in summer or heating in winter. Junior officers shared a room and were provided with coolers and heaters. As their seniority and rank increased, they moved to bigger rooms, with better facilities. Clearly, this concept was not consistent with the objective of building teamwork and making employees believe that they were all equally important. We believed that all the extra facilities which came with higher positions in the hierarchy were really not required for doing one's work. Everyone needed to have a clean and comfortable environment in which to work. The quality and quantity of output was not related to the size of the room, or the dimensions of the table or the number of air-conditioners in the room. Thus

Maruti decided to follow Suzuki's advice and have open offices. It not only reduced cost and space requirements but also led to much better discipline and transparency in working. While the officers could see what the clerical staff was doing, the officers themselves could not use office time to do private work, or call colleagues over for a gossip session over coffee. Since all visitors were met in the meeting rooms, it also meant much less disturbance.

However, initially when the furniture was designed and placed in the open offices, we made a mistake. Four tables were put together, to seat four persons, but each table was separated from the other by chest high partitions. This meant that a person was not visible to even the person sitting next to him. This arrangement was made as a kind of compromise between having separate rooms or cubicles and an open office. When Suzuki came on his next visit, he rejected this arrangement outright. There were to be no partitions at all. All the partitions were torn down, despite lakhs of rupees having been spent on them.

The redesigned office areas in the factory comprised seemingly endless halls with lines of T-shaped tables at right angles to the corridor. The halls were divided into sections by several glass-panelled rooms—reserved strictly for meetings. The head of a section sat at the head of each table, facing the corridor and with his back to the window, while those who reported to him sat on both sides of the T. This made it easier for subordinates to discuss matters with their seniors, unlike in offices where the managers sat in a room. The change was particularly striking for S. Maitra, who had joined Maruti from Tata Motors, and where it was common to wait for two days to speak to his senior manager. At Maruti, all he had to do was walk up to the head of the table and discuss whatever issue he wanted to.

This obsession with transparency and efficiency carried over to the layout of racks in the stores as well. The normal practice was for racks to be placed along the length of a room, with one rack behind the other. This meant that a person entering the storeroom could not see the racks at the rear, or what was going on behind even the first rack. Suzuki insisted that all racks be turned 90 degrees so that when one entered the store it should be possible to see all the way to the back of the store. By walking down the length of the store, it would be possible to see what was going on in the entire store and nothing would be hidden. It was a very simple, but effective, control system which cost nothing to implement.

Most of the persons recruited by Maruti gradually adjusted to these conditions of work. Some did not and they left the company. Krishnamurthy and I felt that this was a small price to pay for bringing in a work culture which would enable Maruti to achieve high standards of quality and productivity.

~

Though blue-collar workers have the greatest role to play in improving productivity and quality, because they are the ones who are actually involved in running the machines and working on the lines, yet, in most companies, white-collar workers have better conditions of work. We decided that this would not be replicated in Maruti. Working hours were, therefore, kept at forty-eight per week in both the factory and offices. The number of holidays was the same for everyone. Air-cooling was provided in the factory, not only for the comfort of the workers but also as a means of reducing dust levels. All employees were entitled to similar medical facilities, with a worker also being eligible to get a heart bypass operation done in the Escorts Heart Institute, a premier hospital which would normally have been within the entitlement of senior managers.

Krishnamurthy was very clear that top management, by its actions, should convey to workers that they were considered to be very important for the success of the company. This message was frequently given to union members. If increments or promotions were to be announced, this was first done for the workers and later for the managers. I continued this approach after Krishnamurthy moved to the Steel Authority of India as its chairman in April 1985. At the same time, this policy was linked to bringing in a strong work discipline. There was no compromise on matters like punctuality, wearing uniforms, working according to the prescribed systems and following instructions. The workers soon realized that while the management would be fair and transparent, and take care of their genuine needs, it would not allow wrong things to be done.

~

It was realized that continuous training of workers was necessary if their attitude towards work, the company and its management was to be changed. This is what the Japanese had done and their advice to Maruti was that communication with workers and explaining the rationale behind policies and actions was of critical importance. The management should not be disheartened if results were not visible in the short term, and instead of taking punitive action if some workers did wrong, it should continue educating them. Krishnamurthy decided that this could best be done through a union which had a positive approach.

The trade union movement in India had developed believing that the interests of the working class and that of the capitalist owners of companies were in conflict. As such, managements could be expected to give only the minimum possible benefits to labour, and it was necessary to fight for every facility. Union activists believed it was not the role of the union, or workers, to get involved in trying to improve productivity or quality. If workers were required to produce more, they should be paid extra for this. The union's job was to fight for the workers and to protect their jobs at all costs. Large companies usually had multiple, politically affiliated unions whose office-bearers were mostly outsiders. Strikes were quite common, and at times these could turn violent.

Immediately after the war, trade unions in Japan functioned in the same way. However, industrial and governmental leaders there quickly saw the fallacy and futility of such a confrontational system and understood that workers could only prosper and have job security if their company was generating profits and growing. At the same time promoters and managers had to ensure that they were fair to workers and gave them an equitable share of the benefits of higher growth, productivity and profits. The Japanese worked to bring this about and succeeded. We understood the logic of their system and so wanted to completely reverse the traditional culture and bring about a mutually beneficial relationship between workers, the union and the management.

As a first step, Krishnamurthy promoted a trade union at Maruti, before political parties and outsiders could establish one. K.K. Datta, who was a union leader at BHEL, was given employment in Maruti, and became general secretary of the Maruti Udyog Employees Union (MUEU), which was affiliated to the Indian National Trade Union Congress (INTUC), the trade union wing of the Congress party. Workers were encouraged to become members of this union and they were told that the management would encourage the union to effectively interact with it so as to best protect the interests of workers. But first the credibility of the union had to be established, and this was done by consulting the union and involving it in framing policies and taking decisions in matters affecting the workers. Thus, the policy regarding uniforms, and its colour and design, was settled in consultation with the union. The union was involved in the functioning of the canteen, the arrangements for providing bus transport for employees, medical treatment issues, and fixing the shift hours. It was also the agency which discussed any problem of workers and was involved in finding solutions which were fair to them and to the company.

The fact that Datta knew Krishnamurthy from before and had been brought to Maruti by him, helped increase the belief that he could get workers a fair deal. The importance of the union was highlighted by ensuring that the president and general secretary of the union were seated on the dais at every Maruti function. They would, along with the top management of Maruti, receive all VVIP guests and garland them. Very soon most employees became members of the MUEU.

The various policies introduced to make workers feel that they were part of the company and would be treated on par with managers greatly helped in creating the belief that Maruti was different from other companies. However, this was obviously not going to be enough if the right values were to be created and sustained. This could be only done through continuous education and good communication. Unfortunately, managements in India spend very little time and resources on this.

I decided to take on this task. Monthly meetings were held with the union, which I chaired, even when I was the managing director, and most directors were also requested to participate in these. This raised the status of the meeting, and conveyed that the management was serious in having talks with the workers. Before the meeting, a note was circulated to the union executives giving information on important developments in the company, and the main tasks and problems ahead. Progress against targets was reported. At the time when the business plan for the next year was to be planned, goals and targets were suggested. At the meeting, the first hour or so was spent in discussing the contents of the note. Not only were the union executives thus kept fully aware of what was happening in the company, but they also felt that they were contributing to its progress. Gradually these union executives, who were all regular workers, became much more aware of various aspects of running a company. This gave them a better understanding of the operations of the company and the considerations involved in decision making, and made them more responsible when raising demands. After the union meetings each executive was required to interact with his constituency and share the information and ideas gathered with the workers. The management believed that this would be the most effective way of reaching all the workers, and this could not be done successfully by the management trying to interact directly with them.

After the general discussions at the union meetings, the MUEU raised issues regarding the workers and suggested how working conditions could be improved. Matters which were regulated by government orders or regulations were outside the scope of the agenda. We did find that if the reasons why a particular suggestion could not be accepted or needed to be modified were explained properly, the union representatives would understand.

Among the matters discussed were the pros and cons of

having multiple, politically affiliated unions, with outside office-bearers. Instances were given of how workers had suffered due to factories being closed, or even police firing taking place, as a result of inter-union rivalry and political interventions. The workers were shrewd enough to understand that outsiders would not work for the Maruti union unless they stood to benefit in some way. This could only be political gain or some financial advantage. Securing these objectives could sometimes be in conflict with the real long-term interests of workers. As a result of these discussions, a large part of the workforce accepted the need for a single union, with none of the office-bearers being from outside Maruti.

Not long after, in 1987, the union also decided to end its affiliation with INTUC. The workers and the union realized that if it remained affiliated to INTUC, and another political party came to power in Haryana, there would be enormous pressure for a second union affiliated to that political party to be formed and this would open the doors for multiple unions with all the dangers inherent in such a situation. Since a Congress government was in power at the Centre, the INTUC complained to the industry minister, N.D. Tiwari. I had to explain to him, and later to the INTUC president, why a non-affiliated union would be better for the long-term success of Maruti. Fortunately, both these gentlemen appreciated my reasoning and did not pursue this matter any further. Later, when Om Prakash Chautala, then of the Janata Dal, became the chief minister of Haryana, he did get a union registered, and it was supported by his party. This was easy, as only seven workers were required to form a union. There was considerable pressure on me to recognize this union, and attempts were made to coerce workers to join and support it. However, the workers were very clear as to what was in their interest and the new union got minimal support. I took the view that the new union could not be recognized unless it had significant membership support. I argued with Chautala that trying to politicize the workers of Maruti would hurt the company, which was already a showpiece of Haryana, and would affect investments to the state. We both agreed that the results of the elections that were due would determine whether the new union had support or not. The workers voted heavily in favour of their existing union. Chautala was gracious and accepted the verdict. His party union was dissolved.

I also decided that it would be useful to occasionally communicate directly with all the employees. Thus, when a very important issue came up, and it was necessary that everyone be aware of all aspects of that matter and its relevance to the company, I would write to the employees on the subject. This would inevitably lead to a debate among them, creating a sense of participation.

The impact of this effort at education and better communication with all employees, when coupled with other actions and decisions to create trust in workers, paid off—Maruti becoming a highly productive and low-cost manufacturer. It would be hard to find any manufacturer in India who has higher labour productivity or greater participation of workers in making improvements. This happened because a large number of workers came to believe that their future, in terms of job security and quality of life, was linked to that of Maruti.

The union-management relations did not always run very smoothly. By 1986, Datta had become unpopular. This was partly due to his behaviour, which alienated many workers, and partly because many workers felt that he was too close to the management. In 1988, Mathew Abraham was elected president of the union for one year. While he agreed that workers should cooperate in increasing productivity and improving quality, he wanted to establish his leadership by trying to secure additional benefits for the workers. In this effort, I believe, he often became unreasonable.

The first major issue he picked was housing for workers. The guidelines issued by the government for public sector undertakings stipulated that they should build a housing colony for a part of the workforce. The Maruti management was aware of this. However, during the preparation of the project report, SMC flatly refused to provide funds for housing. This was partly to keep down project costs and the amount which SMC would have to invest. In addition, SMC wanted the management to concentrate on learning how to make good cars and not how to manage a township. Krishnamurthy was also aware that often issues relating to the management of a township trigger industrial relations problems. So he was happy to accept the view of SMC. Hence, the cost of housing was not included in the project, and it was decided to explore other avenues for providing housing. To this end, in November 1984, the board even considered issuing preference shares to finance a housing project. However, even that would have thrown the economics of the project out of gear.

The union, led by Mathew, however, was adamant on Maruti adhering to public sector guidelines and building a housing colony. Several discussions were held with the union to find a viable alternative. For example, public sector personnel rules also stipulated that employees could be given house building loans. Maruti suggested that such loans would be arranged from a bank, and the interest on these loans could be subsidized. The workers could form a cooperative housing society and build the houses inside the factory premises, provided the houses were used only by employees and ex-employees. The housing colony would have to be managed by the society. In June 1986, the board gave in-principle approval to this idea. However, the union would not agree, and wanted Maruti to build a housing colony, manage it and rent out flats to workers. The issue dragged on for two years.

In 1988 Abraham upped the ante on the issue of housing and the union included a production incentive in its demands. It initiated a tool-down strike, starting with one hour on the first day and increasing progressively by an hour on each subsequent day. This continued for a few days, with the tool down reaching four hours a shift. At this stage, the management sent notices to all workers, saying the tool down was illegal, as no proper notice of a strike had been given, and asking them to show cause why eight times the salary for the period work was not done should not be deducted from their wages. In due course, I went ahead and deducted this amount from all those who had participated in the tool down. For many years the union pleaded for restoration of the deduction. Ultimately only half of the deduction was restored. It was meant to be a message that while the management would be very worker friendly, illegal actions would not be tolerated.

Simultaneously with the notice, I also started talking directly to the workers and explained that under the scheme being followed in PSUs, when a worker retired, he had to vacate the rented house and he had nowhere to live. I showed calculations which established that the amount of rent paid during the service of a worker was several times the cost of the house he was living in. On the other hand, the alternative of a housing cooperative would result in the workers owning their houses and having a permanent asset, where they could live after retirement. The workers wanted to know how they would pay the instalments of the housing loan. I explained that the instalments would be so fixed that they could be paid from the house rent allowance. This allowance would rise as salary levels increased, and workers would not face any hardship. Maruti would get involved in finding a good contractor for building the colony, and provide the engineering supervision free of cost, so that the cost of construction was as low as possible. Maruti would also help in getting land allotted by the Haryana government, since by that time it was not possible for land to be given inside the factory.

In reality, this scheme was far superior to the practice being followed in public sector undertakings and the workers were smart enough to realize this. A majority of them agreed to try out the scheme. The tool-down stir had in any case been given up after the notice of wage deduction and our talking to the workers. Mathew found that he was in a minority on this issue of a housing colony.

I was able to persuade the Haryana government to allot land at the government price, at Chakkarpur village, not far from the factory site. Raj Chopra, a Maruti dealer who also owned a construction company, agreed to build the housing colony without charging any profit. Loans were arranged from public sector banks and Maruti agreed to pay the instalments directly to them from the salaries of the loan takers. Maruti's civil engineering department undertook the supervision of the work. It was decided that double-storeyed houses would be constructed, though the workers wanted independent plots. I explained that this would drastically reduce the number of flats and many workers would have to go without a flat. Nearly 1,000 one-bedroom and two-bedroom houses—the cost ranging between Rs. 125,000 and Rs. 175,000—could be built on the land.

The idea of workers owning and managing their own housing colony was quite novel. The Prime Minister, the late

Chandrashekhar, thought this development was important and agreed to come to Chakkarpur to inaugurate the colony. The scheme was a huge success, with twenty-five-year-olds finding that they owned flats. Soon after the colony was built, the development of the Gurgaon area started in real earnest and property prices started shooting up. These flats, being quite centrally located, appreciated sharply in value. Some of the workers started renting out the flats and the rentals were far more than the instalment of the loan.

Even as the Chakkarpur colony was being built, those who had stayed away from joining the scheme saw its benefits and wanted Maruti to develop another colony. By then, the Haryana government had no more land to allot to Maruti, and suggested that land should be bought by negotiation. Accordingly, about 107 acres of land was purchased at Bhondsi village in 1989, and a second cooperative group housing society formed in 1991. Houses in the new colony were allotted and occupied in 1994. However, purchasing this land, even on behalf of the workers' cooperative, showed how difficult it was to operate as a public sector undertaking.

The party in power in Haryana changed. The district magistrate of Gurgaon, who had helped Maruti in buying the land, was apparently not in the good books of the new government, and was charged with corruption and suspended, only to be found innocent many years later. One of the allegations related to the purchase of the Bhondsi land. Some other district-level officers were also included in this charge. Attempts were made by the Haryana vigilance to also start inquiries against me and other Maruti officers. This was perhaps necessary as otherwise the case against the Haryana officers would not stand. The CBI was also given a complaint. The workers, who were paying for the land, had no complaint, and only wanted the houses to be built fast. When the full facts of how the transaction was made, including the basis of the pricing, were made known to the authorities, the inquiries against Maruti personnel were dropped. The houses were built, but there was no good school in the area. We then formed a Maruti Employees Educational Trust in 1994 and were able to persuade Delhi Public Schools Society, which ran some of the best schools in Delhi, to enter into an agreement with the Trust in 1995 and start a branch in Bhondsi. Maruti provided financial support to the trust, on the condition that children of Maruti workers would get priority in admission to the school. Workers, who always struggled to get admission for their children in a decent school, could now educate them in one of the best schools in the region.

The Chakkarpur and Bhondsi projects solved the issue of Maruti having to provide a housing colony. But a much larger benefit, of permanent value, came in the form of the management winning the trust and confidence of the workers.

~

The need for establishing good communication, and changing traditional ways of thinking, could not stop only at the level of workers. It was also equally important and necessary that supervisors and junior as well as senior management should all share a common vision of how the company should be managed and a new work ethos developed. Unless all these levels of employees were fully involved in the process, it could never succeed. The key was a good system of communication. One initiative taken was to establish a Sahyog Samiti, which consisted of representatives from all levels of employees, coming from all the work areas. This samiti met at regular intervals, and like the union meetings, discussed both general issues of policy as well as specific problems. Individual grievances were outside the scope of the meeting. I would preside over these meetings and frequently reiterate the basic concept of the Japanese system of harnessing human potential to overcome a multitude of handicaps. The members of the samiti were expected to convey the gist of the discussions to their colleagues after the meeting.

A few times in the year, I would also meet with a group of supervisors and listen to them. They would have their own set of grievances. I realized that supervisors often had a problem of identity—they were not workers and were rarely treated as part of the management. The graduate engineers were always treated as being in a different class. It was necessary to address this. These meetings with them, where issues relating to company policy were also discussed, helped them feel more involved with the management. We also had to find ways in which they could upgrade their technical qualifications and have prospects of moving into management levels.

Meetings were also held with the department managers. In the initial years, one concern was that managers tended to work in compartments and were very reluctant to share information with their colleagues, or consult even those departments that would be later involved with implementing a decision taken by them. Managers resented a manager from another department sending for and talking to one of their subordinates. They wanted all such requests for a meeting to be routed through them. Information would only be given to another department if a written request was sent. Such practices often led to poor and delayed implementation of decisions, as those who were not involved in the process of decision making created hurdles by raising objections. They did not feel any ownership for the decision and resented not having been consulted. The Japanese advised us to break down these barriers and create more extensive and open communication between, and even within, departments. The open office system was one way of achieving this. This subject would often figure in the meeting of department managers. Over the years, slow but substantial progress was made.

At these meetings of department managers, they were also encouraged to take decisions and shoulder more responsibility and assured that bona fide mistakes would not lead to adverse consequences. There were complaints from them that powers were not adequately delegated and this led to delays and a feeling of lack of empowerment. However, I sensed that there was a general reluctance to exercise the powers that had been delegated, and most managers—coming from a public sector background—did not want to be in a situation where they would be clearly responsible for a decision. Our exhortations to them to be fearless were probably not really believed. Even after Maruti ceased to be a public sector undertaking in 1992, managers still did not feel confident enough to take responsibility for decisions. I often had to return files saying that the proposal sent to me for approval was within the powers of the concerned officer. This shakiness of managers pointed to a larger human resource development issue which needed to be addressed.

Training managers to become capable of shouldering higher responsibilities is obviously one of the main tasks of any management. A second and third line of succession should be available for all key jobs. However, only a few companies are able to achieve good results in this area. Public sector undertakings are not amongst them. I would discuss this shortcoming with senior managers from SMC to understand how companies in Japan were able to accomplish this task.

In Japan, after an executive had worked for a few years in a job, had acquired good knowledge of that area and it appeared that he had the potential for higher general management, he was rotated through different departments. This gave him a broader understanding of the working of the company and the ability to take decisions which reflected more than the interests of one department. On the other hand, public sector executives rarely ever changed the department in which they worked, and they reached senior positions with knowledge of only one area of the company. For example, a production engineer would stay in production all his life and would not work in other departments, including marketing or supply chain. As a consequence, when he was promoted as a general manager, and later to the board, he would work more as a specialist than a person who had a complete view of the business and could contribute to effective management of the company, including formulation of strategy and long-term plans. In most cases, such a person would also have limited experience of human resource development, as this is a specialized area, and managers from other disciplines never get to work in the human resource development division, since they believe it only deals with recruitment, transfers and postings, pay scales and increments, keeping leave accounts, conducting disciplinary proceedings and so on. Since one of the important requirements of senior management is motivating employees and getting the best out of them on a sustained basis, lack of experience in this area becomes a big handicap.

I soon realized that job rotation as a means of training for higher management responsibilities was not limited to Japanese companies but was also followed in well-managed firms in the west. I decided that Maruti should also introduce job rotation and started by asking Bhaskarudu, who had been working in the production area both in BHEL and now in Maruti, to consider moving to another discipline. His first reaction was to ask if he had done something wrong, for which he was being punished! He found it difficult to understand the value of rotation and felt that moving from production would adversely affect his future career prospects. It took several meetings and discussions, spread over more than a year, for him to agree to move. He was given charge of the supply chain function. I encountered similar resistance when a few good managers in production and materials were asked to move to do human resource work.

Despite misgivings on the part of many managers, a policy of job rotation was introduced and implemented. The results at first were not at all satisfactory. Virtually all the divisional managers would not release their good managers, pleading that their work would suffer. The persons who were released for being rotated were those who were dispensable—quite the opposite of what should have happened. Worse, the divisional managers in the department to which they were transferred gave them stepmotherly treatment, because they were 'outsiders'. They ended up getting almost the worst grades in the division. That was not totally surprising, as they were generally average grade officers. Seeing this happening, the good executives became very apprehensive of being rotated, as they did not want to risk getting bad grades in the new department. After I retired in 1997 the policy of rotation was not implemented. I think the fault was mine in that I had not spent enough time educating the managers on the need for a rotation policy, and how it would help both the company and their careers.

In 2004-05, after I had rejoined the board, and was associated with the human resource work, intensive training was imparted to the divisional managers to make them understand why this policy was necessary and the message trickled down to others. The head of the human resource function, S.Y. Siddiqui, prepared a policy document which laid down that persons with uni-dimensional experience would not be eligible for higher posts in general management, and this document was widely circulated. The rotation policy was implemented thereafter and has been working well since then.

~

The importance of good communication with subordinates, and particularly workmen, was frequently discussed with the departmental managers. It was emphasized that communication could only be said to be good when it was both ways. Merely lecturing to workers was not adequate. Supervisors and managers must also listen to workers with an open mind and respect their views. Merely because a worker was less educated did not mean that he could not have valuable ideas. The success of the Japanese in making continuous improvements in quality and productivity and reducing costs consistently over several decades was based, to a large extent, on ideas generated by workers through the suggestion schemes and quality circles.

From the beginning, the SMC experts emphasized the importance of following the Japanese system of involving workers in making continuous improvements through the suggestion and quality circle schemes. Individuals derive much greater satisfaction from their work if they feel that they are actually helping in adding value, instead of merely carrying out instructions in a mechanical manner. Maruti realized that if workers could become actively involved in making improvements to the company, it would greatly help in creating a new work culture. Accordingly, a suggestion scheme was introduced in 1984 and Maruti paid Rs. 2 for every suggestion made, irrespective of whether it could be implemented or not. Initially some frivolous suggestions were made, probably just to earn the money, but the workers gradually became more involved in making practical and sensible suggestions. After a few years, the scheme was modified and workers were paid only for suggestions which were implemented.

A financial reward system was developed, where the person making a suggestion was given a part of the savings arising from the implementation of the suggestion. In addition, the names of those making large numbers of suggestions were displayed on the notice board. The person making the most suggestions in the company each month had lunch with the Japanese joint managing director in the canteen. At the end of the year, the person making the highest number of suggestions was invited, along with his family, to have lunch with me in a five-star hotel.

The quality circle scheme was based on the belief that workers who were involved in a particular shop-floor activity would be in the best position to know the problems in that area and would also be best placed to provide solutions. In some cases cross-functional teams could be formed. Initially, managers were sceptical of the scheme, despite SMC managers telling them how this activity had led to enormous benefits in Japan. Our engineers and managers thought that since SMC had laid down all the processes in consultation with them, how could less educated workers make improvements to them? SMC insisted that we should try the scheme. Maruti started to form quality circles from 1985 and gradually extended them to all the work areas. Each circle usually consisted of between four and ten workers and included supervisors. Managers were expected to guide the working of the quality circles so that workers understood the methodology of identifying and solving problems.

Over the years, Japanese companies, including SMC, had standardized how quality circles should proceed to identify problems and find solutions to them.

In Japan, the quality circles met after a shift was over. This was not found to be practicable in Maruti because the workers did not have their own transport and needed to leave for home with the other workers in the buses. However, so much importance was attached to promoting quality circles that the company decided to allow one hour a month of working time to be used for this activity, with managers helping identify the problem to be tackled and then systematically finding the correct solution. A scheme for financially rewarding quality circles, based on the quantum of financial benefits accruing from their work, was introduced. Maruti also decided to start a competition between all the quality circles in the company. The winning team would go to SMC, Japan, to take part in an event for quality circles from all the overseas plants. The runners-up and third-placed teams were given good prizes.

Thus, the incentive structure for the quality circles was attractive. Nevertheless, the results in terms of savings were not as much as was hoped for. Till 1990, annual savings were under Rs. 2 crore a year. Between 1991 and 1995, savings increased to an average of Rs. 7 crore a year. I made a far more detailed study of how the quality circles were actually working. I realized that managers were not giving the programme as much attention and importance as was required, perhaps because it did not influence their performance assessment for the year. I told them that in future, their ability to motivate and educate workers to do better in quality circles would be an important factor in evaluating their performance.

The company had far less quality circles than it should have had. With around 3,500 workers, Maruti should have had close to 500 quality circles, but that was not the case. Moreover, the active ones, who were generating savings, was less than eighty. This needed correction. I wanted all workers to actively take part in quality circle activities. After all, company time was being allocated for this purpose. Accordingly, I put a full-time manager in charge of this activity. All the managers were required to get quality circles formed so that all workers under them were a part of one circle. Details of each circle were entered on a computer file maintained by the manager in charge of this activity. Every time the quality circle met, the progress made in that meeting had to be entered into the computer. The manager in charge would monitor progress and would report to me about those quality circles that were not meeting or were not making satisfactory progress.

The results were immediately noticeable. Savings in 1995-96 jumped to Rs. 34 crore. In the next two years, they were Rs. 51 crore and Rs. 78.5 crore. Thereafter, annual savings of about Rs. 70 crore are being achieved each year, with the savings touching Rs. 479 crore in 2008-09 as a result of one quality circle, Uday, alone saving Rs. 429 crore through improvements in the service bay.

~

The management structure in public sector undertakings is very hierarchical. The usual pattern is for a fresh engineer or management graduate being designated as an executive. The next levels are usually senior executive, deputy manager, manager, senior manager, deputy general manager and general manager. The numbers who get promoted each year to the next level depend on the vacancies at that level. In the decision-making process, each level reports to the next higher level. This structure at times leads to persons stagnating for many years without getting promoted. It hampers decision making as there are so many levels which have to be crossed. Experience also showed that in this system, very few persons actually added value and improved the quality of decision making.

We discussed the organizational system in Japan with SMC and it was agreed that Maruti should have a much flatter structure for purposes of decision making. Being a public sector undertaking, we had no flexibility regarding pay scales—we had to follow what was applicable to all public sector firms—but we could determine our organizational structure and decision-making process. The government had determined that workers would have seven scales of pay, with the first two levels being for unskilled persons. It was decided that workmen in Maruti would be recruited from those who had passed the high school examination and had also got a certificate from an ITI in certain specified disciplines. Maruti wanted workers to be literate and have some knowledge of technical working. This would be similar to Japan, where all workers were recruited after passing high school. Literate workers were required so that they could read and understand the operating procedures for the workstation, and also be able to benefit from our communication and educational efforts. In addition, prescribing these qualifications helped in restricting the number of individuals who could be recommended for jobs by politicians. Maruti had very few jobs where unskilled workers were required, and we had inherited many such people who had been employed in Sanjay's company.

The practice in the public and private sector was to recruit diploma holders in an engineering discipline to work as supervisors. Maruti adopted the same system and this continued till it was changed after several years. Salary scales 8 to 10 were meant for supervisors. Engineering graduates, chartered accountants and those who had an MBA degree were recruited as executive trainees and after completing the prescribed training period, were placed in the first level of the managerial scale. These started from 11 and went up to 18. Those with an MBA were given a higher start in scale 11. In accordance with the public sector system, the scales went up to the level applicable to general managers. Campus recruitment was done from a few of the top business schools and engineering colleges, and the balance requirement of fresh engineers was met on the basis of a competitive examination conducted by an outside party. We could tell politicians, who recommended engineers and graduates for jobs, that we could not make any recruitment in violation of this system.

Having complied with the public sector system till this point, Maruti made a few important changes. Firstly, it decided that the pay scale of a person would not be related to his or her functional responsibilities. Thus, movement from one scale to the next one would not be a promotion in the sense that it meant higher responsibilities. There would also not be any fixed number of posts in any scale, and employees would move from one scale to another based on their length of service as well as quality of work. This principle was applied at all levels, including workers. Thus a worker could move to a pay scale equivalent to that of a supervisor, without actually becoming one.

This change was made for a number of reasons. It would enable the company to select people for posts with higher decision-making responsibilities based only on their suitability for the job. In the public sector system, where pay and decision-making responsibilities are linked, and promotions are based on seniority subject to rejection of the unfit, a vacancy in a higher post is usually filled by the next person due for promotion, irrespective of that person's past experience and suitability. This often leads to good officers being selected to do jobs for which they are really not suitable. Their past experience and skills are lost by being placed in a wrong job. Apart from addressing this issue, the system adopted by Maruti ensured that no person stagnated at the top of a pay scale, and salaries increased with age and greater family and other responsibilities. This prevented demoralization, which accompanies stagnation. I had come to know that many progressive private companies also followed the same system.

The annual work assessment forms the basis of all promotions in the government and public sector undertakings. Maruti wanted the assessment to be made more objectively, and more importantly, persons to be graded relative to others in the department or division. In the absence of a relative grading system, persons are assessed according to what each reporting officer has in his mind as the standard of 'outstanding performance'. The best officers are given this grade, and the numbers considered to be outstanding, sometimes, was quite large. Besides the fact that this went against the definition of outstanding, it made it virtually impossible to pick the best person for higher responsibilities. Maruti decided that based on a system of evaluating both achievement against targets and other qualities of a person in quantitative terms, all the persons would be graded so that the best 5 per cent would be classified as A+, 20 per cent A, 50 per cent B, 20 per cent C and 5 per cent C-. A prescribed number of marks were scored depending on the classification secured. Each year the marks obtained were added to those earned in the previous years and when the stipulated level was reached, the person moved to the next level of pay. Thus persons who were graded as A or A+ would move up the levels much faster than a person who scored B or C. In that way a fast track was provided to the more outstanding employees. This arrangement did not fall foul of any government rule, was more transparent, and we hoped, would encourage better performance.

The decision-making system adopted by Maruti provided for only three levels, against the normal six or seven. This was our attempt at a flatter organizational structure. The company was divided into a number of functional divisions. Each division would be headed by a divisional manager, who was the equivalent of a general manager in a public sector undertaking. Below the divisional manager would be departmental managers, who would head a department. Usually a division would have three or four departments. If a department was very large, it could have section managers. Otherwise, the persons below a department manager would be called 'staff'. No pay grades were prescribed for the staff. At times persons in supervisor grades could also be staff. Equally, engineers and graduates in level 11 to level 14 could also be staff. Files moved from a staff member directly to the department manager, and not through another person who was in a higher grade in the same department. This was a departure from the public sector system and speeded up decision making and also reduced manpower needs. It also made the functionaries feel more responsible as they were dealing directly with the department manager and had to make sure that their proposals were well thought out and backed by data.

One of the major concerns of executives in a company, and particularly in a PSU, is their designation, which is seen as determining their status in society and respect within the family. When it was decided that executives would be known as staff, department manager and divisional manager, there was an immediate objection from the employees that these designations would lower their status as these were not known outside Maruti. Outsiders would not be able to gauge their seniority and status in Maruti. If an executive's visiting card described him as 'staff' or a 'department manager', he may not even get to meet his counterpart in other organizations, as they would not know his level in Maruti. It was then decided that while the designations in Maruti would remain for internal purposes, executives would be allowed to use the standard designations, associated with their pay scales, for external purposes.

People were selected as divisional or department managers purely on the basis of their suitability for the post. The salary level for the higher responsibility job would not change, though some of the facilities made available to him would improve. The logic was that the salary level was not linked to the post held, and would change only on the basis of the total points earned through annual assessments and classifications. Persons who were not appointed as department or divisional managers, even though they were senior, could not really complain that they were losing out on emoluments by being superseded.

The grading system worked reasonably well but was also distorted by some of the senior managers, including full-time directors. In an effort to ensure that the maximum number of persons working with them were promoted to the next pay level, the grading and classification was not done objectively in all cases. If a good worker could get promoted by getting a B in a year, because of having been graded A or A+ earlier, he was given that grade, even though he deserved an A or A+. The higher grade was given to another person, who did not deserve it, to ensure that he too was able to meet the criterion for moving to the next grade. My efforts to persuade senior managers to be objective met with very limited success.

There was also constant pressure from directors and divisional managers to increase the number of departments and divisions so that more persons could be appointed to these posts. To an extent, this was done to reward good workers and maintain their motivation levels. At the same time, there was also the belief that the divisional manager who could get most persons promoted, and had the largest number of departments under him, was the most powerful in the company!

In a manufacturing company, involving sophisticated technology, it was necessary to have specialists in various areas, like maintenance of electronic and other complicated electrical and mechanical equipments, and those who were in R&D and engineering. It was necessary to encourage bright engineers to opt to work in these areas and develop specialized skills. They would be demotivated if they felt that they were losing out on salary, status or perquisites by our system of designations. The problem was that generally positions of power and authority in general management were coveted by all because of the perception that persons holding such positions were more important. Companies encouraged such a feeling by giving higher salaries and perquisites to those in senior positions in general management and such persons also enjoyed greater public exposure and recognition. Specialists, on the other hand, worked in the background and were rarely recognized. Because of the nature of their work and experience, we realized that they could not really become department or divisional managers. In such posts we would lose the value of their skills and the chances were that they would not do very well in general management. Maruti decided to have designations of 'specialist' and 'senior specialist' and at the appropriate time, they were given all the financial benefits of people in positions of general management. They could not get the kind of authority which general managers have. This worked reasonably well, though the feeling persisted in many of the specialists that a general manager was a better designation than a senior specialist.

~

One of the interesting lessons learnt during discussions with the Japanese experts was the importance of supervisors in the production system. The workers hired in the Japanese factories were required to have passed high school but were not required to have undergone any further formal education, unlike in Maruti, where they also had a certificate in a technical discipline from an ITI. The new entrants in Japan were all trained on the job, and the task of training them was that of the supervisors. Thus, supervisors had not only to be specialists in some area of the production process, but also had to have the ability to teach newcomers. Supervisors were responsible for maintaining high quality levels and solving problems in the production process. They maintained discipline and ensured that work continued smoothly. They were the key persons on the shop floor, and the Japanese management relied heavily on them to achieve targets and to make continuous improvements.

When any production facility or equipment was installed in Maruti, SMC sent experts to commission the machines and train our workers on operation and maintenance, so as to get the required levels of productivity, quality and output. These experts were all highly experienced supervisors. The credit for Maruti achieving 100 per cent and more capacity utilization in short periods of time, and achieving and exceeding production targets year after year, goes to the efforts and quality of our workers and their managers. But all of them would agree that this success would not have been possible without the inputs from the Japanese supervisors. They spent long hours every day, for months on end, bringing in a new shop-floor work culture.

Unlike India, where supervisors were freshers who had acquired a diploma in an engineering discipline, all the supervisors in Japan were chosen from workers, based on the skills they had acquired and the ability to provide leadership. The many years of experience of working on the lines gave them the required depth of knowledge. Managers evaluated the ability of workers to teach, solve problems and provide good suggestions for improvement. Those with the best record were picked to become supervisors.

The Japanese system gave much more importance to experience and on-the-job learning than to academic qualifications. I believed that there was much merit in the Japanese system. The supervisors in Maruti, who were diploma holders in an engineering discipline, had worked on the production lines for very short periods during their initial induction training. They did not really have any hands-on practical experience of assembling cars, or working in weld, paint or machine shops. They could not be classified as specialists and were only generalist administrators. They could hardly be expected to teach new workers or solve problems on the production lines or on machines. It had become evident that the workers did not really respect their supervisors because of their superior knowledge, but only obeyed them out of fear. The Japanese system of selecting supervisors would not only improve the contribution which supervisors could make to the working of the company, but would also provide an opportunity for good workers to get promotion and motivate all workers to perform better.

I discussed the idea of promoting workers as supervisors and stopping the recruitment of diploma holders with SMC personnel as well as with my Indian colleagues. The Japanese were quite happy to introduce this concept in India. Our own managers apparently also agreed to my view, but I realized later that that they had reservations which they were reluctant to voice before me. During discussions we agreed that since very few workers had been in the company long enough to have reached even the pay scale level just below that prescribed for supervisors, we would initially promote workers as assistant supervisors. Those workers who were in the two pay levels just below the supervisor level would be considered for promotion. Amongst them, the eligibility would be restricted to those who had gone to SMC for the six-month training, had done well there, and had shown leadership skills. It was also decided that about 25 per cent of the vacancies of supervisors would continue to be filled from diploma holders. However, they would be initially placed in a lower scale and be required to work on the lines, doing the same tasks as workers for four to five years. Those who showed qualities required of a supervisor would be given that responsibility. The scheme was then discussed with the union and met with wholehearted support. The union had never believed that workers could become supervisors, as there were no precedents in India, and our willingness to try this out would give it brownie points with the workers.

However, the scheme could not be implemented for the next two years, as it faced stiff resistance from managers on the shop floor. They argued that if workers, who were union members, got promoted as supervisors, they would not be able to maintain discipline, even if they gave up membership of the union. Making a change of this magnitude apparently made managers nervous, and the traditional suspicion which existed between workers and managers had obviously not totally gone away. I was not convinced that these fears were justified, bided my time, and did not approve any new recruitment of diploma engineers as supervisors. As production volumes grew and the workforce expanded, there was a need for more supervisors, and the shortage on the shop floor became acute. The managers relented and agreed to try out the new system. In a few months they found that the promoted assistant supervisors were giving better results, and the system was accepted without reservation.

~

The employees in Maruti were repeatedly told that their future was linked to that of the company, and both would prosper or sink together. Consequently, management and workers needed to work to grow the company and make it as competitive and profitable as possible. This message had been reinforced by the various schemes and policies to convince workers that management respected them and they were an important part of the whole team. At the same time, it was necessary to provide a scheme by which the workers could have an incentive to increase productivity, reduce costs, improve quality and share in the prosperity of Maruti. An incentive scheme, linked to productivity, was one obvious answer. A bonus linked to profitability was another option. The problem was in getting a satisfactory scheme approved by the government. Under the law, workers had to be paid a minimum bonus of 8.33 per cent of salary every year, even if the company was making a loss. In addition, the government had laid down that all kinds of bonuses, excluding the statutory bonus, would have a ceiling of 12 per cent of basic salary, which could be relaxed to 15 per cent for companies who signed a MoU with the government. The union wanted an incentive scheme to be implemented within these parameters. This was also one of the demands during the tool-down agitation during Mathew's first term as union leader. However, I felt that this would limit the incentive to increase productivity as the ceiling would be reached quickly.

In consultation with senior managers, I worked out a productivity-linked incentive scheme. The base level of productivity would be 25 vehicles per employee per year. This was derived from the government-approved project report which had projected a production of 100,000 vehicles a year with 4,000 employees. Thus no one in the ministry could argue that the number was low. It was unusual for any PSU to achieve peak production within the limits of the projected manpower. The pool of money to be distributed as productivity incentive would be two-thirds of the labour saving arising from a production higher than 25 vehicles per employee. Production meant saleable vehicles. It was also provided that if any substantive capital investments were made, which resulted in higher productivity, the scheme would be reviewed. The money accruing to the pool from higher productivity would be distributed to all employees, including those in the management, but directors were excluded, as they were not eligible for any productivity bonus under government rules. A formula was devised for dividing the money between workers and management. At the worker level, those on the production lines would get 115 per cent of the average amount available for each worker, direct workers would get 100 per cent and the indirect and white collar workers would get 85 per cent of the average amount. Employees with low attendance would lose the bonus amount, which would be distributed to the others. This was our attempt to recognize and reward the efforts of those working in the production lines, and also to encourage high attendance.

The scheme was discussed and explained to the union in several meetings. One main concern it expressed was that workers had no control over the number of cars which could be sold, and it would be unfair for their bonus to be reduced because of poor sales even if they had produced more cars. It was explained to them that while this was correct, the marketing and sales people were also entitled to the bonus and would certainly make their best efforts to sell cars. At the same time, the workers needed to fully recognize the reality that in order to give a bonus the company had to earn money, and that could only be done by selling vehicles. The workers understood this logic and did not press the point again. It was also made clear that the productivity bonus was not part of the wage agreement, and did not require the consent of the union. The management was discussing the scheme with them only to make them fully aware of what was planned, and to get suggestions for improvement.

The broad outlines of this scheme were included in the proposals sent to the government for approval of the MoU. As expected, the first reaction was that there should be a limit to the amount to be paid. I argued that doing so would be counterproductive, as workers would stop increasing productivity once the ceiling was reached. Since Maruti was benefiting to the extent of one-third of wage-cost savings, plus all the savings on fixed overheads, the company would lose as a result of any ceiling on bonus. The ministry officers agreed to our proposal, perhaps thinking that productivity could not increase much more that 30 or 35 vehicles per employee.

The scheme was notified in November 1989. Productivity levels and sales started to rise rapidly. The bonus pool grew and in a few years the workers were getting a bonus which was approximately one and a half times their basic salary. One benefit of the scheme was that workers never opposed automation or other methods to improve productivity.

More importantly, the incentive scheme convinced workers that the management had made good on the promise to link their prosperity with that of the company. Getting worker cooperation on contentious issues, therefore, became easier, as the management found in the mid-1990s. The company had a large number of casual/temporary labourers on its rolls and Abraham, who had again become the general secretary of the union, insisted that their services be regularized. Since these people were doing work which was not related to the main activity of the company, like cleaning, sweeping and unpacking crates, and outsourcing was the accepted way of getting such tasks done, it would not have been in Maruti's interest to regularize them. The management talked to the other union leaders, and the managers also talked directly to employees on the shop floor, and pointed out that accepting this demand would lead to a larger number of employees, hence lower production of vehicles per employee, lesser labour savings and a drop in the bonus pool. This smaller pool would have to be shared between larger numbers. Hence each regular worker would see a big drop in his take-home pay. With the majority of the workers unwilling to let this happen, the union quietly dropped this demand.

In March 1992, the original incentive scheme expired, since we had specified a three-year term for it, but as a new one had not been formulated, the company had continued to operate it without any modifications. In March 1995, however, the management found it was necessary to revise it, with the second plant coming up in Gurgaon. Over the years, a considerable amount of capital had also been invested in the company, which had led to a substantial improvement in productivity. In the offices, for example, the old-fashioned typewriters had been replaced, first by word processors and then with computers and printers. This enormously reduced the workload of office support staff. Increased computerization in finance and other areas of work also resulted in the need for lesser people, even though the production and sale volumes had increased significantly. Vehicle despatch planning and documentation, and spare part operations were now all using technology to reduce manual work. As a result, while production volumes were set to reach about 300,000 units with the new plant (which would have greater automation) becoming fully operational, the white collar staff would be less than what was needed when production was 100,000 units. Further, more automation had been introduced in production areas, both to improve quality and reduce worker fatigue. If the old incentive scheme had continued in this changed situation, it would have resulted in the incentive amount becoming several times the basic wage. This would have been an unacceptable distortion, and it was necessary to make suitable corrections.

The management started talks with the union and explained the need to make changes. Abraham just would not agree to make modifications. He was obviously aware of the huge increase in production bonus which would result when the second plant was commissioned. It was explained to him that having an incentive scheme was entirely at the discretion of the management and did not require union approval. Discussions were being held with the union only out of goodwill. The scheme in any case had provided for corrections to be made if capital investments were made, which had been done. The company was not willing to continue the old scheme, as the results would be quite unreasonable. However, the union continued to raise objections and called for a strike for two days in April 1995, though this was in response to a call by many trade unions for a strike in all PSUs. Normally Maruti workers never joined such strikes and clearly the union was trying to pressurize the management. The union was warned that the strike would be illegal as proper notice had not been given and consequences would follow. Many workers did not participate in the strike and production lines continued to be operated during these two days. In addition, some of the union executives belonging to the group opposed to Abraham told me that they were quite happy with the modified scheme and it should be implemented. The management then went ahead and, in January 1996, notified a new scheme that was to last till 1999.

Under the new scheme, which used the production and productivity levels of 1994-95 as the base, incentives were not given on the basis of cars produced but, instead, on the number of working hours required by the direct and line workers to produce cars—Rs. X per man hour saved. The role of indirect workers in determining the bonus pool was eliminated. The incentive amount being paid till 1994-95, on the basis of the then productivity level, was protected provided productivity did not fall below this level. In addition, an amount would also be paid based on the company's profit ratio as compared to that in 1994-95. This was the first time that the incentive payment to workers was linked, though to a small extent, to profitability. Even earlier, I had talked to the union about linking bonuses to profitability, but in 1989 it was thought that it was too early to bring in this concept. The workers better understood payments related to production.

The scheme worked well and every year the number of hours required to produce a vehicle declined. At the same time the controversy relating to appointing my successor had started. Bhaskarudu was supported by Abraham and his group. Abraham had also sought and obtained the support of Gurudas Dasgupta, a Member of Parliament belonging to the CPI. After

Bhaskarudu demitted office in 1999 and Khattar took over as managing director, Abraham felt threatened. He needed to show his strength, I felt. He started demanding that the incentive scheme be revised. On 23 March 2000, the union served a sixteen-point charter of demands. While many demands were raised, the main focus was on the revision of the incentive scheme. Abraham wanted 1988-89 as the base year (when one worker produced twenty-five cars a year) while the management wanted it to be 1998-99 (when one worker produced seventy cars a year), the year when the revised scheme had ended. The union also wanted the incentive to be linked to production volume only, while the management wanted to link it to capacity utilization, quality and individual performance. Long-drawn negotiations were held, but they led to no solution. This was but to be expected, as Abraham was clearly itching for a showdown with the management.

Through June and July 2000, the union resorted to agitational tactics and, even as the company prepared for the launch of the Alto, workers started a relay hunger strike in September, which escalated into go-slow, dharna, and gherao of the canteen in October.

When the management realized that the union would not concur with the new scheme, it went ahead and notified it on 11 October. This was similar to the earlier scheme, but the base became 1998-99 and it was to come into effect from 1 April 1999. The management also agreed to revise the conveyance allowance and provide avenues for promotion in non-production areas. The union objected to two key features of the incentive scheme. One effectively meant that the bonus would be cut if production lines were idle because of a slowdown in sales. This was nothing new as even the original incentive scheme had based the payment on the number of saleable vehicles produced.

If there was a slowing of demand, production would naturally be reduced. The objection to this provision was not justified.

Even though an incentive scheme did not require any consent of the union, and consent had not been taken even in 1996, the union decided to have a staggered two-hour tool-down strike, moving from department to department. This brought the production down to a mere 299 vehicles a day. The union action was illegal and the management suspended nearly eighty workers and declared that from 12 October, only those workers who signed a good conduct undertaking would be allowed in. Those who did not sign it would be considered to be on an illegal strike.

The union challenged this in court, which rejected the union case and said that the undertaking required was in consonance with the provisions of the certified standing orders of the company framed under the Industrial Employees (Standing Orders) Act, 1946 as well as in terms of the settlement arrived at between the management and the union in February 1998. The management also received a setback—the Haryana government did not agree to its request to declare the strike illegal. There had been minor labour troubles earlier, but this was the first full-fledged strike that Maruti faced in the seventeen years of its existence. Few public sector companies had this record.

The stand-off dragged on for three months, with over 2,400 workers, out of a strength of 4,254, staying away from work. The matter was raised in Parliament and the Central government tried to broker a truce. The Ministry of Heavy Industries was being pressured by some MPs to compel Maruti to accept the union's demands. The Haryana government, to its credit, was ensuring that law and order was maintained, and the striking workers could not indulge in coercive tactics. This support was crucial and enabled the management to keep production lines running with the help of temporary and contract workers (besides taking workers on loan from its vendors), putting them up in the factory premises under tents, providing them food and even television for entertainment. The company would put out daily press releases about the number of cars produced the previous day. This was designed to lower the morale of the workers and it worked. At the same time a number of workers were dismissed after following a summary procedure. The management was firm on four points—the union would have to accept the 11 October incentive package, it would help restore normalcy at the factory, the dismissed employees could appeal against their termination but would have to agree to be tried under relevant labour laws, and the union would sign an undertaking on behalf of the workers that they would abide by the certified Standing Orders.

Three months is a long time for workers to be on strike, especially when production was continuing, and the management had no real pressure to make unreasonable concessions. SMC was also clear—there would not be any settlement which compromised on the basic principles underlying the incentive scheme and maintaining discipline. By December, some 1,600 workers had signed the good conduct undertaking and returned to work. Finally, on 9 January 2001, the union buckled and called off the strike. It accepted the 11 October incentive package and agreed to sign the good conduct undertaking. The management also bent a bit—it agreed to take back half the dismissed workers, after they signed the good conduct undertaking. However, forty-one were not taken back. Cases were framed against them, an internal inquiry conducted and they were dismissed.

~

If the strike was a jolt to Maruti, the financial results of 1999-2000 came as a greater shock. Maruti made the first ever loss in its history. Immediate steps were necessary to return to profitability and rationalizing the workforce was one of the many measures which were required.

A voluntary retirement scheme (VRS) was framed and offered to the employees. The scheme was quite attractive and 1,050 employees took advantage of it. After the strike, the employees were in a chastened mood, and many thought it better to take a good package and find some other work. Many of these persons were supporters of Abraham and were not sure of their future in the company. Managers may also discreetly have advised some of them of the benefits of taking VRS and starting a new career. The result was that the deterioration of discipline, which had taken place between 1997 and 1999, was arrested, and the workers gradually reverted to their earlier attitude of cooperating with the management.

At the same time, the management wanted to restore the cordial relations with the union which had existed before 1995. Periodic communications through department and division heads on what was happening within the company resumed and workers were encouraged to speak about their problems, which the management would try to address. Gradually, the workers shed their fears and insecurities.

The challenge of growing competition had now to be met. SMC had taken over the company by increasing its stake to 54 per cent and wanted that the public sector culture of management should change. I was inducted to the board after the public listing in 2003, and this was one of the tasks entrusted to me by Suzuki. There was no doubt that there were many people at the executive level who were not pulling their weight and were unlikely to conform to the more dynamic private sector style of management. It was decided that a VRS should be implemented at the level of executives and managers and this was offered towards the end of 2003.

This time the management took care to do a lot of counselling on the need for having a VRS, making sure employees understood the benefits being offered, and advising them on how to invest the money and rehabilitate their careers. Human resource consultants were called in to help employees restructure their resumes. Those who took VRS before Diwali were pleasantly surprised when the company sent gift packets of dried fruit to their homes. It also allowed the house leases to continue for several months. It was just as well. Those who took VRS in 2001 as well as some of the disgruntled union leaders tried to foment trouble but the employees could not be swayed. As many as 1,251 employees took the golden handshake and left.

This VRS again created insecurity among the workers as they feared that they may also be asked to go under another VRS scheme. There was no such intention and the company rolled out an ambitious programme of internal communication as well as off-site training with outside faculty. The workers were educated about the external environment in which Maruti was now working and how it needed to respond. Initially, the workers responded with cynical disbelief, but gradually they opened up and a lot of misunderstandings got cleared. The next step was to invite family members of workers over for factory visits. It took two long years, but finally the positive mood returned.

~

Many of these HR management concepts introduced into the Indian industrial environment by Maruti came to be adopted by the private sector. Long after he had left Maruti, Krishnamurthy happened to be on the same flight as industrialist Sushil Poddar, chairman of Gillette India. Poddar came up to him and said he was immensely grateful to him. Krishnamurthy joked that he did not even use Gillette blades. Poddar then told him that when Gillette and he were in talks for a collaboration in 1984, the Gillette management told him that under no circumstances could their blade be manufactured up to international quality in India. Upset by that, Poddar anonymously visited the Maruti factory for some days and observed its working. He then replicated many of the Maruti systems in his factory. Soon, the Gillette India factory was considered the best among all Gillette factories globally. The private sector replicating the public sector is something that is unheard of even now. Unfortunately, within the public sector, there was little attempt to learn lessons from Maruti and this continues till now, when Maruti has a proven track record of twenty-five years.

10

GETTING IT RIGHT

What made Maruti the success it went on to become? Nobody can ever know what Mrs Gandhi had really hoped for when she decided that the assets of Sanjay's Maruti Limited should be nationalized and transferred to a public sector company. She did not live long enough to see the success of the company, though she did see the start of sales. It is most unlikely that she would have visualized that in twenty-five years the company would have a production capacity of a million cars a year, be by far the dominant player in the Indian market, and be used by SMC of Japan to design and manufacture cars for the world markets.

The success of Maruti was undoubtedly beyond the expectations of both the partners when they decided to create a joint venture in 1982. Suzuki, despite his decision to invest in Maruti, was actually quite apprehensive of what would happen in India, partly because of his not-so-happy experience with the SMC project in Pakistan. He initially limited investments in the

Maruti project to create a capacity of 40,000 cars a year and, despite the heavy bookings received for the Maruti 800 on more than one occasion, he was very cautious about expanding capacity. He was undoubtedly aware of the political nature of the project and must have been briefed on how public sector companies were performing in India. His very cautious and step-by-step approach to investments in Maruti was not only because he was Japanese, but also because of all the pitfalls he knew existed in the way of Maruti becoming successful. He frequently cautioned me against underestimating Hindustan Motors and Premier Automobiles, saying that they had over thirty years' experience in the business of making cars, while Maruti was a novice.

As for the government, the best that the Ministry of Heavy Industries could have hoped for was that the targets contained in the project report would be achieved and Maruti would not become another of the several loss-making public sector companies within its charge.

And yet, proving everyone wrong, the sale of Maruti cars crossed 100,000 within five years, and the company continued to grow bigger and more profitable. Maruti was an instance, perhaps an exception, where a public sector company outperformed private sector companies.

Public expectations from Maruti were not high—it was, after all, a PSU. The media and non-Congress members of Parliament were very critical, believing that the project was a political gimmick. Indeed, perhaps one of the factors which led to Maruti outperforming expectations was the fact that its failure would have not surprised many. There are benefits to being an underdog, of whom nothing much is expected and who has nothing much to lose.

Ironically, it was the political background to the project—

which was perceived as a liability—that became one of the reasons why Maruti could be built on a strong foundation, and grow without being weakened by the pressures and burdens put upon all public sector companies.

Everyone knew that MUL had been established as a memorial to Sanjay Gandhi and that Mrs Gandhi wanted the project to succeed. They knew that if she found anyone interfering with the progress of the project, or hurting its prospects of being successful, the consequences could be quite serious for that person. Arun Nehru, in whose judgement she had implicit faith, was appointed to oversee the project's progress and get results. No other public sector project ever had such a powerful godfather, to not only ensure that the management performed, but to also give protection from those who use PSUs for exercising patronage. As a result, even Cabinet ministers never tried to put pressure on the management in all the years when he was in power.

The management had a free hand to select the product to be manufactured as well as the technical collaborator, subject to the basic objectives of the project not being lost. Most people found it hard to believe that Maruti had a free hand in choosing a partner, and that no money was to be paid by the collaborator for being awarded the contract. SMC was finally chosen, not because of any political pressure, but because the Maruti management was convinced that it would be the best partner. The success of any project like Maruti is critically dependent on the choice of the technology partner, who has to not only provide product and manufacturing technology but also all other critical inputs including training, so that high levels of productivity and quality could be attained and effective after-sales systems established. As later events showed, Maruti did pick an excellent partner, and credit goes to all those involved in this process. The company's success owes a great deal to this decision. It is quite possible that if political support had not enabled Maruti to make a choice purely on merits, SMC may not have been chosen.

The political support was also very valuable in the processing of the project report and getting the necessary approvals, so that the extremely tight time schedule for start of production could be met. This not only helped in creating greater credibility for the project and the management, but also prevented cost overruns which delays would have caused. A PSU investment proposal has to pass many hurdles before it can be implemented. Perhaps the biggest hurdle in those days was the Planning Commission, which apart from critically looking at the economic feasibility of the projects also examined them in terms of the priorities of national planning. Almost without exception, this processing took considerable time.

In the Maruti project, not only were questions raised about the demand projection for cars, but there was a fundamental objection regarding making an investment for increasing production of a private transport item, when the national priority was for public transport. While Maruti could satisfy the commission on the demand projections, and the viability of the project, the ideological point could only be dealt with politically. Without strong political support, the project would probably have failed to cross the Planning Commission barrier.

The political support and the immunity from political interference came in handy on a range of other issues—the approvals for the licence agreement and joint venture agreements, the speeding up of various clearances, duty concessions, awarding contracts for civil works, recruitments, appointment of vendors and dealers, among other things.

The importance of political commitment for meeting

deadlines, and for the success of a public sector project—where cost and time overruns are the norm—were highlighted in the case of Maruti. In most public sector projects, many decisions are delayed as a result of the need to reconcile various interests, and to reach acceptable compromises. In the case of Maruti, the management was aware of the importance of meeting targets, and made every effort to do so. The management took the needed decisions, as there was no compulsion to compromise. There was a single goal to get the project started on time. It is doubtful if the same results could have been achieved if we had believed that the government was not serious about the target date and would accept reasonable-sounding alibis for delays.

One of the biggest factors for the success of Maruti was the selection of the right products to be manufactured. Over any reasonable period of time, customers cannot be expected to keep buying products which do not meet their real needs and expectations, especially when the product is a very expensive consumer durable, which, next to a house, would probably be the largest investment made by them. The decision by the Maruti management to commission a market survey to decide what kind of car to produce, and reverse the earlier decision to manufacture the large Renault car, no doubt played a major role in the success of the company. The SMC range of products, even though they were not designed for India, proved to be very acceptable to customers here. The products which followed the vehicles selected initially also proved to be successful, with one or two exceptions which did not do too well.

The success of any joint venture project is very much dependent on the right partner being selected. The choice of SMC turned out to be very much the 'right' one. SMC was the leader in Japan in the small car segment, and this position was attained because it not only designed good products but also had the systems to manufacture them at low cost, while maintaining high quality. Not for nothing was SMC known to be a company which gave the best value for money—the very attribute that a majority of Indian consumers look for in products. Even brand names are less important than the value which a product gives the user, over the life of its usage. The success of Maruti owes a great deal to its ability to give users high value for the money spent by them. The constant emphasis placed by Suzuki on cost cutting and increasing productivity undoubtedly helped us in meeting customer expectations.

Suzuki was the president of SMC when the decision to partner SMC was taken. He had taken charge of the company only a few years earlier, and was very committed to expanding it into a much bigger player in the global car market. He saw, when others did not, that the Indian market offered an excellent opportunity for achieving his ambition. He was also a very hands-on manager, and had an unusually perceptive eye on how to reduce costs and make improvements. This again was exactly what was needed in India, where most companies operated on a cost-plus basis for pricing products. Realizing the long-term importance of India, Suzuki decided that he would personally oversee the Indian project and not leave it to anyone else in the company. This was a very unusual decision, as normally the CEO of a large foreign company would not do this, especially for a fairly small project in a developing country. But it was a very significant decision for Maruti, as its management not only was able to benefit from Suzuki's inputs, but Krishnamurthy and I had direct access to him and important matters could be decided correctly and speedily. The government perhaps also felt more comfortable that the president of SMC was taking so much interest in Maruti. I would certainly consider Suzuki's direct involvement with Maruti as one of the important reasons for our success.

SMC, like most Japanese companies, but unlike many western companies, did not adhere strictly to the letter of the legal documents signed with the government and Maruti, where it believed that by doing so the project would benefit. SMC had a much more long-term perspective about benefits from Maruti than trying to make some money in the short term. For example, it ignored the limitation on the number of Maruti employees to be trained free of cost in Japan and took on more trainees than agreed upon. It recognized that such training would be of long-term benefit for the success of the company, and that if it asked for extra training fees, as was justified in terms of the agreement, the government may not allow so many persons to be trained. This training was of great help not only in making employees technically proficient but also in bringing a different work culture into Maruti.

Since SMC had confidence in the Indian management, the procedures prescribed in the agreement as to how important decisions should be made was ignored. The Maruti management and SMC's despatched personnel had good communication, and first Krishnamurthy and then I were able to take all decisions required for day-to-day working. A very good mix of Indian and Japanese knowledge and experience could be achieved. This not only speeded up the process of decision making but also motivated the Indian management, as we came to believe that we were trusted. Indeed, in any good joint venture, agreement documents should not need to be referred to after they have been signed. If that happens frequently, the chances are that the joint venture will not survive, or at least would not be a real success.

Having the right products for the market, a good partner and political support ensured that Maruti had got off to a good start. However, as the saying goes, well begun is only half done.

Strengths have to be developed and nurtured to provide sustained high performance over a long period of time. The fact that Maruti continues to be the market leader even after a quarter of a century, and in a highly competitive market, is because it institutionalized systems that enabled it to build on the initial advantage of political support and a good partner.

Perhaps the most important factor behind the continued success of Maruti was the work culture which we were able to introduce. This not only resulted in creating a very productive and participative workforce but also extended to dealings with all stakeholders, including vendors, dealers and customers.

Krishnamurthy and I had recognized that making the project a success would be a Herculean task, given government policies and priorities, the limited market and the fact that Maruti was a public sector company. But we were determined not to fail. One of the advantages of having a Japanese partner was that we could get a much deeper insight into how the economic miracle happened in that country. We soon realized that the real reason was the work culture created after the Second World War. Japan sorely lacked natural resources as well as energy sources. Both had to be imported, along with food items. To pay for the imports, goods had to be exported, but the main potential market—the United States—was thousands of kilometres away. The cost disadvantage of importing raw material and exporting products over long distances had to be overcome in order to be competitive in this market. The only resource available was the Japanese people, and they had to work in a manner that manufactured goods could overcome the cost disadvantage and be competitive in terms of both quality and cost. Japanese managers devised ways of making this happen by bringing in a very different work culture and Japanese exports soon dominated world markets.

We came to the conclusion that in order to make Maruti a real success, we had to replicate this productive work culture. We spent long hours discussing the Japanese experiences and the transition towards excellence with SMC executives. We realized that nothing in the PSU system stood in our way, and what we wanted to do was practicable provided all of us were willing to change. In particular, managers had to leave their egos behind at home, and derive their satisfaction from the success of the company rather than from the false trappings associated with senior positions in the government and PSUs.

With long stints in the public sector and the government, both of us understood what could be done even within the public sector style of management. Public sector managements are rarely able to successfully fight for changing rules and procedures governing their working. The decision-making process in the government is very unfriendly towards change. In addition, PSU managers do not have any real motivation to try to make improvements in the work system, and they generally take the line of least resistance. Following precedents and keeping paperwork in order is a safer way of working.

Trying to bring about changes meant a huge increase in workload, possible risk of antagonizing vested interests as well as the chance of failing. Neither of us were typical public sector managers, and we were willing to go the extra mile to achieve our objective of making Maruti different and to reach international levels of performance. This came more from personal motivation than anything in the working environment. At the same time, we had to keep in view the limitations of our position as PSU managers, and realized that we could not seriously ruffle bureaucratic feathers. Our experience of having worked in PSUs and the government was of great help in navigating and implementing our strategy for achieving excellence. We were convinced that nobody in the government would object to our introducing a new work culture, provided it did not create any public controversy or raise difficult questions in Parliament.

I was also helped by the fact that I had spent twenty-six years in the Indian Administrative Service before getting absorbed as a Maruti employee in 1982. Most of my colleagues were then holding important positions in the government. Some of them probably felt I had taken a wrong decision in joining Maruti and that they needed to help me! Whatever the reason, I could, for many years, get solid support from various ministries. This helped in many situations when serious problems arose and which could not have been resolved without intervention by the concerned ministry.

The workers really had no difficulty accepting the outward changes which were a part of the new work culture. They liked the common uniform for all, one canteen, open offices and common toilets and similar actions designed to create greater uniformity among all employees. More difficult was the issue of how to make them change their attitude towards the management and start to act as if they were stakeholders in the performance of the company. We realized that employees would only behave differently from their counterparts in other companies if they came to believe that it was in their interests to accept the new work culture, and that doing so would result in enriching their lives and careers. I believed that most workers were looking for job satisfaction, recognition and financial rewards. In accepting the work culture recommended by us, it was important to ensure that they did not feel that they were being exploited in any manner. In fact, they had to be made to believe that they were becoming partners in creating a great enterprise and that this would not only bring financial benefits but also status and recognition.

A new way of thinking had to be created amongst workers and this could only be done by a continuous process of education. Since this teaching would be done by the managers, it was also necessary to change the negative perception which workers traditionally had about their managers and the management. This meant that policies and all actions of the company and its managers had to consistently, and without exception, reinforce the belief that the management was sincere and meant what it was saying about the work culture and the future direction which the company would take. Managers had really to walk the talk.

Changing the attitude of some of the senior managers who were inducted in the early years was more difficult. Used as they were to a hierarchical organizational structure, they were uncomfortable with the flat Maruti structure, with its emphasis on egalitarianism and frugality. Many of the practices which we introduced to create teamwork and a sense of belonging to Maruti went against all their past experience and expectations of the future when they attained more senior positions. Some managers could not adjust to this changed situation and tried to do things their own way. We had no option but to ask them to look for other jobs. Most managers found that the new approach to team building was actually resulting in the company making good progress, and the success was rubbing off on them. In a short time, there was widespread awareness that Maruti was different from other PSUs and was actually fulfilling promises and meeting all targets. The media and the public recognized this and managers from Maruti were praised for what they were doing. This compensated for the absence of the usual trappings of status, strengthened the new work culture and led to its acceptance by all employees.

Both Krishnamurthy and I understood the importance of the

leadership setting an example for other managers and the workers. The changes we wanted would never be really accepted unless everyone saw that both of us were fully and sincerely committed to them. Our body language had to carry conviction that we actually believed in the changes we were introducing. The hopes created amongst the workers, by the initial pronouncements, would not last unless backed by consistent actions by the top management. This meant that we both needed to follow all rules more strictly than anyone else. Thus we were meticulous about wearing the company uniform, eating with the employees in the canteen, and being punctual, among other things. We were particularly careful about how we used and looked after company assets. When I became managing director in 1985, I had the wooden door to my room replaced by a glass panel. Any employee could walk in if I was not having a meeting, or a visitor. I was usually amongst the last persons to leave office in the evening.

Workers are innately shrewd and good judges of people. The Maruti management's credibility was quickly established, especially after action was taken to ensure that senior managers were not having different standards for themselves and followed all the company rules. The workers saw, and appreciated, that managers were not treated as being more equal than them. They also saw that in framing and implementing various rules and programmes, the interests of workers were always safeguarded. There was also a genuine effort to consult them and to have two-way communication. The change in the attitude of the workers brought about by these efforts was responsible for the success of the suggestion, quality circle and kaizen schemes. Workers became really involved in them and believed that they could contribute to the betterment of the company. Many companies in India have introduced similar schemes, but few have got results anywhere near what Maruti could achieve on a consistent basis. The main reason for the difference was that workers in Maruti believed that they were partners in the progress of the company, while such identification was generally lacking elsewhere.

Besides bringing the Japanese style of people management and motivation, a crucial factor in Maruti's success was its adoption of many of the Japanese systems of work. All the workstations in the factory had boards setting out instructions for the operator. These were detailed step-by-step directions, so that even a newcomer could quickly learn to work correctly. The shop floor area had larger boards with different slogans and messages to educate workers, change their mindset and instil the right attitudes. There was repeated stress, among other things, on cleanliness, punctuality, following standard operating procedures, doing work right the first time, and remembering that the next worker on the line was a customer. Workers were encouraged to come out with new slogans and ways of communicating the required messages to their colleagues.

In addition, SMC introduced concepts never before heard in India. For example, 5S involves organizing the workplace in a way that improves efficiency. It comprises Seiri (proper selection), Seiton (arrangement), Seiso (cleaning), Seiketsu (cleanliness) and Shitsuke (discipline). This is the exact opposite of 3M—Muri (inconvenience), Muda (wastage) and Mura (inconsistency). 'Eliminate them,' the poster listing them exhorts. 3G relates to Genchi (actual place), Genbutsu (actual thing) and Genjitsu (actually). What this simply means is that when there is a problem, the concerned people must go to the place where it has occurred, examine it and take realistic action to solve it. And then there was 3K—Kimeraareta Koto Ga (what has been decided), Kihon Dori (exactly as per standard), Michin to Mamoru (must be followed). Over time, everyone in Maruti understood these systems and how they led to a better way of taking decisions and achieving results.

Following the Japanese way, the Maruti management was very clear that all issues should be discussed threadbare and everyone was free to air his views on each matter, but once a decision had been taken, that could not be changed unilaterally or simply ignored. This attitude was not limited to production techniques but carried over into all aspects of working. In the early days, even after it had been decided that Maruti would recruit only fresh workers and not hire them from other public sector undertakings, it was found that the production department had recruited quite a few workers from HMT and Bharat Electronics. I summoned the general manager production and asked him how this had happened in spite of the instructions being very clear. He said, 'Yes sir, but after all I have to deliver on the production front and I thought we must have some experienced workers here.' This attitude cost the man his job. A general manager not willing to follow company policy was not something that could be taken lightly.

The adoption of the concept of kaizen had far-reaching impact on Maruti's success and gave it the muscle few of its competitors had. The Japanese industry had become highly competitive over the years because of small, but continuous improvements, epitomized by the concept of kaizen (kai or change and zen or good). It is a concept completely alien to the Indian management culture, especially in the public sector, which relies a great deal on precedents. Kaizen activities were taken up by cross-functional teams (CFTs) constituted from time to time and related to issues like improvements in the use of space for storage, reducing the weight of products to save cost and fatigue in handling, and shortening the distance materials had to be moved so as to save energy and cost. The teams would meet frequently till a satisfactory solution had been found to whatever problem they were dealing with, following which it would be dissolved. When another issue arose, another CFT would be set up.

One of the learnings from studying the reasons for the Japanese success in manufacturing was that if a company had good systems, and these were followed carefully by all, the results would be excellent, even if the employees were not brilliant but were only of moderate capabilities. In India, managers had rarely understood the importance of systems for ensuring quality or productivity. As a result, neither had workers been trained to follow systems, nor had managers, in the course of supervising work, insisted that systems should be observed without any deviations. Consequently, once workers thought they had learned how to do a job, they would stop looking at the operating procedures and do their work from memory. They believed that they were capable enough to do so and did not need to look at the operating instructions all the time. As a consequence mistakes were made. In order to change this culture, Maruti decided to get certified under the ISO, even though the Japanese companies did not consider this was necessary in Japan. Maruti got certified under ISO 9000 in 1995.

It was then decided that vendors, who had big problems regarding giving consistent quality, should also get ISO certified. While the larger vendors could do this by getting support from a consultant, the smaller ones could not afford to hire one. I suggested to Kumar that this problem should be overcome by Maruti itself providing consultancy to groups of small vendors. This was done and in the first instance a group of about fifteen small-scale vendors from Faridabad were trained by Maruti managers. The initiative proved successful and these small vendors could get ISO certification. It was a step towards making manufacturers more aware of the need and value of systems. It also led to Maruti partnering with the CII in 1997 to set up the CII-Maruti Quality Clusters scheme, starting with one group of twenty Maruti vendors. Kumar was put in charge of this effort, working closely with Japanese quality management advisor Yoshikazu Tsuda. The idea was to improve the competitiveness of auto component firms through a common learning process. The movement spread quickly and in 2006, there were sixty-four such clusters across India. But long before that, thanks mainly to this effort, India's auto component industry had attained a formidable reputation for quality with several firms winning the prestigious Deming Prize, and this was one of the factors that led auto manufacturers to decide to set up shop in India when the sector was opened up.

SMC brought to Maruti the concept that cost reduction was a continuous process, and that it was always possible to make improvements and reduce costs. Despite being the lowest cost manufacturers of cars in the world, Japanese companies continued to reduce costs every year. Suzuki once told me that they were now wringing water out of a dry towel. In India the towel was dripping! The idea that costs could be reduced was alien to most Indian managements during the days of licences and no competition. Over the years, manufacturers had priced products on a cost-plus basis and had been making good profits. There was no need to worry about cost reductions. Perhaps Maruti would have worked in the same manner, but for the fact that SMC always emphasized the need to control and reduce costs. Since Krishnamurthy and I were determined that Maruti should not make a loss, we recognized that adopting SMC's approach would help in achieving that objective. Minimizing expenditure and reducing cost became a part of the management philosophy.

Often this was at the cost of annoying politicians. For example, the company decided that as a policy no 'with compliments' advertisements would be given—a standard way of giving money for institutions and other projects of politicians. Maruti did not sponsor events even when requests came from important people. At the same time, Maruti also looked for ways to reduce costs in what SMC was doing. I felt that the cost of shipping CKD kits from Japan was too high, largely because of the packing volume. SMC did not think it could be reduced and said that this was the way it had been done ever since it started supplying CKD kits abroad for assembly. I talked to some of my contacts in Peugeot and Volkswagen and felt that improvements might be possible. I decided to visit them and study their CKD operations. As a result I could give evidence to SMC that the Europeans were able to pack the CKD kits in a smaller volume, even though their cars were larger. SMC accepted the point and got the packing system redesigned, resulting in enormous savings for Maruti.

All these inputs from SMC were of enormous benefit in ensuring the long-term competitiveness and profitability of Maruti. We could sail through difficult times without too much difficulty. We funded all our expansion from internal resources and have not only remained debt-free till now, but in fact are a very cash-rich company. However, there were also areas where the Maruti management had to adapt Japanese practices and change traditional ways of working, to ensure good results for the company. The policy for developing vendors and treating them as partners in all respects was innovative and resulted in huge benefits for the company. The Indian automotive component industry developed rapidly because of the support provided by Maruti to a large number of vendors. The Maruti board, which included government officers, provided full support as otherwise it would probably have been too risky for PSU managers to actively go out and support private industrialists.

The policies adopted by Maruti in the area of marketing and sales was based on the Japanese experience but modified to suit Indian conditions. Like in the case of vendors, we took upon ourselves the role of improving the skills and management capabilities of our dealers. They made profits as a result, but we wanted dealers to be profitable. This too was contrary to the norm in the government that officers should not help private people make profits. Maruti also benefited from the decision to keep profit margins very reasonable, especially when the vehicles were in short supply and commanded a high premium. This led to a more rapid growth of demand and also gave Maruti an image of not being a profiteering company.

The wide acceptance of Maruti products all over the country was greatly helped by the establishment of Maruti Authorized Service Stations (MASS), another innovation made to suit the Indian conditions. The policy for spreading awareness of the importance of using genuine spare parts, and making it possible for customers to buy these at reasonable prices, also helped customers get the best value from their cars, and gave Maruti its high reputation for reliability.

The financial independence which Maruti was able to attain, almost from its inception, helped in reducing the scope for any interference or directions from government on how to manage the company. This independence came about largely due to our devising and implementing the scheme for advance booking of cars with a deposit, and selling cars according to the computerized allotment of sale priority. The interest on the large amounts of money collected enabled us to make profits from year one. Many other car companies have since followed this system.

Continuity of management is generally considered as a key factor in the success of any institution. Maruti was fortunate in this respect. Krishnamurthy remained the managing director and CEO only till early 1985, but he continued as the non-executive chairman till 1990, and his experience and wisdom were available to us. By 1985 the success of Maruti was obvious and there were many aspirants, including those with good political connections, for the managing director's post. However, Krishnamurthy believed in the continuity of management and he recommended that I should succeed him, since I had been with the project from the start and Suzuki was comfortable with me. His view was accepted. I remained the government-appointed managing director till 1992, when I reached the government retirement age of fifty-eight. In that year, SMC became a 50:50 equity partner and acquired the right to recommend the managing director. SMC decided that it would like me to continue for another five years—though it could have brought in a Japanese person—and the government agreed to this recommendation. Accordingly I continued as the managing director till August 1997. So for the first sixteen years Maruti was headed by only two persons, and they had been with the company since inception. I believe this was a very important reason for the success of Maruti, and the fact that the new work culture could take deep roots.

A comparatively small, but significant innovation made by Maruti was deciding to use computers and information technology from the very time of starting operations, and at a time when India was far from becoming an IT superpower that it has now become. This idea was supported by SMC and was not resisted by the workers. The IT division of Maruti did remarkable work in developing all the software and the systems, and applying them to all the departments of the company without any outside help. This led to transparency in all transactions, and it was possible to avoid some of the pitfalls associated with manual operations. Manpower could be kept under control, and as time passed, IT was extensively used in quality improvement and cost control. The spare parts operations match those of Suzuki in efficiency and to a large extent that is because of the IT systems. The shop floor of Maruti today has many systems which have been developed in-house and which lead to substantial benefits in giving customers better value for money.

Perhaps the most important reason for the success of Maruti, despite being a PSU, was that both Krishnamurthy and I, even though from a PSU and government background, had the analytical capacity to understand the inherent weaknesses of the system, and the intellectual integrity to act in a manner which could overcome them to the maximum extent possible. Having SMC as a partner, and Suzuki as a person who was willing to provide all support from his company, became extremely useful in this task. Local knowledge, not only of India but of the governmental systems, was combined with the best of Japanese experience and learning, modified as was necessary and used in all areas. Maruti showed that the human mind can overcome most obstacles.

Maruti's stupendous progress was attributed by many people to the fact that the car industry was protected from new entrants by the licensing system till 1993, and to the support which it got from the government. These critics apparently did not realize that all Indian industries got protection because of the licensing policy, and the virtual ban on imports. Yet, not many examples can be identified of industries that, because of protection, grew as rapidly as Maruti, and attained productivity and quality levels which enabled them to export products to even west Europe, as

Maruti did with its cars. In fact, protection usually led to deterioration of quality and service standards. It was also overlooked by these critics that all PSUs not only enjoyed protection but most also had total monopolies in their lines of business. They operated under the same set of laws and rules as Maruti, except that we enjoyed protection from political interference for the first few years. Yet only a few PSUs ever implemented projects on time, and within budget and achieved production in excess of installed capacity No PSU in the manufacturing sector was anywhere near as profitable as Maruti, or grew as fast as we did. The entire growth was financed from internal resources and Maruti did not depend on government funds after the start-up. Probably Maruti had labour productivity which was higher than any manufacturing industry, including private sector companies, and a unique work culture. I believe the credit for this ability to build on the start should be given to SMC and the Indian management.

INDEX

ACKNOWLEDGEMENTS

This book has been written because Maruti, a public sector company, established a unique, highly productive work culture and not only put India on wheels but played a large role in the industrial development of the country as well. I had the good fortune to be closely associated with the company from its start, and for that I am grateful both to the Government of India as well as Suzuki Motor Corporation, and its chairman and CEO, Osamu Suzuki. Without the faith they reposed in me, the experiences that shape this book would not have been possible. Osamu Suzuki supported my idea to write this book, and S. Nakanishi, the then managing director of Maruti Suzuki India Limited, provided many documents and information from Japan, since it was not easy to locate all the necessary information either in the records of the ministry or of Maruti. My grateful thanks to them.

While I wanted to record the history of Maruti, I also realized that I would need help to achieve this task. Aroon Purie, then director of HarperCollins *Publishers* India and chairman of the India Today group, didn't hesitate when I mooted the idea and readily agreed to publish this story. My thanks also to

Krishan Chopra, then publisher, HarperCollins *Publishers* India, who found Seetha, my co-author. He was patient with both of us and gently kept up the pressure.

The way this book has shaped up would not have been possible without a whole lot of people who gave us time to share their memories and insights.

Gulzar Kalra and former minister Arun Nehru, who had worked closely with Sanjay Gandhi, helped us reconstruct the run-up to and rationale for the nationalization of Maruti Motors in 1981 and its reincarnation as Maruti Udyog Ltd. V. Krishnamurthy, currently chairman of the National Manufacturing Competitiveness Council, who had been given the task of heading Maruti and implementing the project, and D.V. Kapur, then secretary, Ministry of Heavy Industries, Government of India, recollected some of the pulls and pressures that they faced in the early days of the project as well as the policy setting of the 1980s. The former Japanese ambassador to India, Y. Enoki, who had been first secretary and then economic counsellor in the Japanese embassy in the early 1980s, gave us a glimpse into how the MUL–Suzuki Motors partnership was viewed in Japan when it was forged.

A number of persons who worked with Maruti in the early days or were associated with it in some manner provided many valuable inputs. These include Vijay Mathur, D.S. Gupta, Raj Chopra, Surinder Kapur, chairman and managing director of Sona Koyo Steering, and Baba Kalyani, chairman and managing director of Bharat Forge. Amitava Nandy's razor-sharp memory provided many amusing and insightful anecdotes of the early years.

We are indebted to a whole lot of people in Maruti itself. Indeed, the story of Maruti's progress may not have been tracked with such details without the help of Krishan Kumar,

S. Maitra, Mayank Pareek, M.M. Singh, Ramesh Krishnan and S.Y. Siddiqui. Many gaps in factual information needed to be filled. Rahul Bharti and his team patiently dug out old records, annual reports and facts and figures we kept asking for.

The perils of trying to reconstruct current history, we found, lay in trying to get old records. After being told by an official of the National Archives that he could get us any document before 1947 and perhaps till the 1960s, but could make no promises about documents after the 1970s, we had almost given up hope of finding any government papers relating to Maruti. Two people came like a godsend. R.C. Joshi, director in the Press Information Bureau, somehow traced the speech Mrs Indira Gandhi had given when she inaugurated the Maruti factory. And Nagesh Singh, advisor in the Planning Commission, remembered where in Yojana Bhavan the Project Appraisal Division's highly sceptical note on the Maruti project could be found.

A book which spans the history of a company for a period in excess of twenty-five years cannot be written without a great deal of help from a large number of people. We seek the understanding and forgiveness of others who have provided help but have not been mentioned here.

ABOUT THE AUTHOR

R.C. BHARGAVA joined the Indian Administrative Services in 1956. After an eventful tenure, during which he had postings in Uttar Pradesh, Jammu and Kashmir and in the Central government, he was deputed to BHEL as its commercial director in 1979. In 1981, he moved to Maruti Udyog Limited, retiring from the IAS shortly thereafter. He was appointed managing director of MUL in 1985. In 1990, he also assumed the responsibility of chairman of the board. Except for a few years following his retirement in 1997, he has continued to be closely associated with the company, from 2007 as chairman once again.

Mr Bhargava is on the boards of a number of leading Indian companies across a diverse range of sectors. He has also been providing advisory and consultancy services to several Indian and foreign companies. The emperor of Japan conferred on him the 'Order of the Rising Sun, Gold and Silver Star', and he received the *Economic Times* Lifetime Achievement Award, both in 2011.

SEETHA is a Delhi-based senior journalist and the author of *The Backroom Brigade: How a Few Intrepid Entrepreneurs Brought the World to India*. She has been a journalist since 1983, and has worked with several reputed publications of the Times group, the ABP group and the India Today group. She has covered the demolition of the Babri Masjid and tracked the political economy. She also blogs at www.beyondlabels.blogspot.in.

HarperCollins *Publishers* India

At HarperCollins India, we believe in telling the best stories and finding the widest readership for our books in every format possible. We started publishing in 1992; a great deal has changed since then, but what has remained constant is the passion with which our authors write their books, the love with which readers receive them, and the sheer joy and excitement that we as publishers feel in being a part of the publishing process.

Over the years, we've had the pleasure of publishing some of the finest writing from the subcontinent and around the world, including several award-winning titles and some of the biggest bestsellers in India's publishing history. But nothing has meant more to us than the fact that millions of people have read the books we published, and that somewhere, a book of ours might have made a difference.

As we look to the future, we go back to that one word—a word which has been a driving force for us all these years.

Read.